# ELEMENTARY PSYCHOLOGY

# ELEMENTARY PSYCHOLOGY

Jadunath Sinha MA, PRS, PhD

New Central Book Agency (P) Ltd
LONDON
HYDERABAD ERNAKULAM BHUBANESWAR
NEW DELHI KOLKATA PUNE GUWAHATI

**NCBA**

**REGD OFFICE**

8/1 Chintamoni Das Lane, Kolkata 700 009, **India**
email: ncbapvtltd@eth.net

**OVERSEAS**

NCBA (UK) Ltd, 149 Park Avenue North, Northampton, NN3 2HY, UK
email: ncbauk@yahoo.com

**EXPORT**

NCBA Exports Pvt. Ltd, 212 Shahpur Jat, New Delhi 110 049
email: ncbaexports@ncbapvtltd.com

**BRANCHES**

212 Shahpur Jat
**New Delhi** 110 049
**email:** ncbadel@ncbapvtltd.com

**Shop** Nos. 3 & 4, Vinayak Towers
**681/B** Budhwar Peth, Appa Balwant Chowk
**Pune** 411 002
email: ncbapune@ncbapvtltd.com

Shop No. 15, Bharati Towers, Ground Floor
**Forest** Park, **Bhubaneswar** 751 001
email: ncbabub@ncbapvtltd.com

House No. 3-1-315, 1st Floor
Nimboliadda, Kachiguda, **Hyderabad** 500 027
email: ncbahydb@ncbapvtltd.com

GSS Shopping Complex, 1st Floor
Opposite College Post Office, Convent Road
**Ernakulam** 682 035
email: ncbaernk@ncbapvtltd.com

Radhamayee Complex (Second Floor)
Opp. SBI, Panbazar, Jaswanta Road
**Guwahati** 781 001
email: ncbaguwahati@ncbapvtltd.com

ELEMENTARY PSYCHOLOGY • Jadunath Sinha



First Published: 1992
Reprinted: 2008, 2013

**PUBLISHER & TYPESETTER**
New Cental Book Agency (P) Ltd
8/1 Chintamoni Das Lane, Kolkata 700 009

**PRINTER**
New Central Book Agency (P) Ltd
Web-Offset Division, Dhulagarh, Sankrail, Howrah

**COVER PRINTER**
Biswanath Studio
3 Garanhatta Street, Kolkata 700 006

**PROJECT TEAM**
Prabhat Jas, Somenath Ganguly

ISBN: 978 81 7381 569 0

Price ₹ 150.00

# PREFACE

This book is an introduction to General Psychology. It deals with the main topics of General Psychology in a very simple and easy language. It deals with the topics in Abnormal Psychology also.

All the topics are explained by means of homely examples of every day experience. Attempts have been made to meet the difficulties of the mere beginners in the study of Psychology. Some diagrams have been inserted to illustrate the different parts of the nervous system, the sense-organs, perception of figure and ground and optical illusions.

The English and American books are not easily intelligible to the Indian students. The instant demand of numerous students has persuaded me to bring out the book for the benefit of the beginners. It covers the syllabi of Council of Higher Secondary Education, Pre-University and Intermediate classes all over India.

My thanks to my daughter Arati, Daughter-in-law Gita and grand-children Aparna, Anjan, Anita and Aniruddha who constantly attended me in my old age while I was busy in writing the manuscripts.

My special thanks to my son Amiya Kumar Sinha, Executive Director, Jadunath Sinha Foundation who prompted me to write the volumes and helped me in preparing the manuscript of the book.

May 15, 1978 Jadunath Sinha

# CONTENTS

# ELEMENTARY PSYCHOLOGY

## CHAPTER I

### *The Definition, Scope and Methods of Psychology*

### Psychology

Psychology (psyche—soul; logy—science) literally means science of the soul. Formerly it dealt with the nature of the soul. But, at present, it deals with the mind. It is a science of mind or consciousness. It deals with mind or mental processes. It is concerned with the experience and behaviour of the individual. Behaviour is the expression of experience. Experience belongs to a mind or subject. An object produces experience in a subject. If there were no subject and object, there would be no experience. So psychology has to assume the reality of the subject or mind as an experiencer. But it does not enquire into the nature of the subject. Modern psychology tries to explain the nature and development of experience and behaviour. Experience is consciousness. Behaviour is its expression in the body. Anger is an experience. But frowning and shouting are behaviour.

### The Place of Psychology among Sciences

There are sciences of matter, life and mind. Physics, Chemistry, Astronomy, etc., are physical sciences. They deal with the phenomena of matter. Physics deals with heat, light, electricity and other physical phenomena. Chemistry deals with chemical combinations of elements. Astronomy deals with the heavenly bodies. These are physical sciences. Botany deals with the phenomena of plant life. Zoology deals with the phenomena of animal life. Physiology deals with the functions of the animal and human body. These deal with the phenomena of life. These are biological sciences. Psychology deals with the phenomena of mind. It is the science of mind. It is a mental science.

## Psychology is a Natural Science

Psychology is not a part of metaphysics. It is a natural science. It treats of a definite subject-matter viz., mind. It investigates mental processes by introspection, and their expressions by observation and experiment, compares them with one another, and groups them under different classes. It seeks to explain mental processes by their concomitant physiological processes and physical stimuli. It tries to explain them by the laws of mind. It makes use of the idea of causation like every other natural science. It believes that all mental processes are determined by their causes. Sometimes it attempts to explain mental phenomena by framing hypotheses. It assumes the reality of mind, the reality of matter, and the mind's capacity of knowing matter. It assumes that mental phenomena are intelligible and can be explained by the intellect. Psychology aims at a systematic and self-consistent body of knowledge relating to mind. So psychology is a natural science.

Psychology is a positive science, which deals with the different kinds of mental modes or consciousness as they are. It deals with them as facts of experience. It tries to explain them by the laws of mind and by showing their connection with the body and the physical and the social environment.

## The Scope or Data of Psychology

Psychology is the science of mind. It deals with mental processes. My mental processes are open to my inner perception or introspection. I can experience my pleasure, pain, joy, sorrow, etc., by looking within. Introspection can reveal my own experience.

But I cannot directly observe the mental processes of others. I can infer their mental processes from their behaviour. The mental processes of others are expressed in their behaviour. I can observe their behaviour directly, and infer from it their inner mental processes. Looks, gestures, postures, language, etc., are the outward expressions of mental processes in the organism. They are their organic manifestations. These are a key to the minds of others. So behaviour also comes within the scope of psychology. Behaviour is known by observation or external perception.

Mental processes are accompanied by physiological processes. They cannot be adequately explained without their concomitant physiological processes. I see light. Light waves strike my eyes and act on the retinas and produce an action there. This is conducted by the optic nerves to the brain. This produces an impression on the mind. Then only I perceive light. If we leave out of account the physiological processes, we cannot account for the sensation of light. So physiological processes also connected with mental processes come within the scope of psychology. It must study the nervous system, sense-organs, muscles and glands, which are intimately connected with mental processes. Physiological processes can be investigated by experiment.

Mental processes are sometimes produced by external objects. Air waves produce sensations of sounds. Light waves produce sensations of colours. External stimuli produce sensations of colours, sounds, etc. Emotions are excited by particular situations. Joy is excited by the sight of a friend. Anger is excited by the sight of an enemy. Fear is excited by the sight of a dangerows object eg., a tiger at large. These mental processes cannot be explained without reference to the external objects. Psychology deals with external objects as related to the mind. It studies them as objects of experience.

Psychology deals with all types of minds—human mind and animal mind. It deals with the different stages of the human mind, the child mind, the adolescent mind, the adult mind and the senile mind. It deals with the normal mind and the abnormal mind. It deals with the individual mind and the collective mind. It studies the customs and manners. myths and legends, religion and folk-lore, language and literature of people in order to infer their mental development from them. These are the objective products of collective minds.

Thus psychology deals with the following: (1) mental processes; (2) their expressions in behaviour; (3) their concomitant physiological processes; (4) their external stimuli or objects; and (5) the objective products of collective minds. These are the data of psychology.

## Definitions of Psychology

Psychology is defined in the following ways:

(1) Psychology is the science of mind.

The definition is open to two criticisms. In the first place, the sciences are of two kinds, positive and normative. Psychology is a positive or natural science. It deals with mental processes as they actually happen in the mind. Logic, Ethics, and Æsthetics are normative sciences. They deal with norms or ideals of Truth, Good and Beauty respectively. They tell us how we ought to think, feel and will. So the word 'science' is ambiguous. It should be specified as a positive science. In the second place, the word 'mind' is ambiguous. It may mean (a) the soul or the mental substance, or (b) the mental processes, or (c) the mental substance together with mental processes. Modern psychology deals with mental processes and their expressions in behaviour. Psychology deals also with behaviour, physiological processes and external objects related to experience.

(2) Psychology is the science of consciousness..

This definition is open to criticism. The word 'science' should be specified as positive. Psychology is a positive science. It is not a normative science. Psychology deals with all mental processes. It deals with different levels of consciousness,—the focus of consciousness, the margin of consciousness, and the subconsciousness. So the word 'consciousness' is ambiguous. Psychology deals also with behaviour, physical processes and external objects which are related to consciousness.

(3) Psychology is the science of behaviour.

This definition is objectionable. Psychology is a positive science. This should be mentioned definitely. Psychology tells us how we *do* behave actually. It does not tell us like Ethics how we ought to behave. Psychology is primarily concerned with experience or consciousness. It is concerned with behaviour incidentally as an expression of consciousness. Behaviour is unintelligible without experience or consciousness. Psychology is the science of experience and behaviour.

You see your enemy and experience the emotion of anger. Your emotion is an experience or a kind of consciousness. You clench your first, grind your teeth, and assume a threatening attitude. These are called behaviour which is an expression of anger.

Behaviourists hold that psychology is the science of behaviour. Behaviour is the response to the organism to the stimulus. There is no mind. There are no mental processes. They are unnecessary and should be dispensed with. Psychology should dispense with introspection altogether. It is a biological science. Its methods are observation and experiment. It should study the behaviour of the living organism. J. B. Watson is an advocate of this view. He wants to reduce psychology to an objective science.

But this is absurd. Behaviour is inexplicable without experience or consciousness. It is the expression of consciousness. Behaviour is not merely a bodily phenomenon. It cannot be explained apart from its context in the mind.

(4) Psychology is the positive science of experience and behaviour.

It is a positive science as distinguished from a normative science. It deals with experience of an individual mind—all kinds of mental modes, knowing, feeling and conation. It deals with the conscious and the subconscious. It deals with behaviour which is an expression of experience. It deals with the behaviour of an individual mind—animal mind, child mind, and adult human mind. It deals with the behaviour of the collective mind. It deals with the behaviour of the normal mind and the abnormal mind.

## Methods of Psychology

Psychology investigates its data by introspection, observation and experiment.

I. Introspection.—Psychology is the science of mental processes. I can observe my own mental processes by introspection. Introspection is inner perception. It is looking inward. To introspect is to attend to one's own experience. This is the characteristic method of psychology. It is not available to other natural sciences. It is the fundamental method of psychology. Observation and experiment are based upon introspection. Introspection has a unique advantage. Our mental processes are always with us and can be introspected at any moment. Introspection gives us direct and immediate, certain and exact knowledge of our own mental processes. But it can give us knowledge of our own mental processes only. So it cannot give us general knowledge of the laws of mind. Therefore introspcetion should be supplemented by observation and experiment.

Introspection is beset with the following difficulties.

(1) Mental processes are vague and obscure in comparison with material objects. It is easy to attend to material objects. But it is difficult to attend to mental processes which are vague. Material objects are clear and distinct. But mental processes are obscure.

This difficulty can be overcome by practice. Introspection requires a power of abstraction which can be acquired by habit. Abstraction is withdrawal of mind from external objects and fixing it on a mental process.

(2) Mental processes are fleeting by their nature. They elude the grasp of internal perception. For example, mild emotions are fleeting. They tend to vanish when we attend to them. Anger, fear, etc., tend to disappear when they are attended to. But physical objects are enduring and can be distinctly perceived.

This difficulty can be overcome by memory. If some mental processes vanish when we attend to them, we may call memory to our aid. We can easily retrospect or remember what we failed to introspect. If we cultivate the habit of mental alertness, we can introspect even the fleeting mental processes. Moreover, the difficulty can be overcome by the co-operation of experts. If many expert psychologists investigate their own similar fleeting mental processes, they may record their experiences and compare notes with one another.

(3) Two scientists can observe the same object in other natural sciences. But two psychologists cannot observe the same mental process, e.g., fear. They can observe the similar emotion of fear in their own minds and compare their experiences with one another.

Two psychologists can never observe the same mental process. This is impossible from the nature of the case. But still this difficulty can be decreased by the co-operation of experts. Many expert psychologists may introspect similar mental processes, e.g., anger, fear, etc., and compare notes with one another[1].

(4) Introspection requires that the same mind be the observer and the observed. But how can the same mind turn back upon itself and make itself the object of observation ? The same mind cannot divide itself into two parts—the knower and the known, subject and object. Therefore Comte holds that introspection is impossible.

This theoretical objection contradicts the direct evidence of our experience. We do introspect our mental processes, e.g., joy, sorrow, etc. These are facts of experience. I feel joy. And I know that I feel joy. I am conscious, and sometimes I know that I am conscious. Thus I am self-conscious. Self-consciousness is a special privilege of the human mind. It is consciousness of consciousness. In introspection the mind is the subject or knower and its mental process is the known object. So there is some difference between the knower and the known in introspection. We may calmly attend to a mental process without destroying it.

Introspection gives us knowledge of our own mental processes. It gives us knowledge of the individual mind. But psychology is a science of mind, not of any individual mind. It seeks to arrive at the general laws of mind which hold true of all minds. So introspection of one's own mind must be supplemented by the observation of other minds. Every individual has certain peculiarities. So unless we observe the minds of others we cannot ascertain the general truths about the mind. Psychology cannot be a science unless it supplements introspection by observation.

II. Observation.—We can infer the mental processes of other persons through their behaviour. My friend is angry with somebody. I observe his behaviour. He frowns, howls, grinds his teeth, closes his fist, and assumes a threatening attitude. I observe these organic expressions collectively called behaviour. I infer from them that there is anger behind them ; these are the expressions of anger. I interpret his behaviour in the light of my own experience. When I got angry I found that my anger was expressed in such behaviour. So I infer from my friend's behaviour that he is angry ; inference may not be conscious. I interpret the behaviour of others in the light of my own experience, which I know by introspection.

Thus observation of other minds includes the following factors : (i) perception of behaviour ; and (ii) inference of a mental process from the behaviour. We interpert the behaviour of other persons in terms of our own experience. In order that we may be able to interpret the experience of others, it is necessary that we have similar experiences. Observation is based on introspection.

Observation is beset with the following difficulties.

(1) There is a tendency in the human mind to read its own thoughts, feelings and tendencies into other minds. A pious man is apt to think every other person to be pious. A rogue has a tendency to think that every other person is a rogue. The interpretation of other's behaviour rests on the analogy of one's own experience. Stout says, "Interpretation becomes more difficult in proportion to the difference between the mind of the psychologist and the mind which he is investigating.[2]" The greater is the difference between the observer's mind and the observed mind, the greater is the difficulty in studying the mind of the latter. It is very difficult to know the

child mind, the animal mind, and the abnormal mind because they are different from the normal, adult, human mind. It is difficult for a cultured and educated man to interpret the mind of a savage correctly.

The difficulty can be overcome by constructive imagination and the power of inference. The psychologist has in his own experience all the constituent elements by which he can interpret others' behaviour. Only he will have to analyse his complex consciousness into its constituent elements and re-compound them in such a way as to explain the behaviour of others correctly. He should adopt a principle of caution. In order to explain the behaviour of a lower and simpler mind, he should appeal to a lower kind of experience. For example, he may explain the actions of insects and birds by instincts rather than by intelligence.

(2) Bias and prejudice affect our interpretation of others' behaviour. They vitiate our observation of other minds. We do not find fault with our friends. We always find fault with our enemies. The mother cannot easily find defects in the conduct of her son.

This difficulty can be overcome by cultivating an impartial attitude of mind. The psychologist's mind must be free from all biases and prejudices. He should cultivate a dispassionate attitude.

(3) Hypocrisy of the person whose mind is observed is an obstacle to the correct interpretation of his behaviour. This difficulty may be remedied by close observation of various kinds of his behaviour. The psychologist can effectively overcome all the difficulties of observation by constructive imagination[3].

III. Experiment.—Experiment is observation under prearranged conditions. It eliminates irrelevant circumstances and isolates relevant ones. Experiment is the observation of the behaviour of other individuals under test conditions. An experiment requires two persons, the 'experimenter' and the 'subject' or the person whose mind is observed. The experimenter gives a stimulus which acts on the mind of the subject. He has an experience. He introspects his experience and tells the nature of his experience to the experimenter. Thus the

2

subject has introspection of his experience. The experimenter has observation of the subject's behaviour. Thus experiment involves introspection and observation,—introspection on the part of the subject and observation on the part of the experimenter [4].

In an experiment we observe the causal relation between two phenomena, keeping all other conditions the same. Interest remaining the same, we observe the relation between the number of repetition of the stimulus and recall of its impression.

Experimental psychology is engaged in qualitative analysis of consciousness. It investigates different kinds of consciousness and their relation to one another. Sensation, perception, memory, imagination, thought, emotion, and volition are the different kinds of consciousness. Experimental psychology also investigates the quantitative relation between mental processes and physiological processes. It also determines the quantitative relation between mental processes (e.g., sensations) and physical stimuli. Thus experiments have made psychology a more or less exact science. By experiments we can measure the intelligence of individuals, their personality traits, abilities, etc., determine the modes of learning among animals and so on[5].

But the experimental method has its own limitations. (1) Some mental processes occur only under normal conditions of mental life. In experiments on association of ideas isolated words are presented to a person successively, and he is called upon to name the first idea which each of them suggests to him. Continuity of interest, which determines the association of ideas in normal mental life, is excluded. Thus experiments interfere with the normal flow of ideas in the mind. (2) Sometimes they modify the mental process of the 'subject' under artificial conditions of observation. If a teacher's teaching method is inspected by an inspector in his class, his teaching is often modified and becomes artificial. So the 'experimenter' must be very cautious and circumspect in observing the behaviour of the 'subject', and the subject must have great mental alertness in introspecting his mental processes as they occur normally in his mind[6].

Experiment has many advantages over observation. It can multiply instances as often as we like. It can study a mental process under a variety of conditions. It can eliminate irrelevant circumstances and isolate relevant ones. It can study a mental process or behaviour coolly and circumspectly. It can measure the quantitative relations of mental processes to physiological processes and physical stimuli. It attempts to make psychology an exact science. Experimental psychology is called "New Psychology". Thus introspection, observation and experiment are the methods psychological investigation.

## Branches or Fields of Psychology

(1) **General Psychology.**—It studies the mental processes of the normal adult human mind, and explains them by the laws of mind and rational hypotheses. It studies sensation, perception, memory, imagination, thought, feeling, emotion, volition, and various kinds of action. It makes use of introspection, observation and experiment as methods of psychological investigation. It makes use of analysis and synthesis.

(2) **Genetic Psychology.**—It is a branch of psychology which traces the growth and development of mind in the individual and the race. It includes animal psychology, child psychology, psychology of adolescence, psychology of the adult mind, etc. Sometimes it means a branch of psychology which traces the unfolding of the powers of the human mind. Mental development is akin to organic growth. It is not of the nature of accretion or addition from without but growth from within. Genetic psychology traces the development of human mind and the animal mind.

(3) **Animal Psychology : Comparative Psychology.**—It deals with the animal mind. It is sometimes called comparative psychology, because it compares the developed mind of man with the lower manifestations of animal life, and these with one another. It compares the behaviours of the different species of animals. The special problems of animal psychology are instincts and modes of learning. What are

the instincts of animals? Are they blind? Or are they modified by experience, intelligence, and habit? Do animals learn movements by trial and error method? Or do they learn them by insight? In the investigation of the animal mind we should adopt the following principle. In order to explain animal behaviour, we should always have recourse to the simplest explanation possible. We should try to explain animal behaviour by instincts rather than by intelligence, by association of ideas rather than by logical reasoning, by simple memory rather then by constructive imagination. If a simpler mental process can cope with the situation, a higher process will not emerge. More and more complex mental processes emerge as the environment becomes more and more complicated. We can investigate the animal mind by observation and experiment. We observe the behaviour of the animal under a variety of conditions. When we observe its behaviour under the test conditions, we are said to experiment with it.

(4) **Child Psychology.**—It deals with the child mind. It specially traces the development of the child mind. It studies the genesis and growth of elementary mental processes of sensation, perception, simple memory and imagination in the child. It also studies the contribution of heredity and environment to the growth of the child mind. What is the original endowment of the child? How far is it impoverished or enriched by the action of the environment? What are the instincts of the child? How are they modified by experience? What is the nature of intelligence? How are instincts modified by intelligence? How does the child learn? Does he learn by the trial and error method or by imitation or by insight? Child psychology also studies the adjustment of the child to the social environment—the home, the school, the wider community. We can observe the child mind by observation and experiment.

(5) **Individual Psychology.**—It deals with individual differences of different persons. It investigates the personal peculiarities of different types of persons. Some persons have visual imagery, others have auditory imagery, others have

motor imagery. Jung divides persons into two types—introverts and extraverts. Introverts are the persons whose life-energy is directed inward. Mystics, poets, thinkers, etc., are introverts. Extraverts are the persons whose life-energy is directed outward. Men of action are extraverts. Jung recognizes ambiverts also who are midway between the two types. Their life-energy is turned both inward and outward. The study of such personal traits is the task of individual psychology.

(6) **Dynamic Psychology.**—It studies the motives of the normal human minds. It is the psychology of motivation. It studies the conscious and the unconscious motives of normal human behaviour. It is of recent origin.

(7) **Social Psychology.**—It deals with the group mind or collective mind. It investigates the mental attributes of crowds, mobs, deliberative group minds (e.g., assemblies, councils, etc.,) and other social groups as contrasted with the characteristics of the individuals composing them. Social psychology deals with the psychological principles which govern social relations, organisations and practices. The group mind is distinct from the individual minds composing it. Social psychology investigates the peculiar traits of the group mind, psychological interrelations of persons forming familities, crowds, mobs, etc., and of their leaders. For example, the mob mind is the least intellectual, excessively emotional and impulsive, and highly suggestible,, fickle, and irresponsible. Social psychology deals with the different grades of the group mind, and the laws that govern their behaviour. It studies social conflicts, race prejudices, public opinions, fashions, riots, mass hysteria, etc., It studies social cohesion and social disintegration,

(8) **Abnormal Psychology.**—It deals with the unusual phases of the normal mind such as illusions, hallucinations, day-dreams, dreams, sleep, lapse of memory, slips of the tongue, slips of the pen, hypnotism, trance, etc. It also deals with the abnormal states of mind or mental diseases such as obsessions, phobias, delusion, hysteria, double personality, and multiple personality. It deals with temporary mental disorders and permanent

mental derangements, and explains them by laws of mind. It offers physiological and psychological explanation of mental disorders. Psycho-analysts seek to explain all mental disorders by mental causes. Abnormal psychology is allied to psychiatry.

(9) **Physiological Psychology.**—Psychology deals with mental processes or functions of the mind. Physiology deals with physiological processes or functions of the various organs of the body. Physiological Psychology deals with the relations between mental processes and the nervous system. It studies the connection between various kinds of consciousness and the functions of the brain, the spinal cord, the nerves, the sense-organs, and the muscles and glands. It investigates the connection between psychoses and neuroses. It is different from psychology which studies mental processes primarily, and also from physiology which studies all physiological processes. Physiological psychology deals only with those physiological processes which accompany mental processes. It makes use of experiment.

(10) **Psycho-Physics.**—It deals with the quantitative relation between mental processes, especially sensations, and physical stimuli. The greater is the intensity of the stimulus (e.g., light), the greater is the intensity of the sensation (e.g., sensation of light) up to a certain point. (Chapter VIII. Weber-Fechner Law). Psychology studies not only the relation of mental processes to physiological processes, but also to external stimuli.

(11) **Applied Psychology.**—The theoretical principles of psychology are applied to different spheres of practical life. So we have now many branches of applied psychology.

(1) Educational Psychology.—Education is the harmonious development of the powers of the individual. Educational psychology deals with the natural relations among these abilities, the laws of their unfolding, and the judicious methods of their cultivation or repression. It applies the general principles of psychology to the art of education. Especially child psychology is the fundamental basis of educational psychology. It also takes the help of dynamic psychology.

(2) Commercial Psychology.—It deals with the psychology of salesmanship, the psychology of advertising and the like problems connected with commerce. It applies the general principles of psychology to the practical problems of commerce. For example, the art of advertisement makes use of the general conditions of attention.

(3) Industrial Psychology.—It deals with the problems of fatigue, mental traits of workers, managers, and clerks, and business organisation. It makes use of mental tests, interviews and other methods for the selection of different categories of persons engaged in an industrial organisation. It applies the general principles of psychology to the practical problems of industry for its efficient work.

(4) Legal Psychology.—It deals with the mental traits of judges, lawyers and witnesses. It deals with the psychology of testimony, the psychology of handwriting, and the psychology of the criminal mind. It applies the general principles of psychology to the legal profession.

(5) Medical Psychology or Psychiatry.—It deals with the mental causes of mental disorders and functional disorders of the nervous system and the psychical methods of curing them. It suggests some psychical methods of treatment such as hypnotism, suggestion, auto-suggestion, rest-cure, free talking, and re-education. Psycho-analysis is an effective method of psychical cure of neuroses, insanity, and the like[7].

## Schools of Psychology

**(1) Introspective Psychology.**—Formerly psychology was introspective. Wundt in Germany and Titchener (1867—1927) in America were exponents of this school. They made use of experiments. But their main task was to describe experiences as facts and analyse them into their simple elements and explain how complex psychoses were formed by their fusion with one another. They mainly made use of introspective analysis.

**(2) Associationism.**—Hume, Bain, J. S. Mill, Herbert Spencer and others built up associationist psychology in Great Britain. They explanied complex cognitions as compounds of simple sensations, and complex voluntary actions as complex wholes of simple reflex actions. They explained mental combination by association. Associationism is no longer in vogue.

(3) **Functional Psychology.**—William James (1842-1910), John Dewey (1859-) and J. R. Angell (1869-) in America are the exponents of functional psychology. Psychology is the science of human abilities. Mental functions are the devices for the effective adjustment of the organism to the complex environment. Sensation and perception adjust the organism to the present stimuli, memory, to the past, imagination, to the future, and thought, to a complex situation. If simple mental modes can cope with the environment, complex mental modes do not emerge. Functional psychology has been replaced by behaviourism in America.

(4) **Behaviourism.**—J. B. Watson (1878—) in America is the founder of behaviourism. It is a reaction against introspective psychology. It has banished the mind and mental modes or conscious processes from psychology because they serve no useful purpose. It has dispensed with introspection. It regards psychology as the science of behaviour. Behaviour is the response of an organism to a stimulus. So behaviourism is called stimulus—response psychology. Though behaviour is inexplicable without experience or consciousness, many American psychologists are under the dominant influence of behaviourism.

(5) **Gestalt Psychology.**—Max Wertheimer (1880-1943), Kohler, etc., in Germany are the pioneers of Gestalt psychology. It makes use of the concept of 'gestalt', form, whole, configuration, in explaining perception and behaviour. We perceive an object as a figure in a ground, as a whole unit and not as an aggregate of parts as associationism holds. Our behaviour is a whole movement in response to a whole situation. We pass from an unorganised whole movement to an organized whole movement. Apes learn by insight, and not by trial and error. Gestalt psycholoy is a revolt against associationism. It brands associationism as 'brick and mortar' psychology. It is dead against analytical method.

**Hormic Psychology.**—McDougall is the founder of hormic psychology. Its central concept is purpose. Every striving has a goal, a purpose. It involves foresight of the purpose. McDougall makes too much of instincts. They are the basis of primary emotions. Emotions are organized into sentiments. Intelligence serves the ends of instincts. Character is built on the sentiment of self-regard which organizes all other sentiments. Hormic psychology is a reaction against associationism and intellectual psychology. It has fallen into disrepute. The term 'instinct' also is in bad odour at present.

**Psychoanalysis.**—Freud is the founder of the school of psychoanalysis. It is a branch of abnormal psychology. It seeks to cure hysteria by psychoanalysis, free association, or free talk. It tries to unearth the complexes formed by the repressed desires (e.g., sex wishes). Sex desires are banned by the society. They are not allowed gratification always. The ungratified desires are repressed and become unconscious wishes and form complexes. They are directly or indirectly expressed in dreams. The interpretation of recurrent dreams is an important method of treatment of hysteria and other mental disorders. Psychoanalysis is psychology of abnormal motivation. It regards all mental disorders as caused by mental causes. It is allied to psychiatry or psychotherapy. Psychiatry seeks to cure mental disorders by psychical methods. Jung and Adler differed from Freud with whom they collaborated and founded rival schools of psychoanalysis. Freud made too much of sex wishes (*lidido*). Adler laid stress on the mastery motive. Jung emphasized the will-to-live from which self-assertion and sex wish emerged in the course of evolution. Psychoanalysis, in some form or other, has come into vogue.

## REFERENCE

[1] Stout, *Manual of Psychology*, Ch I
[2] *Ibid.*
[3] Sully, *Outlines of Psychology*.
[4] Stout, *Manual of Psychology*, Ch. I.
[5] Angell, *Psychology*, Ch. I.
[6] *Manual of Psychology*, Ch. I.
[7] Boring, Langfeld & Weld, *Foundations of Psychology*, 1948, pp. 11-13.

# CHAPTER II

*Psychology and other Sciences*

## The Place of Psychology among Sciences

There are three kinds of sciences ; physical, biological, and mental. Physical sciences deal with the phenomena of matter. Physics, Chemistry, Astronomy, etc. are physical sciences. Biological sciences deal with the phenomena of life. Botany, Zoology, Physiology, etc. are biological sciences. Mental sciences deal with the phenomena of mind. Psychology is a mental science. It is a positive or natural science. It tells us how the mind actually works—how it actually knows, feels and wills. Logic, Ethics and Æsthetics are normative mental sciences. Logic tells us how the mind ought to think. Ethics tells us how the mind ought to will. Æsthetics tells us how the mind ought to feel. They are concerned with norms or ideals which regulate our life. Hence they are also called normative or regulative sciences. Logic seeks to determine the ideal of Truth. Ethics seeks to determine the ideal of Good. Æsthetics seeks to determine the ideal of Beauty.

## Psychology and Physical Sciences

Psychology is a science of experience of an individual mind. But experience depends upon interaction of subject and object, both of which are real. Psychology deals with mental processes such as knowing, feeling and willing. In order to account for them adequately it must study the nature of physical objects in relation to knowing, feeling and willing. But there is a difference between psychology and physical sciences in the treatment of physical objects. Physical sciences investigate the nature of physical objects apart from their relation to an individual mind. But psychology studies the nature of physical objects as related to an individual mind—

as objects of its knowing, feeling and willing or as objects of experience. It is not connected with the nature of physical objects in themselves apart from their relation to an individual mind. It does not deal with objects. Psychology is primarily concerned with mental processes ; it is indirectly concerned with their objects inasmuch as they help it explain mental processes. Physical sciences investigate the nature of the environment. So they help psychology explain the experience and behaviour of the individual, which are its reactions to the environment.

## Psychology and Biology

Psychology is a science of the mind. But the mind is intimately connected with the body. Mental processes cannot be adequately explained without the concomitant psychological processes. The environment acts on the mind through the sense-organs and the mind reacts to the environment through the muscles. The sense-organs and muscles are organs of the body. So mental processes are closely related to bodily processes. In fact, they are regarded by many psychologists as functions of life. They are devices for better adaptation of the psycho-physical organism to the environment. Many modern psychologists approach psychology from the biological point of view. They hold that consciousness emerges when the innate reactions fail to adapt the organism to the environment, and higher mental processes are evolved in order to adjust the organism more effectively to the environment. They believe that all mental processes have useful functions in life.

## Psychology and Physiology

Psychology is a science of mental processes. Mental processes are intimately connected with physiological processes especially of the nervous system. So psychology studies these physiological processes in order to adequately account for mental processes. It does not investigate those physiological processes, which are not related to mental processes, because it is primarily concerned with mental processes. Psychology deals with the nervous system.

Psychology is not to be confounded with physiology. Psychology is a science of the mind. It deals with experience viz., knowing, feeling and willing. These are connected with physiological processes which are, therefore, studied by psychology. Psychology deals with behaviour which is an expression of experience. Behaviour is bodily reaction of an individual mind to the environment. So psychology studies the nature of the different kinds of behaviour. It does not study the nature of all kinds of physiological processes. Physiology, on the other hand, studies the nature of all kinds of physiological processes. It studies the functions of all the organs of the body. It studies the functions of the heart, the lungs, the liver and the like. Psychology does not deal with them.

### Psychology and Normative Sciences

Psychology is a positive science of the mind. It deals with mental processes as they actually occur. It tells us how an individual mind actually knows, feels and wills. It does not tell us how the mind ought to know, feel and will. Logic, Ethics and Æsthetics, on the other hand, are normative sciences. They are concerned with norms, ideals or standards of life. Logic is concerned with the ideal of Truth. Ethics is concerned with the ideal of Good. Æsthetics is concerned with the ideal of Beauty. Logic tells us how the mind ought to think. Ethics tells us how the mind ought to will and act. Æsthetics tells us how the mind ought to feel. Logic is based on the psychology of thinking. Ethics is based on the psychology of will. Æsthetics is based on the psychology of feeling. Psychology is a positive science. It is not a normative science.

### Psychology and Logic

Psychology is wider in scope than Logic. It deals with all kinds of mental processes, viz., knowing, feeling and willing. It enquires into the nature of all these mental processes. But Logic deals with thinking only, which is a kind of knowing. It does not deal with feeling and willing. It deals only with thinking i.e., conception, judgment, and reasoning.

But Logic is not identical with the psychology of thinking. Psychology is a positive science, while Logic is a normative science. Psychology tells us how we actually think. Logic tells us how we ought to think in order to arrive at truth.

Psychology is concerned with mental processes, e.g., conception, judgment, and reasoning, while Logic is concerned with mental products, e.g., concepts, judgments and inferences.

Psychology deals with concrete mental processes, viz., conception, judgment and reasoning as attended with feeling and willing, while Logic deals with the abstract mental products, viz., concepts, judgments and inferences divorced from feeling and willing.

### Psychology and Ethics

Psychology is wider in scope than Ethics. Psychology deals with all kinds of mental processes, viz., knowing, feeling and willing. But Ethics deals with willing only. It does not deal with knowing and feeling.

But Ethics is not identical with the psychology of will. Psychology is a positive science, while Ethics is a normative science. Psychology tells us how we actually will. But Ethics tells us how we ought to will. "Ethics enquires how we ought to will, not how we actually do will. Psychology, on the other hand, deals only with the process of volition as it actually occurs, without reference to its rightness or wrongness, or to the ultimate conditions which make rightness or wrongness possible[1]." Psychology is a science of the actual, while Ethics is a science of the ideal. Psychology, as a positive science, studies all the mental processes as they actually occur. It deals with knowing, feeling, and willing as facts. Ethics, as a normative science, seeks to explain the facts of moral life by reference to an ideal or standard according to which we ought to live. It tells us how we ought to will.

### Psychology and Æsthetics

Psychology is wider in scope than Æsthetics. It deals with all kinds of mental processes, viz., knowing, feeling and willing. But Æsthetics deals with feeling only. It does not deal with all kinds of feelings and emotions. It deals mainly with the aesthetic emotions of the sublime and the beautiful. It deals with the aesthetic emotions only.

Psychology is a positive science. But Æsthetics is a normative science. Psychology tells us how we do feel. Æsthetics tells us how we ought to feel. It enquires into the conditions of beauty and ugliness. Stout observes, "Psychology has nothing to do with this distinction as such. It only enquires how things actually come to appear beautiful or ugly; it has no concern with such questions as whether what appears beautiful really is beautiful, or how the distinction between beauty and ugliness is constituted[2]."

## Psychology and Metaphysics or Ontology

Psychology deals with knowing as a fact. Epistemology deals with the validity of knowledge. It enquires into the conditions which make knowledge valid. Metaphysics or ontology enquires into the nature of the reality that is known.

Metaphysics or Ontology deals with the nature of the self, the external world, and the Absolute. Psychology is not concerned with the Absolute at all. It assumes the reality of mind or self and the external world or not-self, and the possibility of knowledge or the mind's capacity to know the world. Metaphysics proves the reality of the self, the world, and the knowledge of the world by the self. It cannot assume any thing. Metaphysics tests the validity of the fundamental assumptions of psychology.

Formerly there was rational psychology. It was a part of metaphysics. It was metaphysics of the soul. It dealt with the nature, functions and destiny of the soul. But now psychology has become empirical. It is a science of mind or mental processes. It enquires into the nature of mental processes. It does not consider metaphysical questions. Most modern psychologists think that psychology can do without the concept of the self or subject. But we think that it is not possible. Psychology is a science of experience of an individual subject. Experience is due to the interaction between subject and object. It would not be possible if there were neither subject nor object. The existence of the self or subject as an experient is presupposed by psychology. Psychology does not enquire into the nature of the self or subject. Metaphysics deals with this problem.

## REFERENCE

[1] *Manual of Psychology*, 1910, p. 6.
[2] *Ibid*, p. 6.

## CHAPTER III

## The Nervous System

### I Structure and functions of the Nervous System

The individual knows the environment though the receptors, and acts on it through the effectors. The nervous system is the adjustor mechanism through which he knows and acts on the environment. He sees, hears, tastes, smells, touches, learns, remembers, thinks, wills and acts through it. His experience and behaviour depend on his nervous system. Hence the study of it is absolutely necessary for investigating the nature of experience and behaviour.

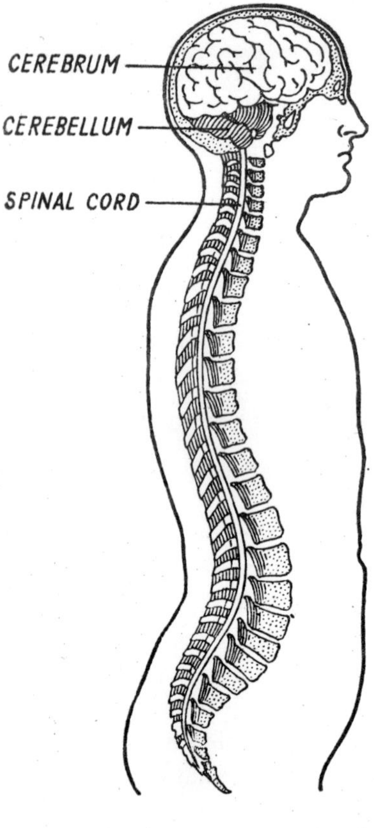

The Cerebro-spinal Axis.

The Nervous System mainly consists of two parts ; (1) the Cerebro Spinal Axis ; and (II) the Nerves.

1. The Cerebro-Spinal Axis consists of the following parts :—

(1) Spinal Cord.—It is a white soft cord-like substance running through the spine or back-bone. It is composed of a grey central core of nerve-cells, and a thick outer layer of white matter which consists of nerve-threads. It is the centre of reflex actions. It converts sensory impulses

directly into motor impulses, because in the spinal cord sensory and motor neurons, connected through their nerve-fibres with the sense-organs and the muscles respectively, are in very close proximity to one another. Therefore an incoming sensory impulse easily finds its way out over motor nerves and produces reflex actions in immediate response to sensory stimulations, without passing to the brain. The spinal nerves are given off from the spinal cord on either side at regular intervals. There are thirty one pairs of these nerves. Each nerve has two roots, an anterior and a posterior root, which unite with each other. The spinal cord is composed of the grey matter and the white matter. The grey matter consisting of nerve cells lies inside and the white matter consisting of nerve fibres lies outside completely covering the grey matter. The spinal cord is the channel of communication from the brain and to the brain.

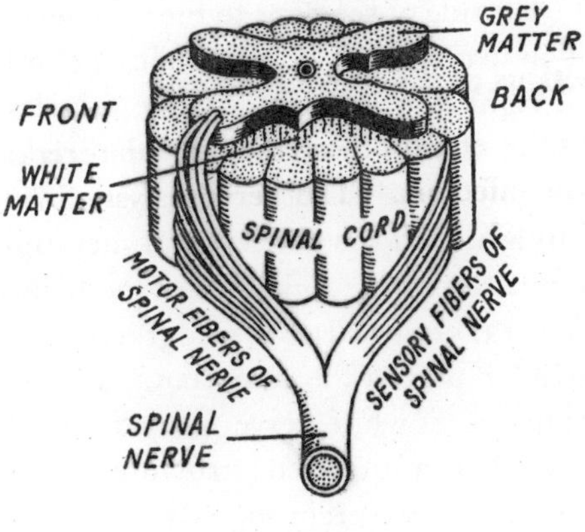

The Spinal Cord.

(2) The Brain or the Encephaton within the skull consists of the following parts :—

(i) Medulla Oblongata.—It is the prolongation of the spinal cord, called also the Bulb or the Stem which connects the brain with the spinal cord. It acts as a conductor between the spinal cord and the brain. All the nerve fibres passing from the spinal cord to the brain pass through it. It controls heart rate, respiration circulation, etc. It lies between the two hemispheres of the cerebrum. It is composed of the grey matter and the white matter. The grey matter lies inside the white matter which covers it. In this respect, the medulla resembles the spinal cord.

(ii) Pons Varolii.—It is a bridge-like band of nervous substance above the medulla oblongata. It connects the two lobes of the cerebellum. The nerve-fibres from the cerebrum pass through it to the lower parts of the body. As they pass they cross one another. The nerve-fibres from the right cerebral hemisphere pass through the left side of the pons to the muscles of the left side of the body. The nerve-fibres from the left cerebral hemisphere pass through the right side of the pons to the muscles of the right side of the body. Thus an injury to the right cerebral hemisphere brings about paralysis of the muscles of the left side of the body, and an injury to the left cerebral hemisphere causes paralysis of the muscles of the right side of the body.

(iii) Cerebellum or the little brain.—It is a wedge—shaped body situated below the hinder part of the cerebrum. It consists of two hemispheres composed of white nerve-fibres covered by a thin layer of grey cells. It is a furrowed structure. The furrows are much deeper than in the cerebrum. Its functions are the co-ordination of muscular movements and the maintenance of the balance of the body. It controls co-ordinated and balanced movements such as walking, sitting, standing, etc., and preserves the equilibrium of the body. In it the grey matter encloses the white matter. The two hemispheres are connected by a broad band of fibres called the Pons.

(iv) Mid-brain or inter-brain.—It is above the cerebellum and forms the base of the brain. It contains the Thalamus, which controls and co-ordinates the bodily functions involved in metabolism, and the Hypothalamus, which controls the expressions of emotions. It contains the lower centres which are connected with the sense-organs by nerve-fibres. Other nerve-fibres lead from them to the sensory areas of the cortex. There are different lower centres for the different sense-organs. The cortex of the cerebrum is not directly connected with the sense-organs.

(v) Cerebrum.—It is the upper brain, and consists of two hemispheres called cerebral hemispheres separated by a fissure. The right hemisphere is connected with the left side of the body and the left hemisphere with the right side of the body. There are folds and furrows in the cerebrum, called the convolutions or gyri and fissures of the brain. The greater is the number of convolutions in the cerebrum, the greater is the intelligence. The fissures of Rolando and Sylvius divide each cerebral hemisphere into four lobes. The brain consists of the grey and the white matter. In the cerebrum, the grey lies outside and encloses the white matter which lies inside. The grey matter is called the Cortex which consists of collections of neurons. The white matter consists of nerve-fibres. The grey matter consists of nerve cells.

The cerebrum controls the higher forms of actions, viz., voluntary actions. It regulates and inhibits the actions of the lower centres. It is the sovereign of the whole nervous system and the organism. It is the seat of sensation, perception, memory, imagination, thought, emotion, and volition. It contains the different sensory centres which are the seats of different kinds of sensations. It contains the different motor centres through which it controls muscular movements or voluntary actions. It enables us to learn, remember, think, judge, and understand things. It is the seat of the intellect. Different portions of the cerebrum are connected with different kinds of consciousness. Some of them are sensory areas which receive sensory impulses from the sense-organs. Others are motor areas which send out motor impulses to the muscles. Others are association areas which are co-ordinating centres. The cerebrum controls, arrests, separates and combines the activities of the lower centres in the spinal cord, the medulla oblongata, and the cerebellum. It receives sensory impulses from the sense-organs through the lower centres, and sends out motor impulses to the muscles through them.

### II. The Nerves and their Functions

The nerves appear like fine white threads. They are bundles of extremely thin nerve-fibres. Some of them issue directly from the brain and are called cranial nerves or cerebral nerves ; and some of them issue from the spinal cord in the back-bone, and are called spinal nerves. The cranial nerves run into the sense-organs in the head, viz., the eyes, the ears, the nose, and the tongue. The spinal nerves run into the skin, viscera, and muscles.

The nerves are of two kinds : (1) Sensory or Afferent or In-carrying Nerves and (2) Motor or Efferent or Out-carrying Nerves. The former carry nerve currents from the sense-organs inward to the sensory centres in the spinal cord and the brain. The latter carry nerve currents from the motor centres in the spinal cord and the brain outward to muscles and glands. The sensory nerves are the axons of sensory neurons situated in the sense-organs and other internal organs. The motor nerves are the axons of motor neurons situated in the motor centres of the spinal cord and the brain. The former carry nerve-currents inward from the sense-organs and the internal organs to the sensory centres and produce sensations. The latter carry nerve-currents outward from the motor centres to the muscles and glands, and produce muscular movements and glandular secretions. The nerves are conductors of nerve-currents.

### The Elementary Structures : Neurons

The nervous system is made up of cells. A nerve-cell with all its filaments is called a neuron. Its filaments are really a part of the cell. It has a tough coat called cell-wall, and contains a white liquid called protoplasm like the white albumen of an egg. It has a cell-body containing a thick liquid called neucleus, and often within this nucleus smaller bodies called neucleoli, and its branches or filaments radiating from it. Two types of branches are connected with each nerve-cell. One is the receiving type and is called dendrite. The other is the sending type and is called axon. An axon transmits the nerve current away from the cell-body. A dendrite transmits the nerve current towards the cell-body. An axon has a myelin or medullary sheath which insulates it. A dendrite has no medullary sheath. An axon is long while a dendrite is short. The grey matter of the brain is composed of cell-bodies and dendrites while the white matter is made up of the axons. There are millions of neurons in the nervous system. They are the elementary structural units, which are separate and distinct. Each neuron consists of the nerve-cell and dendrities and axon. The dendritis look like the branches of a tree. The axon looks like a long slender thread without branches and ends in an end-brush.

The junction of two neurons is called the Synapse. Here the axon of one neuron breaks up into an end-brush of fine

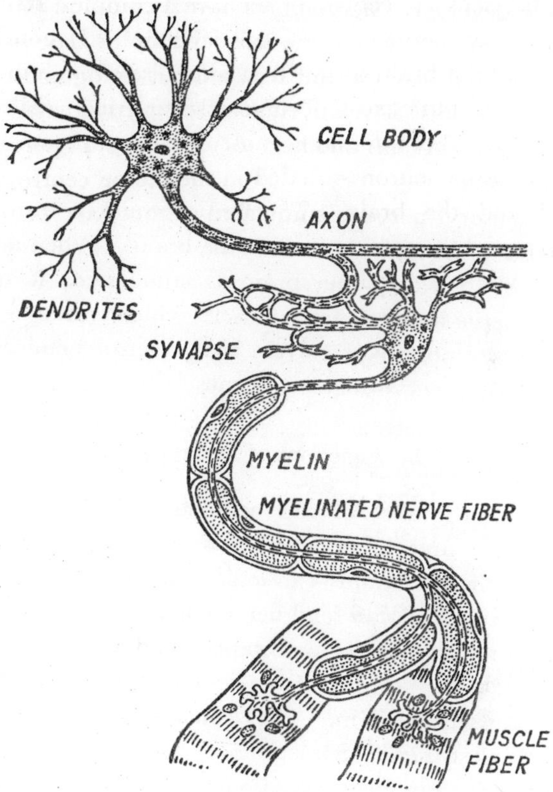


Neuron.

branches which interlace with the dendrites of the other neuron. The dendrite in a synapse is a receiving organ, while the axon end-brush is a stimulating organ, and not a receiving organ. At the synapse the axon end-brush of one neuron stimulates the dendrites of another neuron, but there is no continuity between the two processes. Nerve-currents are conducted from the ends of the sensory axon to the dendrites of the motor cells. They are not conducted from the latter to the former. There is inhibition of nerve-currents in the Synapse. They flow freely through the nerves. But there is a greater delay in the passage of nerve-currents through the synapse. So it obstructs the flow of nervous energy.

The fully-developed nerve-fibres have a complex structure. The central strand is called the axis cylinder. It constitutes the true nerve and carries the nerve-impulse from one point to another. It has a relatively thick covering called the medullary sheath. It has another membranous sheath called the neurilemma.

When a sensory nerve is stimulated it quickly transmits a nerve-impulse to the spinal cord or the brain. When a motor neuron in the cord or the brain is stimulated, it quickly transmits a nerve-impulse to a muscle which makes a movement. A nerve-impulse or current is an electro-chemical wave which can move a nerve centre or a muscle to action.

## The Functions of Neurons

The neurons consist of the cell-bodies and nerve-fibres. Both cell-bodies and nerve-fibres possess irritability and conductivity. A slight stimulus can make it active. This is called irritability. A neuron can send nerve-currents from one part of the organism to another. This is called conductivity. The cell-bodies have also the power of either reinforcing or inhibiting the nerve-impulses sent to them. They can strengthen the impulses received or arrest them. Sometimes their action is automatic ; they send out nervous excitation along the nerve-fibres without any external stimulation. They interconnect the neurons with one another. The cell-bodies supply nutrition to the nerve-fibres. The function of inhibition formerly ascribed to the cellbodies is now ascribed to the Synapses or junctions of neurons.

## Three types of Neurons

There are three kinds of neurons. The first is the sensory neuron, the second the motor neuron, and the third the central neuron. The third type is often called the association or correlation neuron. The sensory neuron connects a sense-organ with a sensory centre. The motor neuron connects a motor centre with a muscle. The central neuron connects a sensory neuron with a motor neuron. It is the co-ordinating neuron.

The neurons are of three kinds according to their functions. The sensory neurons conduct nerve currents from the sense-organs to the sensory centres. The motor neurons which terminate in muscles carry nerve currents from the motor centres to the muscles. The central neurons connect sensory neurons with motor neurons.

## The Nerve Current

The nerve current is an electro-chemical wave which is transmitted through a nerve fibre. Its nature is not precisely known. It cannot be discharged by a week stimulus. A stimulus must have minimum intensity to excite the nerve impulse. But its greater intensity does not excite a more intense nerve current. This is called the all-or-none-law. If a nerve fibre responds at all, it responds completely. But this does not mean that a more intense stimulus does not produce a more intense sensation. In fact, a more intense stimulus does produce a more intense sensation. It is due to the facts : (1) that it increases the frequency of response in each nerve fibre ; and (2) that it stimulates more nerve-endings at the same time.

All nerve currents are not of the same size. A nerve current is large in large nerve fibres, and small in small nerve fibres. The size of the nerve current also depends upon the condition of the nerve fibre, fresh or fatigued. But a nerve fibre always responds according to the all-or-none-law. Either it does not respond, or responds completely. A nerve impulse travels along a nerve fibre from about 1 to 100 meters a second[1].

## Localisation of Mental Functions in the Brain

Each cerebral hemisphere is divided into four lobes. The frontal lobe extends from the front of the brain in the forehead to the central fissure. The parietal lobe extends behind the central fissure and passes over into the occipital lobe which lies at the back of the head. The temporal lobe lies below the fissure of Sylvius in the region of the temples and rearward.

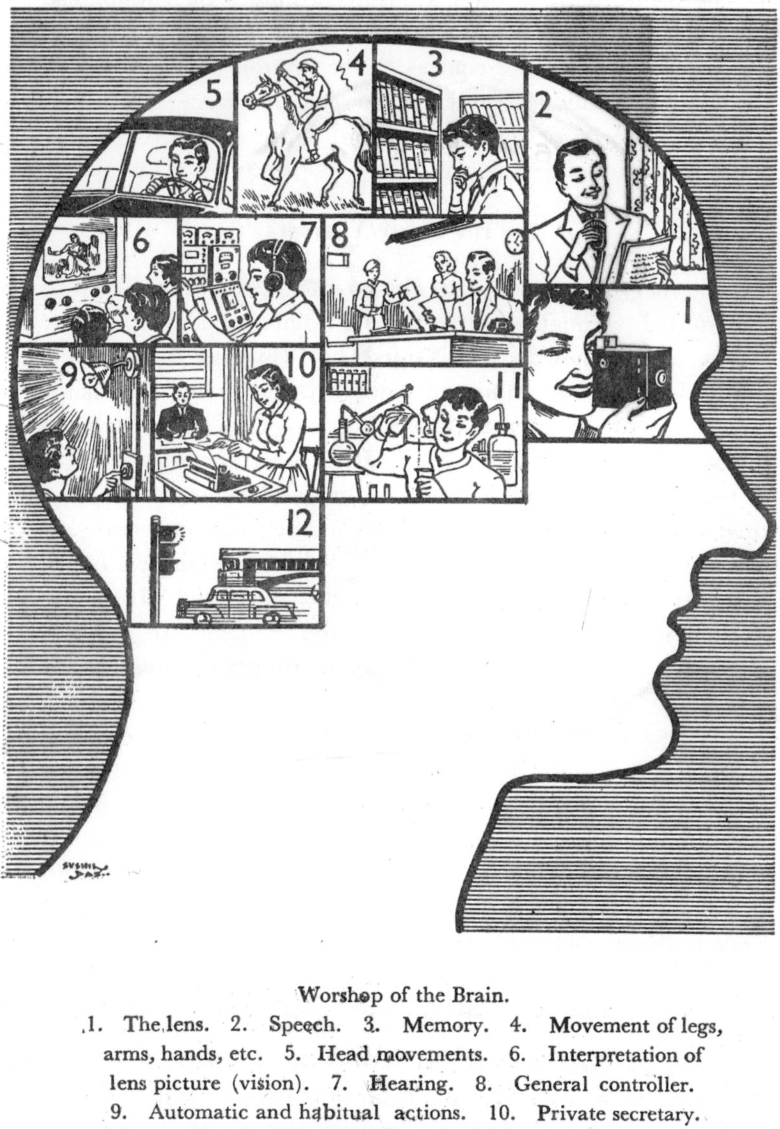


Worshop of the Brain.
1. The lens. 2. Speech. 3. Memory. 4. Movement of legs, arms, hands, etc. 5. Head movements. 6. Interpretation of lens picture (vision). 7. Hearing. 8. General controller. 9. Automatic and habitual actions. 10. Private secretary. 11. Taste and smell. 12. Reflex actions.

The different parts of the cerebrum are connected with different mental functions. The visual area lies in the occipital lobe at the rear of the brain. It is connected with the visual organs or eyes through the optic nerves. It is the seat of visual sensations. The auditory area lies in the temporal lobe where it dips into the fissure of Sylvius. It is connected with

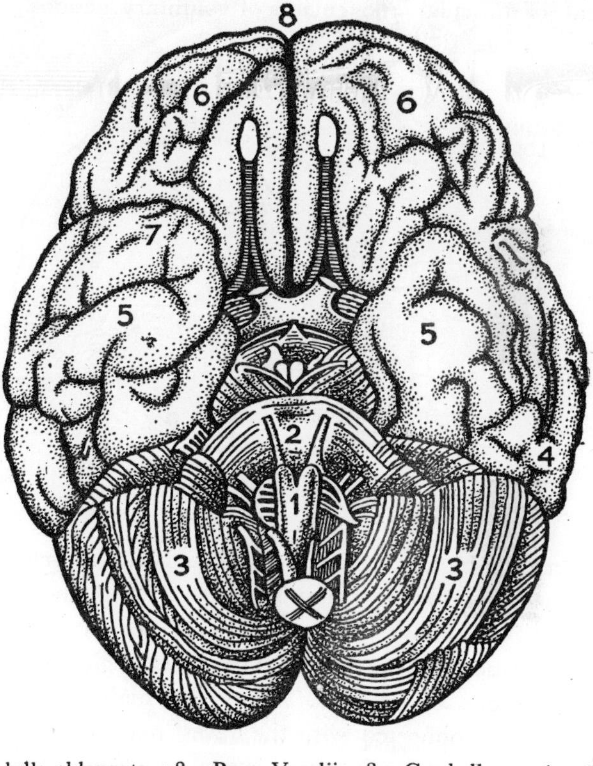


1. Medulla oblangata. 2. Pons Varolii. 3. Cerebellum. 4. Occipital lobe. 5. Temporal lobe. 6. Frontal lobe. 7. Parietal lobe. 8. Longitudinal Fissure. 4—8. Cerebrum.

the auditory organs or ears through the auditory nerves. It is the seat of auditory sensations. The olfactory area and the gustatory area are not visible from the surface. The olfactory area lies in a secluded position covered by the temporal lobe.

The somesthetic area lies just behind the central fissure. It is connected with the tactual organ or the skin through the tactual nerves. It is also connected with the muscle senses through sensory nerves. It is the seat of tactual or cutaneous sensations. It is also the seat of muscular or kinesthetic sensations.

The motor area lies just in front of the central fissure. It is connected with the muscles through the motor nerves. It is the seat of muscular movements of voluntary actions. In the

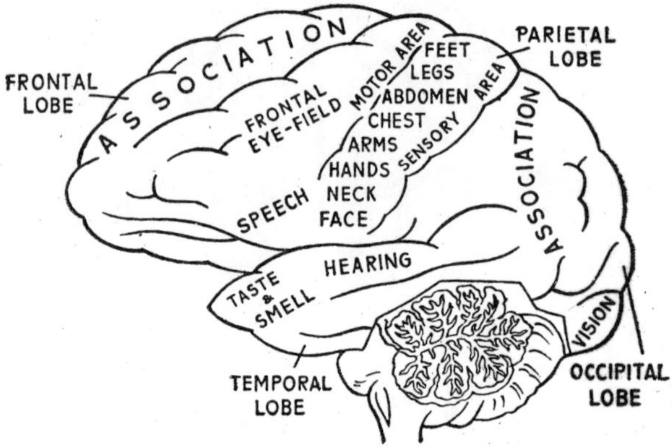


Localisation of mental functions in the Brain.

motor area the highest region is connected with muscles of the legs. The next lower region is connected with the muscles of the trunk of the body. The next lower region is connected with the muscles of the arms. The lowest region is connected with the muscles of the face. Thus the highest part of the motor area is connected with the lowest part of the body, and the lowest part of the motor area is connected with the highest part of the body. The motor centres of speech lie in the lowest part of the motor area.

There is one large area in the parietal, temporal, and occipital lobes, lying between the several sensory areas. There is another large area in the frontal lobe lying forward of the motor area. These are called association areas. They have a synthetic function, and combine the activities of the sensory areas and the motor areas. These association areas are supposed to be the seats of higher mental processes, e.g., reasoning, volition, learning by experience, etc. So the different parts of the brain are connected with different kinds of consciousness. Different mental functions are localised in different parts of the brain.

## The Reflex Arc

The reflex arc is the physiological mechanism of a reflex action. A sense-organ is stimulated by a stimulus. A sensory neuron carries the nerve impulse from the sense-organ to a sensory centre or nerve-cell in the spinal cord or the brain stem. There is a synaptic connection between the sensory neuron and a motor neuron. The motor neuron carries the nerve current from the central switching station to a muscle or a gland. The muscle or the gland acts according to the impulse received through the motor neuron. This combination of a sensory neuron with a motor neuron through a synaptic junction in the grey matter in a lower centre is called the 'reflex arc'. The nature of reflex action will be considered later. We see a flash of lightning. At once our eyes closed. It is a reflex action.

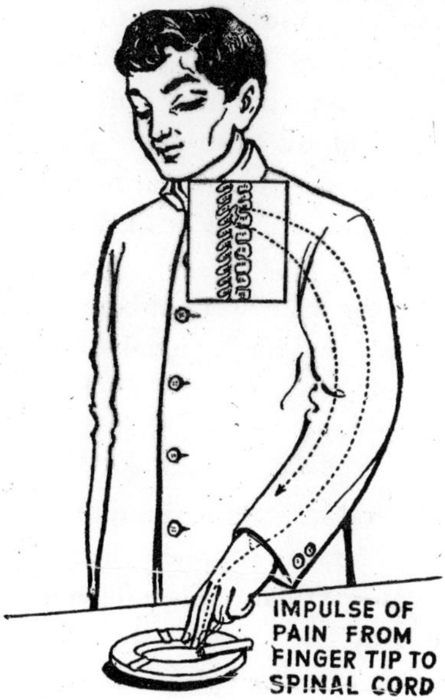

The Reflex Arc.

## The Receptors

The environment acts upon the individual through the sense-organs, and the individual reacts to the environment through the muscles and glands. The sense-organs are at present called 'receptors', because they receive forces from the environment. The muscles and glands are at present called 'effectors', because the individual reacts to the environment through them.

### The Muscles

There are two kinds of muscles, voluntary and involuntary. Voluntary muscles are under the control of the will. The muscles of the limbs, trunk and face are voluntary. Involuntary muscles are not under the control of the will. The muscles composing the wall of the stomach, intestines, and the heart are involuntary. The voluntary muscles are long drawn out and marked across or striped. The involuntary muscles are shorter and taper at both ends, and are unstriped. But the muscles composing the heart, though involuntary, are striped ; but they are very much shorter than ordinary striped muscle fibres.

Striped muscles are attached to the framework of bones, and so called skeletal muscles. They are chiefly involved in all overt actions. They are supplied chiefly with nerve fibres from the cerebrospinal system, and react more quickly than smooth muscles.

Smooth muscles are called visceral muscles because they are attached to the internal organs. They are supplied with nerve fibres from the autonomic nervous system. They have to do with internal adjustments of the body.

Contraction is the function of all muscles, smooth or striped. The excitation comes from the cerebrospinal system to the muscles, and releases the energy stored in them in the form of a contraction. Muscular contraction determines the behaviour of an organism. The muscles are one kind of effectors.

### The Glands : Duct Glands and Endocrines

There are two kinds of glands, viz., duct or exocrine glands and ductless glands or endocrlnes. The former are glands of external secretion while the latter are glands of internal secretion. The former discharge their products through ducts or little tubes into a body cavity or on to the surface of the body. They secrete chemical substances from the body fluids and form new chemical compounds. The process is called secretion. Salivary glands, liver, pancreas, other digestive glands, tear glands, and seveal glands are important duct glands. Saliva is secreted by the salivary glands in response to the taste or smell of food. The liver gland secretes bile ; the pancreas gland secretes the pancreatic juice. The other digestive glands secrete other digestive juices. They respond to the presence of food. The sweat glands secrete sweat in response to heat and to the excitation of the autonomic nervous system. The tear gland secretes tears.

Ductless glands or endocrines discharge their products directly into the blood stream through the walls of the blood vessels which interpenetrate the glands. Their secretions are called hormones. The adrenal glands, the thyroid glands, the pituitary glands, and the sex glands or gonads are ductless. They are intimately connected with emotions.

There are two adrenal glands, one lying close to each kidney. Each adrenal gland consists of two parts, a central core or medulla and a cortex surrounding it. The medulla produces the hormone called adrenalin. The cortex produces the hormone called cortin. The adrenalin hastens and strengthens the heartbeat, increases the blood pressure, stimulates the circulation, removes the fatigue of muscles, arrests the digestive activities of the stomach, expands the pupil of the eye, and produces perspiration. Excessive secretion of adrenalin produces excessive muscular activity, emotivity, and restlessness. Deficient secretion of adrenalin produces fatigability of muscles and weak responsiveness. Cortin acts as a general stimulant. Its deficiency produces weakness and languor, aversion to activity, and loss of sex interest. Its overactivity produces increased masculinity in both sexes.

The thyroid gland lies at the base of the neck in the front of the windpipe. It secretes the hormone called thyroxin, the main constituent of which is iodine. It speeds up metabolism and stimulates the growth of the body and the development of the mind. If the gland is defective, growth is stunted, and intelligence is impaired. Overactive thyroid brings on irritability. Defective thyroid brings on sluggishness.

Near the thyroid glands there are parathyroid glands which have something to do with the removal of toxic products from the body. The parathyroid hormone is a quieter, while the thyroid hormone is an exciter. The absence of the parathyroid hormone makes the nervous system overexcitable. The presence of this hormone restores the nervous system to relative calm. Excessive parathyroid hormone produces lassitude and lack of interest. Deficient parathyroid hormone produces muscular tenseness, and quick and intense response to stimuli.

The pituitary gland is attached to the under side of the brain. It is called "the master gland" because its hormones affect most of the other glands. It has an anterior lobe and a posterior lobe. The former produces hormones that stimulate the thyroid, the adrenal, and the sex glands. The latter produces hormones which regulate blood pressure. The former has great influence on the growth of bones. Its overactivity produces a giant, and its underactivity produces a dwarf.

The sex glands or gonads are vitally connected with sex emotions. The male sex hormones produce development in the direction of masculinity. The female sex hormones produce development in the direction of feminity. The lack of gonadal hormones tends to make a person of either sex neutral or devoid of sex characteristics.

The hormones produced by the endocrine glands are carried by the blood stream throughout the whole body. The functions of the different ductless glands are interrelated to one another. A disorder in the function of one gland may cause disorders in the functions of others. The functions of the endocrine glands have not yet been determined precisely. The science of endocrinology is still in an infant state[2].

### The Relation between Mind and Body

The mind is intimately connected with the body. (1) It knows external objects and their qualities through the sense-organs. It acts upon them through the muscles. The sense-organs and the muscles are parts of the body. (2) Mental development depends upon brain development. The larger and the more complex the brain, the greater the intelligence. A man is more intelligent than a monkey because he has a larger and more complex brain. A monkey is more intelligent than a dog because he has a larger brain. (3) A severe injury to the brain brings about unconsciousness. (4) Impairment of the different parts of the brain leads to the loss of particular kinds of consciousness. Visual sensations are lost if the visual area is impaired. Auditory sensations are lost if the auditory area is impaired. The muscles are crippled if the motor area is injured. If the association areas are injured, there is loss of memory. (5) If the optic nerves are cut or injured, visual sensations are lost. If a motor nerve between the motor area and a particular muscle is cut or injured, the muscle is crippled or paralysed. Thus there is an intimate relation between body and mind. The physiological processes in the nervous system only are attended with mental processes.

### Theories of the Relation between Body and Mind

(1) Interaction.—According to this theory, the body or the brain acts upon the mind in sensation, and the mind acts upon the body in volition. An external stimulus acts upon a sense-organ, which sends a nerve-current to a sensory area. The vibration in it produces a sensation in the mind. The mind makes a volition, which produces a vibration in the motor area ; it is conducted through a motor nerve to a muscle which contracts. This is a common sense view. Descartes was an advocate of it.

But it is open to objections. Interaction generally takes place between two similar things. But body and mind are dissimilar. Body is extended and unconscious. Mind is conscious and unextended. How can they interact upon each other ? Further, in sensation physical energy is lost and converted into sensation ; in volition mental energy is lost and converted into physical energy. But, according to the law of Conservation of Energy, physical energy can neither be lost nor created.

(2) Parallelism.—According to psychophysical parallelism, neural processes and mental processes are attended with each other. They do not act upon each other. They run parallel to each other.

This theory also is open to objections. It is a statement of fact but does not explain it. Through-going correspondence between neural processes and mental processes is not proved. Interaction is a fact of experience. When the body is strong, the mind is active. When the body is weak, the mind is weak. They do not belong to the same order. The mind is higher than the body, and can control, regulate and use it as its instrument. A strong mind can activate even a weak body and make it execute its will. Mahatma Gandhi could use his frail body by the resolution of his strong mind. These facts are not confirmed by psychophysical parallelism. But it works as a provisional hypothesis.

## REFERENCE

[1]T. Morgan, *Introduction to Philosophy*, pp. 532-33 ; Boring, Langfeld & Weld, *Foundations of Psychology*, pp. 27-30.

[2]Woodsworth, *Psychology*, 1955, pp. 125-133 ; Bridges, *Psychology : Normal and Abnormal*, pp. 32-36

# CHAPTER IV

## Consciousness

Consciousness cannot be defined because it is an elementary quality. It can be described by enumerating its constituent factors, viz., knowing, feeling, and willing in their various forms ; or it may be described by contrasting it with the attribute of matter. The essence of mind is consciousness, while the essence of matter is extension.

### The levels of Consciousness

There are three levels of consciousness, viz., (1) the focus of consciousness, (2) the margin of consciousness, and (3) the subconscious or the unconscious.

(1) There is the focus of consciousness in which there is clear and distinct consciousness of objects. It is called the field of attention. It is filled with focal or attentive consciousness. In this region mental activity is intense. Gaze at the moon attentively. You have clear and distinct consciousness of the moon. The impression of the moon is in the focus of your consciousness.

(2) Then there is the margin of consciousness lying round the focus of consciousness. It is the region of vague and indistinct consciousness of objects. It is called the field of inattention. It is filled with marginal consciousness. When you gaze at the moon, you are not absolutely unaware of the surrounding stars ; you are vaguely aware of them ; they produce vague impressions in the margin of your consciousness. Marginal impressions are vague and indistinct.

The focus and the margin of consciousness together constitute the field of consciousness. The expression is borrowed from the field of vision. The farther from the focus, the less clear the impressions ; the nearer the focus, the more clear the impressions. We cannot define the limit of consciousness.

(3) There is the level of the subconscious below the

threshold of consciousness. We are neither distinctly nor indistinctly conscious of it. We have indirect evidences for its existence. It is an under-ground chamber of the mind, as it were, in which all past experiences are treasured up and from which they are revived. It is the repository of all mental dispositions. Some call the level below the threshold of consciousness the unconscious. But this is inappropriate. The 'unconscious' is equivalent to 'nonmental'. But what is below the threshold of consciousness does not cease to be mental. Hence we prefer to call it the subconscious. Freud, Jung and Adler call it the unconscious[1].

## The Margin of Consciousness

While you are reading a book attentively by a candle light, you are clearly conscious of the contents of the book. Their impressions are in the focus of your consciousness. But while you are reading, you are not entirely unaware of the candle light, your clothes, the ticking of the clock, etc. You are vaguely and indistinctly aware of them. They produce vague and indistinct impressions in the margin of your consciousness which surrounds the focus of consciousness. The margin of consciousness is the region of dim and indistinct consciousness. Stout erroneously calls it the subconscious.

There is no absolute demarcation between the focus of consciousness and the margin of consciousness. What is in the margin of consciousness now may come to the focus of consciousness the next moment. You may be vaguely aware of the candle light, while you are reading. But if the light becomes very dim suddenly, you become fully conscious of it. Likewise you may be vaguely aware of the ticking of the clock while you are reading, but when it stops suddenly you become fully conscious of it. Again, what occupies the focus of consciousness now may recede into the margin the next moment. You are reading a book. Suddenly you find that your mind has wandered away from the book and is thinking of the dinner to which you have been invited. Thus there is no absolute line of demarcation between the focus and the margin of consciousness[2].

### The Subconscious

We understand by the subconscious a state which lies below the threshold of consciousness. It should not be confused with the margin of consciousness. We are vaguely aware of the margin of consciousness ; but we are quite unaware of the subconscious. We cannot perceive it either clearly or indistinctly. Freud, Jung and Adler call the Subconscious the Unconscious. We have indirect evidences for the existence of the subconscious. They are the following :—

(1) Memory.—Memory is not possible without retention. We can remember the things which we perceived in the past and which are retained in our subconscious level. If they go out of the mind they cannot be remembered. Therefore we must admit that our past experiences are preserved in a store-house called the subconscious level, which are brought up to the level of consciousness in future. Recall depends on retention. Past experiences are retained in the subconscious level of the mind.

(2) Recognition.—You meet a person to-day. You do not think of him at all till you meet him again after a week. You at once recognize him, because your experience of him a week before has left an after-effect in the form of a subconscious trace which persists and produces recognition. In recognition there is a fusion of a percept with an image brought up to the level of consciousness. Therefore recognition presupposes the existence of the subconscious.

(3) Sudden recollection.—Sometimes we try to remember the name of an acquaintance. We try and try again, but fail to remember the right name. Then we stop thinking and think of something else. Very often we find that the name suddenly flashes in our minds. This is the work of subconscious mind.

(4) Dreams.—Dreams are the manifestations of the subconscious working of the mind. During dream the subconscious level of the mind works. The subconscious traces of past experiences are revived and combined together in a fantastic manner. Some dreams, according to Freud, are fulfilments of the repressed desires or wishes which are unsatis-

fied during waking life. A child is forbidden to take a large quantity of sweetmeat. His desire to take it is repressed ; and the repressed desire is satisfied in dream. He dreams that he is eating a heap of sweetmeat. Thus dreams prove the existence of the subconscious. During dream the mind is influenced even by external objects. If there is a bright light in the room in which you sleep, this may produce a dream of conflagration. In the state of dream we have an intermediate state between purely conscious states ; sleeping and waking are meditated by dreams which generally occur during light sleep[3].

## Consciousness and Self-Consciousness

Consciousness is awareness or objects. It is directed towards external objects of mental processes. Generally it is directed outward. You see a tree. You are conscious of the tree. This is called consciousness. You are angry. You feel an emotion. This is also a mode of consciousness. Both these are experiences.

But when you refer the perception of the tree or the experience of anger to yourself, you have self-consciousness. Here consciousness of a physical or psychical object is referred to the self or subject. This is a higher degree of consciousness. You are conscious of the fact that you perceive the tree or feel the emotion of anger. This is self-consciousness ; it is consciousness of consciousness. Man is self-conscious. We do not know if animals are self-conscious.

Object-consciousness is psychologically prior to self-consciousness. Self-consciousness is developed through social intercourse. A baby is not capable of self-consciousness. But he can have consciousness. So we must not confound consciousness with self-consciousness.

## REFERENCE

[1]Stout, *Manual of Psychology.*

[2]*Ibid.*

[3]Hoffding, *Outlines of Psychology* ; Flower, *Simple Psychology.*

# CHAPTER V

*Analysis of Mental Processes*

## Fundamental Modes of Consciousness

There are three fundamental modes of consciousness : knowing, feeling and willing. They are called cognition, affection and conation. Consciousness is normally concerned with an object. There are three ways in which our consciousness is related to its object. (1) The mind has some kind of cognition of the object. (2) It feels pleased or displeased with it or is otherwise emotionally affected by it. (3) It experiences a tendency in some way to act upon it—to alter or transform it, to appropriate or reject it. Thus there are three ultimate modes of consciousness : knowing or cognition, feeling or affection, and conation or mental activity. You see a flower. You have a cognition of it. You feel pleased with it. You experience a feeling or affection. You feel an impulse to pluck it. You experience a conation or mental striving. These three mental processes are the ultimate modes of consciousness. They are all elementary psychoses. They cannot be reduced to more elementary mental processes.

Every concrete mental process or psychosis involves three mental factors, viz., cognition, feeling or affection, and conation. These mental factors are inseparable from one another. But sometimes cognition is more predominant in a psychosis, and therefore it is called a cognitive state. Sometimes feeling is predominant in a psychosis, and therefore it is called an affective state. Sometimes conation is predominant in a psychosis, and therefore we call it a conative state. But we must remember that in each of these psychoses all the three elements are present.

Cognition gives rise to feeling ; and feeling gives rise to conation. You see a flower ; you have a cognition of it. The cognition gives you pleasure. Pleasure is a feeling. Thus cognition is prior to feeling; feeling arises from cognition. The feeling of pleasure gives rise to an impulse to act on the flower. Thus conation arises from feeling; feeling is prior to conation. Thus at first there is cognition, then feeling, and last of all conation; this is the order of experience. But sometimes feeling arises from conation. When conation is fulfilled, there is pleasure; when it is baffled, there is pain. When we successfully attend to a game, we feel pleasure; when we fail to do so we feel pain.

### Kinds of Cognition

(1) Sensation is the bare impression produced in the mind by a stimulus. Its meaning is not interpreted. A baby sees a patch of light. He has a sensation of light. But he does not know that it is light.

(2) Perception consists in the interpretation of a sensation. It brings out the meaning of a sensation. When the baby knows that he sees light, he has perception of light. In perception a sensation is referred to an external object in a point of space. Perception presupposes a sensation.

(3) Memory is the reproduction of past experience in the same order. You learnt a poem. You remember it now. This is memory. It presupposes previous perception. It involves retention and recollection.

(4) Imagination is the rearrangement of the contents of past experiences into a new pattern. You imagine a golden mountain. You remember gold and a mountain, and join them together. Imagination presupposes memory. It is mental manipulation of past experiences.

(5) Thinking is mental exploration of past experiences to master a new situation. It involves memory of past experiences and grouping them into new patterns to solve a problem. You lose your way. You go this way and that way. You sit and think of the known data, inter relate them, and find a key to the new situation. You think out your way. Thinking presupposes memory and imagination.

## Kinds of Feeling

(1) Feeling is simple pleasure or pain which arises from a sensation. You see a patch of yellow or blue colour. It gives you pleasure. You hear a noise. It gives you pain.

(2) Emotion is a complex affective attitude which arises from the perception, memory, or imagination of a situation. which excites an instinctive tendency. You perceive a tiger at large in front of you which threatens your life, and you are seized with fear which is an emotion. You see your intimate friend after a long time, and you are filled with joy.

(3) Sentiment is a permanent emotional disposition. Love or hatred is not always felt as an actual mode of consciousness. It is a parmanent tendency to feel the emotion of love or hatred on appropriate occasions. You have deep love for your friend. But you do not always feel it. It is a sentiment or permanent emotional tendency. But when you meet him after a long time, you feel the emotion of love.

## Kinds of Conation

(1) Attention is conation or mental act. It consists in focussing the mind on an object or an idea. You make an experiment and attend to its results.

(2) An action involves practical conation. It consists in some form of interference with external objects. Attention involves no such interference.

(3) A sensori-motor action or sensation-reflex is an immediate motor or glandular response to an external stimulus which produces a sensation. A stimulus is applied to sense-organ ; it produces a sensation in the mind ; then it is followed immediately by a response. Something obstructs the throat, and it is immediately followed by coughing.

(4) An ideo-motor action is an action which follows an idea of a movement. You clap your hands in a crowd while listening to a lecture, and others will clap their hands. Here the idea of an action automatically passes over into action.

(5) An instinctive action is an innate response of the organism to a total situation. It is effective on its first appear-

ance ; it is not learned, though it is modified by experience. A young lizard comes out of an egg, and falls upon an ant and devours it. A bird builds its nest before it lays eggs. Bees build hives. Spiders build cobwebs. These are instinctive actions. They are purposive actions without any clear consciousness of the ultimate purpose.

(6) A voluntary action is a purposive action. It is an action to realise an end or purpose consciously. It involves anticipation of an end, the choice of means, deliberation, choice, and resolution. You work hard to pass your examination with distinction. This is a voluntary action.

(7) A habitual action is the result of repeated voluntary actions. It is mechanical in nature. It dispenses with the guidance of consciousness and attention. Our sitting, walking, talking, writing, etc, are habitual actions. Habitual actions may be the results of repeated non-voluntary actions also.

# CHAPTER VI

## *Attention*

### Attention and Inattention

The 'field of consciousness' is divided into two parts : (1) the 'field of attention' and (2) the 'field of inattention'. The field of attention is the focus of consciousness. It is the region of clear and distinct consciousness. The field of inattention is the margin of consciousness. It is the region of vague and indistinct consciousness. Impressions are discriminated from one another in the focus of consciousness. Impressions in the margin of consciousness are not distinguished from one another. The 'field of attention' is the high light of clear and distinct consciousness. But the 'field of consciousness' contains vague consciousness of objects, of which we are not distinctly aware. The farther from the focus of consciousness, the more indistinct the consciousness ; the nearer the focus of consciousness, the more distinct the consciousness.

Sometimes 'inattention' is used in the sense of attention to an undesirable object. A student is rebuked by his teacher for his inattention in the class-room. Here the student is not attentive to the lecture to which he should attend ; but he attends to other things to which he should not attend at the time, e.g., the noise in the compound, the passing motor car, the trees and birds outside, or music in a neighbouring house. This is the popular meaning of 'inattention'. In psychology we take it in the sense of vague and indistinct consciousness. Titchener rightly observes, "In the normal waking life, there is, in strictness, no such thing as inattention. We give that name to an attention which is directed upon what we regard as an improper object. The inattentive person is merely attending to something else ; the pattern remains the same[1]".

## Nature and Characteristics of Attention

Attention is the act of fixing or focussing the mind on an object. It consists in the direction of mental activity to an object or content of consciousness. It is of the nature of conation or mental activity. It is the cause of clear and distinct consciousness. You look at the sky and see a star dimly. You fix your attention on it and observe it closely. You become clearly consious of it.

(1) Attention is conation or mental activity. It consists in focussing the mind on an object or an impression. It consists in direction of mental activity. It is adjustment of the mind to an object, which is either physical or mental.

(2) Attention is selective. At any moment numerous stimuli act upon the sense-organs. Many stimuli act even upon the same sense-organ. All these things make a bid for our attention. We select some of them and attend to them, and reject others and take no notice of them. Thus attention involves selection of some object to the exclusion of others. When you attend to your teacher's lecture, you select the lecture and reject the noise in the street, talking in the verandah, music in the adjoining house, etc.

Thus attention has two aspects, positive aud negative. When you attend to a thing, you focus your mind on it, and withdraw it from other things. Focusing of mind is the positive aspect of attention. Withdrawal of mind is the negative aspect of attention. When you are attentive to one thing, you must necessarily be inattentive to other things. The objects attended to produce distinct impressions. But the objects to which we are inattentive produce vague and indistinct impressions in the margin of consciousness.

(3) Attention at any moment has a narrow range. Attention is selective. So it must have a narrow range. We can attend to a limited number of objects at a time.

(4) Attention is mobile. It flits from one object to another. Attention cannot be fixed on a particular object for more than eight to ten seconds. Sometimes it shifts even more quickly. Attention constantly fluctuates. This shifting of attention can be proved by a simple experiment. Hold a

watch near your ear. Hold it at such a distance that its ticking is scarcely audible. The ticks will appear to you to be louder and fainter and then disappear altogether. The sounds themselves do not actually become louder and fainter, or appear and disappear. These are due to the shifting nature of attention.

(5) Attention is exploratory. Sometimes we attened to a new object. Newness is favourable to attention. When we attend to a new object, we explore its qualities. We can attend to it so long as we can explore some of its new qualities. Even when we attend to a familiar object, we alway attened to its new qualities. If there be no novelty in the object, it no longer makes a bid for our attention. Woodworths says, "Attention is mobile because it is exploratory; it continually seeks something fresh for exploration."

## Span of Attention

How many things can be attended to at once? We can attend to only one thing at a time. Angell says, "We never have more than one mental object before the mind at any one moment. This object may be complex or simple, but if it is really present in its entirety to consciousness it is cognised mentally as a single thing". When we perceive a table, we attend to it as a complex single object; not as four legs, plus four sides, plus a top, etc.

We seem to attend to a number of things at a time. But this is wrong. Here there is a rapid shifting of attention from one thing to another.

Experiments are made to measure the span of visual attention. A number of simple objects are presented to the eyes. The time of exposure is very short. It ranges from 1/100 to 1/3 of a second. The objects exposed to the eye are simple. Dots, lines, letters or digits are exposed. Complex objects like words or triangles are exposed. The mind perceives each object as a whole or unit. It can attend to only four or five separate units. If the items are not grouped into familiar units, only four or five units can be perceived accurately at a single glance. But if the items are combined into meaningful wholes, for instance, if letters are combined into words, a large number of items can be perceived at once.

Experiments have been made to measure the span of auditory attention. The number of auditory impressions perceived at once is slightly larger. An adult subject can perceive eight sounds given in rapid succession. But when sounds are given in a rhythm, a much larger number of sounds can be perceived.

How many acts can be attended to at the same time? How many things can be done at once? The answer is simple. We can do one voluntary act at the same time. We cannot do two or three voluntary acts at one time. But we can quickly shift our attention from one voluntary act to another. We can dictate two letters to two persons by quickly shifting our attention from one letter to another. But we can carry on a habitual action and a voluntary action at one time. A weaver goes on weaving and talking at the same time. A typist can type and pick up conversation to a certain extent. A girl can knit wool and carry on conversation.

## Kinds of Attention

I. Non-voluntary, Voluntary, and Involuntary Attention.

(1) Non-voluntary Attention.—It is spontaneous or effortless; it does not involve an effort of the will or volition. It is determined by the object. It is not determined by the subject or mind with its volition. When we attend to an object spontaneously or in an effortless way but not against the will, we have non-voluntary attention. When your mind is diverted to a piece of music in a neighbouring house, while you are occupied in reading a book, your attention to the music is spontaneous or non-voluntary. Or while you are listening to a lecture in the class, you unconsciously fall into a reverie and build "castles in the air" about your future career. This is non-voluntary attention. The mind always attends to something or other. Whenever our attention to an object flags, it is at once diverted to some other interesting object or idea.

Non-voluntary attention appears early in life, because it does not involve an effort of the will, and it is directed generally to interesting objects.

(2) Voluntary Attention.—It is determined by the subject or mind ; it involves a conscious effort of the will or volition. It is the result of mental activity. It always involves mental exertion or effort. It is not effortless or spontaneous like non-voluntary attention. In voluntary attention an effort of the will is directed towards an object or idea. When you attend to a passage with a mental strain to understand its meaning, you put forth voluntary attention. When you attend to a lecture in the class in spite of some noise in the verandah, you have voluntary attention. When you solve a difficult problem in the examination hall in spite of the invigilators coming and going and occasionally talking to one another, you have voluntary attention.

(3) Involuntary Attention.—It is attention paid to an object against the will. It is not effortless or spontaneous like non-voluntary attention. It involves a deliberate effort of the will like voluntary attention. But it differs from voluntary attention in an important respect. In involuntary attention the will is directed against the object to which it is paid, while in voluntary attention the will is directed towards the object to which it is paid. Thus, if the door slams violently while you are engaged in writing, you are compelled to attend to the sound against your will. Here you put forth involuntary attention. When you are engaged in answering questions in the examination hall, you are compelled to attend to any sudden noise in the hall against your will. This is involuntary attention.

Stout distinguishes the three kinds of attention, thus : "Attention, so far as it follows upon an express volition to attend, is called voluntary attention. All attention which is not so initiated is non-voluntary or spontaneous. When we attend not merely without an express volition to attend, but in opposition to such a volition, attention is in the strictest sense involuntary, and not merely non-voluntary[2]." Non-voluntary attention precedes voluntary attention in mental development.

Involuntary attention and voluntary attention appear later, because they presuppose the power of controlling the will.

II. Sensory and Ideational Attention.—Attention is divided into sensory and ideational attention according to the nature of its object. Sensory attention is attention to sensible objects. When you attend to a tree, a house, or a book, your attention is sensory. Ideational attention is attention to ideas, thoughts, emotions, and volitions. It is attention to mental contents. When you attend to the image of your absent friend, or to the grief excited by the death of your dear friend, you have ideational attention. Sensorial attention precedes ideational attention in the life of the child, because his attention is first directed outward to external objects and then inward to mental processes.

III. Immediate and Derived Attention.—Attention is immediate, when its object is interesting in itself. Attention to music is immediate, because it is interesting in itself. But when you are sick and do not like music, your attention to it is not immediate. When you attend to a sumptuous feast which evokes your interest, your attention is immediate. But attention is derived or apperceptive, when it is directed to an object which is not interesting in itself, but which owes its interest to something else. When you attend to a lecture in mathematics without feeling any interest in it, but only for the purpose of passing the examination, your attention is derived or apperceptive. Immediate attention precedes derived attention. The child attends to an interesting object spontaneously. He learns to attend to uninteresting objects later, when he acquires some control over his will.

James says "Voluntary attention is always derived, for we never make an effort to attend to an object except for the sake of some remote interest which the effort will serve[3]". Non-voluntary attention is in most cases immediate, because it is directed to objects which are interesting in themselves. The distinction between immediate and derived attention is drawn by William James.

IV. Analytical and Synthetical Attention.—Attention is divided into analytical and synthetical attention according to its function. When by attending to an object the mind analyses it into its component factors, the attention is analytical. When you attend to a tree and analyse it into its component parts, e.g., roots, trunk, branches, leaves, etc., your attention is analytical. When by attending to an object the mind combines the component parts or properties of an object into a complex whole, the attention is synthetical. When you attend to the roots, trunk, branches, leaves, etc., and combine them into a complex whole (e.g., tree) your attention is synthetical[4].

## Conditions of Attention

Attention depends upon objective conditions and subjective conditions. These are determinants of attention. They are the factors of advantage in attracting attention.

I. Objective Conditions are the following :—

(1) Strength or intensity of the stimulus.—Other conditions being equal, a strong stimulus attracts attention before a weak one. A bright light attracts our attention easily, but not a faint one. A loud sound attracts our attention more than a faint sound.

(2) Size of visible objects.—In the case of visible objects, a big size has an advantage over a small size. The full moon easily attracts our attention ; but the small stars may escape our attention. The advertiser uses large type to attract the attention of the prospective customers. Full-page or half-page advertisements in the newspaper easily attract our attention. But small advertisements escape our notice. So big posters are used to advertise plays by owners of cinemas, theatres, etc.

(3) Striking quality of the stimulus.—It has a distinct advantage apart from its intensity. Saturated colours attract our attention easily. But pale colours escape our notice. High notes are more attractive than low notes. Sensations of itch, tickle, and pain catch our attention more easily than a sensation of bare contact. The advertiser uses coloured lights and pictures to attract the attention of customers.

(4) Definite form.—A definite form of an object arrests our attention easily. But a vague and indefinite form does

not attract our attention. The full moon which has a definite and regular form easily attracts our attention. But the vast expanse of the sky does not catch our attention.

(5) Change.—If there is a change in the stimulus, it is likely to attract attention. But the change must not be too gradual if it is to be effective ; it must have a degree of suddenness. A steady noise may cease to be noticed after sometime. But a sudden noise is sure to arrest attention. If a noise suddenly drops into a calm, it is sure to attract our attention. But if it gradually subsides, it may escape our notice.

(6) Movement.—Movement involves change. It is a distinct factor of advantage. A moving object easily attracts attention. A motor car or a railway train is more likely to arrest attention while running than when it is standing. Advertisements by means of moving electric lights easily catch our attention. The movements of a hunter easily catch the attention of the wild animals. But if he is perfectly still, he may not be noticed by them. A horse shies if a piece of paper is blown across his path. But he does not shie if it lies in his path[5].

(7) Novelty.—Novelty is a condition of attention. The child is attracted by a new toy, a new coat, a new book, a new tricycle, etc. We are attracted by a new building. When a new teacher is appointed, all students want to see him.

A strange object awakens our curiosity. A Negro in England, or an Englishman in an Indian village, is sure to catch the attention of the people. Sometimes cinema posters are carried by men of multi-coloured dress in order to attract the attention of the people. Strangeness involves an element of newness.

A rare thing is sure to arrest attention. A tourist coming to India is sure to see the Tajmahal, because it is one of the wonders of the world. We attend to a comet, but not to the sun, because the appearance of the comet is a rare phenomenon. The solar eclipse is a rare phenomenon. So it arrests our attention. Rareness also involves an element of novelty.

(8) Duration.—If the stimulus lingers for some time, it is very likely to catch our attention. A song, if continued for a minute, may escape our notice. But if it is continued for fifteen minutes, it is very likely to arrest our attention. But attention cannot be fixed on an object for a long time on account of its monotony.

(9) Repetition.—If a stimulus is repeated, it is likely to draw our attention. You call a man once or twice, it may escape his notice. But if you call out to him several times, he is sure to attend to the call. The teacher repeats the same lesson over and over again to attract the attention of all the students. But too much repetition will cease to attract attention on account of its monotony.

(10) Contrast.—A two-storeyed building in the midst of many one-storeyed buildings is sure to catch our attention. A tall man in the midst of short men easily arrests attention. A brick-built house in a village in the midst of many mud houses with thatched roofs draws our attention.

II. Subjective or mental conditions are the following :—

(1) Interest.—Interest is a main determinant of attention. We attend to those things which interest us. You are interested in games. You will naturally attend to the news of matches in a newspaper. Your friend takes great interest in current politics of India. He will attend to the news of the political affairs of India. A person is interested in vacancies of employments. He attends to advertisements of vacant posts in newspapers. A musician attends to music. A merchant attends to merchandise. An artist attends to pictures. So we should develop a strong interest in an object to which we desire to attend.

(2) Disposition and temperament.—A person of religious disposition and temperament naturally takes a keen interest in religion, and attends to religious discourses. An optimistic person attends to the bright aspect of things. A pessimistic person attends to the dark aspect of things. Thus disposition and temperament determine interest which is a condition of attention.

(3) Instincts.—Attention follows the lead of instincts. A

cat is hungry. Hunger is an instinct. It will lead the cat to attend to mice. You are hungry, and you will attend to bread and rice. A bird attends to the materials of a nest for nest-building before laying eggs. The nest-building instinct compels it to attend to them and build a nest. Thus instincts determine attention.

(4) Emotions.—Attention is determined by emotions. A lover attends to the good qualities only of his beloved. A person attends to the bad qualities only of his enemy. A person in joy attends to the bright aspect of a situation. A person in grief attends to the dark aspect of a situation. Thus emotions determine attention.

(5) Habit.—Habit and education determine attention. A student of Botany attends to peculiarities of plants owing to habit. A student of Zoology attends to peculiar animals. A chemist attends to chemicals. Thus attention is determined by habit.

### Attention and Interest

Attention is the selective activity of the mind. It is a process or function. It is determined by interest. Interest is an affective disposition. It is not an experience. It is an enduring disposition of the mind. McDougall says, "Interest is latent attention ; attention is interest in action[7]". Interest means what 'matters'. It is the enduring mental system that sustains attention. It not only generates the force that makes attention possible, but also sustains attention.

Interest may be either temporary or permanent. Sometimes we speak of interest not as a fleeting process but as a stable condition or bias of the mind. Some have permanent interest in football ; some have such interest in music ; some have such interest in gardening, etc. These permanent interests also determine attention. Not only interest at the moment is a condition of attention, but also a permanent interest determines attention.

Thus interest is a subjective condition of attention. It is always accompanied by attention. If you have interest in music, you are sure to attend to it. The greater is the interest, the greater is the attention. But attention is not always accompanied by interest. We attend to many things in which we do not find any interest. We add up figures in the office, though we do not take any interest in them. Nor is it true that the greater is the attention, the greater is the interest. Attention and interest do not invariably go together. They are not identical with each other. Interest is a condition of attention. But attention is not a condition of interest. Nor is it invariably accompanied by interest.

The object of attention may be related to the subject or mind in different ways. It may further its ends and evoke pleasurable interest in it. Or it may thwart its ends and evoke painful interest in it. The account of a battle may evoke a pleasurable interest in a soldier of an optimistic disposition, who looks for his promotion. The same account may evoke a painful interest in another soldier of a pessimistic disposition, who is overwhelmed by the fear of death.

## Motor Adjustments in Attention : Attentive Attitude

Attention involves certain motor adjustments. First, there is the general attentive attitude. In attention the whole body becomes motionless and is oriented to the object of attention. In sensory attention the whole body is adjusted to the object. When we watch a game, we stand erect, lean forward, crane our neck, and adjust the whole body to the object of attention. In ideational attention also we assume a similar rigid attitude. The body leans forward, the neck becomes stiff, and the eyes gaze at vacancy. The whole body is oriented to the idea attended to.

Secondly, there is the motor adjustment of the sense-organs. In sensory attention there is the adaptation of the sense-organs to the objects. In vision, the eyes converge upon the object, and the lenses are accommodated to the distance of the object. In hearing, the ears are adapted to the sounds. In touch, we explore the object with the hand. In smelling, we inhale in order to bring the odorous particles into contract with the olfactory membrane at the upper part of the nasal cavity. In tasting, we press against the substance in the mouth with the tongue. In all sensations, we adapt the sense-organs to their objects.

In ideational attention also there is slight adaptation of the sense-organs concerned with the objects. If I attempt to recall the image of my house, I find that my eyes tend to turn in the direction of the imagined locality. If I attempt to recall a smell, I tend to make slight movements of breathing. If I attempt to recall a taste, I tend to move the tongue slightly, and my mouth waters.

Thirdly, in sensory and ideational attention both, there are certain inhibitory processes. In very close attention to sensible objects the body remains motionless, breathing is partly arrested, and movements of the body are stopped. These inhibitory processes exclude the disturbing influence of distracting objects, and make attention to the proper object easy.

## Distraction and Attention

When we attend to our task, our attention is often distracted by other things. When we read a book, our attention is diverted to music in an adjoining house or a talk among our friends. Anything that interferes with attention is a distraction. It competes for attention because it has some factors of advantage.

Distraction may be overcome in several ways. First, it may be overcome by throwing more energy into the task. In order to overcome distraction, you may read aloud to drown the distracting noise.

Secondly, it may be overcome by forming a habit of inattention to the distraction which recurs frequently. If you live near a railway station, at first your attention is distracted by the whistle and rattling sound of the running trains. But gradually you become accustomed to these sounds. You cultivate the habit of inattention to them. Do not fix your mind on the distraction. Draw your mind away from it and fix it on your task repeatedly. Thus you form the habit of inattention to a distraction. Thirdly, sometimes distraction may be overcome by linking it with the main task. The beginner at a harmonium finds it difficult to use both hands. When the right hand presses the reeds, the left hands cease to blow. But by practice he can couple both the hands and play upon the harmonium efficiently.

## REFERENCE

[1]*A Beginner's Psychology*, p. 102.
[2]*Psychology*.
[3]*Manual of Psychology*, 1910, p. 629.
[4]*A Brief Text-Book of Psychology*.
[5]Angell, *Psychology*.
[6]Woodworth, *Psychology*, pp. 398-99.
[7]*Outlines of Psychology*.

# CHAPTER VII

## *Sensation*

### The Nature of Sensation

A sensation is the simplest cognition. It is a simple impression produced in the mind by a stimulus. The stimulus acts upon a sense-organ or the peripheral extremity of a sensory nerve ; the impression or nerve-excitation is conducted by the sensory nerve to a sensory centre in the brain ; then a sensation is produced in the mind. This is the case with sensations of colours, sounds, tastes, smells, heat, cold, etc. Stimuli are either external to the organism or within the organism. They are neither extra-organic or intra-organic. Organic sensations of hunger, thirst, fatigue, headache, etc., are produced by the internal conditions of the organism. They have no special sense-organs. Sensations are simple impressions of some qualities. But their meanings are not known. As soon as their meanings are interpreted, they become perceptions. A baby just born will have pure sensations. But adults can never have absolutely pure sensations. They interpret the meanings of sensations and know them to be sensations of qualities (e.g., sounds) of certain objects (e.g., bells) occupying definite portions of space in the external world. But a new-born baby is incapable of interpreting the meanings of sensations. He has pure sensations. But we have no pure sensations. Our sensations at once become perceptions. So pure sensations have a hypothetical existence ; they are abstractions. Ward says, "A pure sensation is a psychological myth.[1]" Sensations are the most elementary raw material of our knowledge. There are no simpler cognitions than sensations.

Woodworth defines sensation as the first response of the brain or the sensory area to a stimulus. A stimulus acts upon the organism which reacts upon it. He expresses it by the formula S—O—R. S—stimulus, O—organism, R—response.

## The Attributes of Sensations

There are certain general distinguishable characters of sensations. They are sometimes called attributes of sensations. Sensations have quality, intensity, duration or protensity, extensity, volume or voluminousness, and local sign, local character, or local signature.

(1) Quality.—Sensations differ in quality. Sensations of colours, sounds, tastes, smells, heat, etc., differ from one another in quality. There is a generic difference among them. They are sensations of different kinds. They have different sense-organs. They are produced by different kinds of stimuli. Sensations of colours are produced by the action of light waves on the retina of the eye-ball. Sensations of sounds are produced by the action of air waves on the auditory organ. Red, green, blue, yellow, etc., differ from one another within the same genus of colour. There is a specific difference among them. Red differs from blue specifically, and from heat and cold generically. In the generic differences of sensations there are different kinds of stimuli, different kinds of sense-organs, and different kinds of sensory or afferent nerves.

(2) Intensity.—Sensations of the same quality may differ in intensity. A light may be dim or bright, a sound faint or loud, a smell mild or strong, a taste weak or strong, a pressure light or heavy. A dim light produces a faint sensation of light. A bright light produces an intense sensation of light. The other conditions remaining the same, greater intensities of stimuli produce greater intensities of sensations.

(3) Duration.—Every sensation has a sensible duration. A sensation may linger in the mind for a certain duration. A sound sensation may last for a shorter or longer duration. This is a difference in duration. Duration is also called protensity or protensive magnitude.

(4) Extensity.—Visual and tactual sensations have extensity. This is admitted by all psychologists. Look at the moon and then at a star. Your first visual sensation has greater extensity than the second. Touch a book with a

finger tip and then with your palm. Your first tactual sensation has less extensity than the second. Extensity is the attribute of a sensation which is due to the area of the sensitive surface affected by a stimulus. Extensity is different from intensity. Put a coin on your skin. Then put another coin beside it. The second tactual sensation will gain in extensity. But put the second coin upon the first coin on your skin. Your tactual sensation will gain in intensity. Extensity is different from extension. Extensity is an attribute of sensations. Extension is an attribute of material bodies. The perception of extension develops out of the extensity of visual and tactual sensations.

William James holds that other kinds of sensations also have extensity. The sensation of loud report of a thunder has greater extensity than the squeaking of a slate pencil. The taste of the solution of quinine in which the tongue is dipped has greater extensity than the taste of a bit of sugar placed on the tip of the tongue. The smell of a bunch of roses has greater extensity than that of a single rose. The pain of cramp all over the body in Influenza has greater extensity than that of a headache. Thus all kinds of sensations have extensity. Extensity is also called volume or voluminousness[2].

(5) Local Sign.—If a person touches your check, forehead and nose successively with the same pencil point with the same degree of pressure, your tactual sensations will differ from one another in local signs. They will not differ in quality or intensity. Local sign is a peculiar attribute which distinguishes a sensation of one part of an extended sense-organ (e.g., skin or retina) from an otherwise identical sensation of another part. It is due to the particular locality of the sense-organ stimulated, while extensity is due to the extent or area of the sensitive surface stimulated. Local sign is also called local signature or local colouring.

Extensity has two peculiarities : (1) A sensation having extensity is made up of a number of simultaneous sensations having different local signs. (2) The constituent sensations form a continuous whole.

## Kinds of Sensations

Sensations are of three kinds: (1) organic sensations, (2) special sensations, and (3) motor or kinaesthetic sensations. Hunger, thirst, fatigue, etc., are organic sensations. Sensations of colours, sounds, tastes, smells, pressures, heat, cold, etc., are special sensations. Sensations of movement are motor sensations. Organic sensations are produced by the conditions of the internal organs of the body. Special sensations are produced by the stimulation of the special sense-organs, viz., the eye, the ear, the tongue, the nose, and the skin. Motor sensations are produced by changes in the organs of movement, viz., muscles, tendons, and joints.

## Organic Sensations

(1) Some organic sensations are not localisable. They are vital feelings, e.g., sensations of comfort or discomfort. They are produced by the general condition of the organism as a whole. These sensations mingle into one total sensation called common sensibility or the coenaesthesis. (2) Some organic sensations are vaguely localisable. Headache, hunger, thirst, etc., are vaguely localisable. Hunger can be vaguely localised in the stomach. Thirst can be vaguely localised in the throat and the palate. Headache can be vaguely localised in the head. (3) Some organic sensations are definitely localisable, e.g., cuts, burns, sores, bruises, etc. They can be localised in particular parts of the body, which are affected.

(1) They have no special sense-organs. They are not produced by external stimuli. They are produced by changes in the internal organs of the organism. (2) They have little cognitive or knowledge-giving value. They do not inform us of anything of the external world. They are 'the barometer of our life process'. They inform us of the sound or unsound condition of the body. (3) They have a tendency to blend into one another. They tend to fuse into a mass. They are not so clearly distinguishable from one another as special sensations are. (4) They cannot be easily revived. It is

very difficult to remember the sensations of hunger, thirst, and fatigue. (5) They are not capable of definite localisation in most cases. Most organic sensations cannot be definitely localised in particular parts of the body. (6) They are important conditions of our pleasure and pain. They have a high degree of affective value. The organic sensations contribute to our pleasure and pain. Bodily comfort and discomfort depend on organic sensations.

### Special Sensations

Sensations of colours, sounds, tastes, smells, temperature, and pressure are special sensations. (1) They have special end-organs or sense-organs, e.g., the eye, the ear, the tongue, the nose, and the skin. (2) They are produced by special kinds of external stimuli. Colour sensations are produced by light waves. Sound sensations are produced by air waves. (3) They are clearly distinguishable from one another. Colours, sounds, smells, tastes, etc., can be distinguished from one another. (4) They are capable of localisation. They can be referred to definite points of space on the body or in the external world. (5) They have great cognitive value. They give us knowledge of the qualities of external objects. (6) They admit of a great variety of kinds and degrees than organic and motor sensations.

### Muscular, Motor, or Kinaesthetic Sensations

Motor sensations are produced by the strain in the muscles, tendons and joints. Their conditions are reported to the brain by sensory or afferent nerves. In motor sensations there is also the compression of the skin. There are sometimes pure tactual sensations of contact. They are often accompanied by organic sensations, e.g., increased circulation of blood, quick breathing, heat, perspiration, fatigue, etc. Sensations of muscles, tendons, and joints contribute important factors to motor sensations. The sensations of the compression of the skin, contact with external objects, and organic sensations of fatigue, etc., accompany motor sensations.

In moving the arm, the skin is pressed in various ways. There are different kinds and degrees of tension in the tendons. The joints slide over one another. There are various degrees of contraction of the muscles. All these tissues are connected with sensory nerves, and contribute to the experience of position and change of position[3]. Sensations of muscles also contribute to the perception of varying position, movement, and tension.

### Value of Motor Sensations

(1) They have a high cognitive value. They give us knowledge of the fundamental properties of matter, e.g., extension, impenetrability, position, distance, and direction of physical things. They are known to be material by virtue of these qualities. So the motor sensations contribute to our knowledge of the external world. (2) They have also a great affective value. Muscular exercise is a source of pleasure and pain. Pleasure of health depends, to a large extent, on the state of the muscles. Moderate exercise of muscles gives us pleasure. Over-exercise or under-exercise of them gives us pain.

### Taste

The stimulus is a liquid substance. Or it is soluble in the saliva of the mouth. It acts upon the taste buds or bulbs within the cavities of the larger papillæ or prominences of the tongue. The taste buds are the proper sense-organ of taste sensations. There is a chemical action between the stimulus and the sense-organ. It is conducted to the brain by the gustatory nerve. Taste sensations are called gustatory sensations.

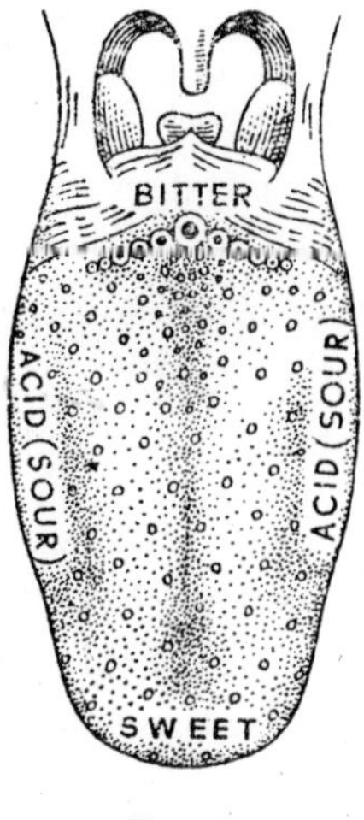

Tongue

Sweet, sour, salt and bitter are the four primary tastes. Wundt adds metallic and alkaline tastes. But the metallic taste is a combination of taste with smell and muscular sensations.

Strong alkalines may make the tongue slippery. They may also produce puckering of the surface of the tongue. So alkaline tastes are combinations of taste with tactual and muscular sensations. The metallic and alkaline tastes are not recognised as primary tastes now. The four primary tastes are sweet, sour, salt and bitter. They cannot be reduced to any simpler tastes. The tip of the tongue is more sensitive to sweet. Its back is more sensitive to bitter. Its sides are more sensitive to sour. Its whole surface is sensitive to salt.

Tastes are mixed with smells in flavours. The flavour of 'polao' is a blend of taste and smell. Juices of onions and potatoes taste alike when their smells are excluded by closing the nostrils. Tastes are mixed with organic sensations of the alimentary canal in relish and disrelish. In disrelish there is a tendency to nausea. Tastes are mixed with touch in tastes of hot and cold. Cold coffee differs from hot coffee in touch, heat and cold. Tastes are combined with pressure sensations. Charged water tastes the same as uncharged water. But the former gives taste sensation combined with pressure sensation, while the latter gives taste sensation only without pressure sensation. Fiery tastes like pepper and mustard are mixtures of tastes with muscular sensations.

There is contrast in tastes. Salt, by a sort of contrast, makes distilled water taste sweet. Sweet tastes sweeter after salt taste. Sweet tea tastes sweeter after tasting salty articles. But salt does not taste more salty after tasting sweet things. Similarly there is contrast between salt and sour, and between sweet and sour. Children taste sour things after taking sweetmeat in order to be able to take more sweetmeat. Bitter does not produce contrast effect. Nor is it affected by contrast.

The sense of taste has a little cognitive value. It gives us little knowledge of the external world. It gives us knowledge of tastes of things. But they are not very important qualities. The sense of taste has a high affective value. It contributes to our pleasure and pain. Tastes can not be revived in memory. It is impossible to remember tastes.

## Smell

The stimulus is some vapour or gas or odoriferous particles carried by the wind. Its organ is a membrane lining the nasal cavity and composed of a layer of cylindrical cells whose outer ends are exposed to currents of air. There is a mechanical or chemical action between the stimulus and the sense-organ. It is conducted to the brain by the olfactory nerve. Smell sensations are called olfactory sensations.

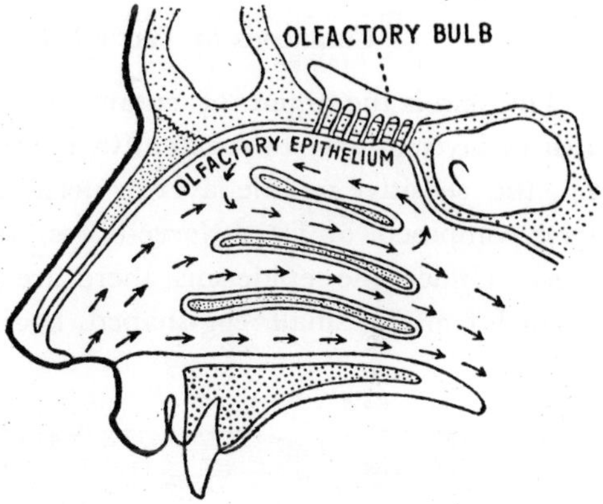

Air-currents thrnogh the nasal cavity

There are six pure sensations of smell : (1) spicy smell, (2) flowery smell, (3) fruity smell, (4) resinous smell, (5) foul smell, (6) and scorched smell. Spicy smell is found in spices. Flowery smell is found in flowers. Fruity smell is found in apples and other fruits. Resinous smell is found in turpentine. Foul smell is found in decaying animal matter. Scorched smell is found in burnt substances. This is not a scientific classification.

Smells are mixed with tastes, e.g., in flavour. They are mixed with touch, e.g., in the smells of snuff, ammonia, etc. They are mixed with organic sensations of the respiratory system, e.g., in choking sensations, etc.

The sense of smell is the oldest sense. It has a prominent feeling tone. It gives pleasure and pain. It is extremely delicate. Camphor can be smelt in a dilution of one part to 40,000 parts of water. Its cognitive value is not very great. Smell sensations are vague and indistinguishable. The sense of smell is easily fatigued. If you continue to smell a good odour or a bad odour for some time, you will cease to perceive it. This is called adaptation. A person living by the side of a drain giving out bad smell fails to perceive it owing to adaptation. Some animals and insects have a keen sense of smell.

## Cutaneous or Tactual Sensations

The skin is the organ of cutaneous sensations. It consists of three layers : (1) the insensitive outer layer or epidermis, (2) the sensitive middle layer or dermis, and (3) the inmost layer composed of fat. Nerve-fibres issue from the middle layer. Under the epidermis there are conical papillae, some of which contain small egg-shaped bodies composed of cells

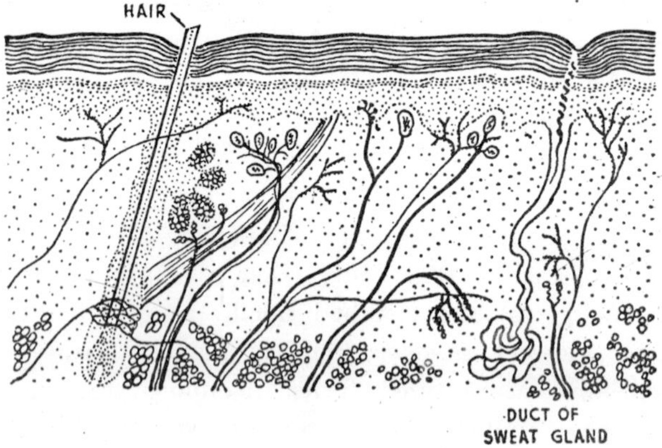


Section of Skin

called touch-corpuscles to which nerve-fibres are attached. There are four distinct organs called cold spots, warmth spots, pain spots, and pressure spots in the skin. If you take a cool blunt-pointed object, like a knitting needle, and explore gently some portion of the skin, such as the back of the hand, you will find that at certain points there flashes out a distinct sensation of cold. They are called cold spots. At other spots nothing but pressure will be felt, and if the pressure be very gentle, no sensation will be felt in many places. If the point be slightly warmed, you will feel warmth sensations at some spots. They are called warmth spots. If a fine broom straw or a horse-hair be substituted for the knitting needle and the skin be explored with a gentle pressure, many spots will yield a distinct cutting pain sensation. They are called pain spots. From some spots will issue sensations of pressure. They are called pressure spots. Cold spots sometimes yield sensations of cold if they are stimulated with slightly warm objects. These are the *'paradox' sensations* of von Frey[4]. The sensation of heat is a blend of warmth and cool. There are no heat spots. Burning hot is probably a combination of warmth, cool and pain.

The tip of the tongue and the tips of fingers are very sensitive to touch ; the cheek and the forearm to heat ; the cornea to pain. A pain spot yields pain sensation, even if it is explored with a cold or hot needle. Cutaneous pain, therefore, is a kind of sensation distinct from the feeling of pain. Pain sensation is different from feeling of pain.

The sense of touch is the primitive sense-organ. The other sense-organs are supposed to have been evolved from it. It has a high cognitive value. It can discriminate different degree of pressure, heat, cold and pain. Active touch, i.e., touch combined with muscular sensations, gives us knowledge of movement, resistance, position, distance, and direction of material objects. Active touch is touch combined with movement. Passive touch or bare contact gives us some knowledge of surface or extension. Active touch gives tactuo-muscular sensations.

## Hearing

The ear is the sense-organ for sounds. The stimulus consists in vibrations of the air. Particles of air are condensed and rarefied alternately, and produce air waves. Any vibrating body can produce air vibrations.

The ear consists of three parts : (1) the external ear or auricle, (2) the middle ear or tympanum, and (3) the internal ear or labyrinth. The external ear gathers the sound waves and transmits them to the middle ear. The sound waves strike the ear drum, called the tympanic membrane, and sets it in vibration. This vibration is conducted by means of three tiny bones, called the hammer, the anvil, and the stirrup, to the membrane at the close of the middle ear. The labyrinth consists of three parts, viz., (i) the vestibule, (ii) the semicircular canals, and (iii) the cochlea. The cochlea contains a membrane called the basilar membrane, on which is seated the organ of corti, consisting of rods and cells. This is the real organ of hearing. The nerve-fibres issuing out of the nerve-cells compose the auditory nerve. The vibration of the membrane at the end of the middle ear sets the membrane in the cochlea into sympathetic vibration. The nerve-cells which are located along the harp of the cochlea translate these vibrations into nerve currents which are conducted by the auditory nerve to the brain. Then sensations of sound are produced in the mind.

Sound sensations are of two kinds, tones and noises. Tones are musical sounds. Noises are non-musical sounds. Tones are produced by regular and periodic air vibrations. Noises are produced by irregular and non-periodic air vibra-

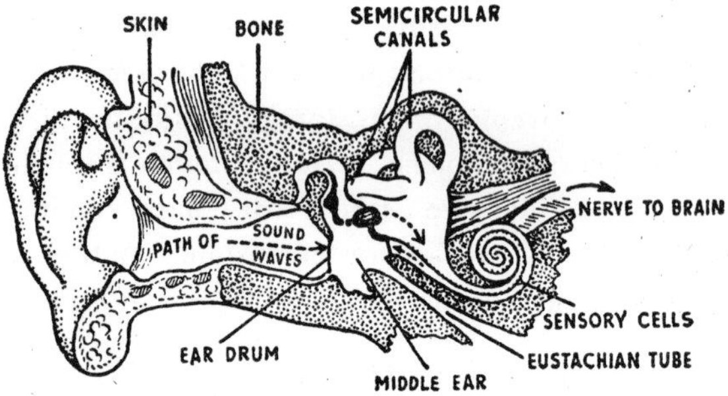


Section of Ear

tions. Tones have pitch, timbre, and harmony or discord. Pitch depends upon the rate or frequency of air vibrations. It depends upon the rate of air vibration. It is determined by the length of the wave. A high note depends upon a short wave length. A low note depends upon a long wave. The greater the number of successive air vibrations striking the drum of the ear in a second, the shorter are the air waves, and the higher is the pitch. The smaller the number of consecutive air vibrations, the longer are the waves, and the lower is the pitch. Timbre is the peculiar quality of a tone produced in a particular musical instrument. A violin, a harmonium, and a piano may all give the same note or pitch with the same loudness, but they have different timbres, and can easily be distinguished by them. Timbre depends upon the complexity of air waves. It is due to the mingling of the fundamental tone (or ground tone) with overtones (or partial tones). Certain tones fuse with one another and produce an agreeable effect in consciousness. This is called harmony or consonance. Other tones refuse to fuse with one another; they are harsh and discordant in their effect upon us. They are disagreeable. They produce discord or dissonance. Loudness or intensity of a sound depends upon the amplitude of air waves; the greater the amplitude, the louder the sound. The volume or extensity of sounds depends upon the area or extent of the sounding object. The roaring of a lion is more voluminous than the voice of a man.

Let us arrange the attributes of sound sensations with their physical antecedents in pairs. Tone—periodic vibration; noise—non-periodic vibration; pitch—vibration rate: timbre vibration composition; intensity or loudness—amplitude of vibration.

The sense of hearing has a high degree of discriminating power. It is probably lacking in local character. It can give us knowledge of succession and help us in perceiving time. It is a great aid to the acquisition of knowledge through language. Its emotive value is very great. The charms of music are derived from it. The semicircular canals in the inner ear are responsible for the sense of balance or equilibrium. They have nothing to do with hearing.

### The Visual Sensations

The eye is the sense-organ for visual sensations. Light waves are the stimuli. The proper sense-organ is the retina within the eye-ball. Light waves act upon the retina, and the photo-chemical action is conducted to the brain by the optic nerve.

The eye-ball is spherical in size. It has three coats. The tough outer coat is called the sclerotic, to which are attached six external muscles that move it. Inside the sclerotic, there is the choroid coat filled with a dense dark pigment. It makes the eye impervious to light except through the cornea and the pupil. Inside the choroid there is the retina made of rods and cones. The retina is the proper sense-organ for vision. There is a round opening in front of the sclerotic, closed by a transparent substance called the cornea. Back of the cornea there is the anterior chamber filled with a liquid called the aqueous humour. Behind it there is the iris, a round black disc with a hole in the centre called the pupil. The pupil contracts and expands to admit more or less light into the eye-ball. In dim light it expands to admit more light; in bright light it contracts to admit less light. Immediately behind the iris there is the double-convex crystalline lens, surrounded by the ciliary muscle and ciliary processes, which accommodate it to objects at different distances. The lens with its attachments constitutes the mechanism of accommodation. Behind the lens there is the large main chamber of the eye, filled with a liquid called the

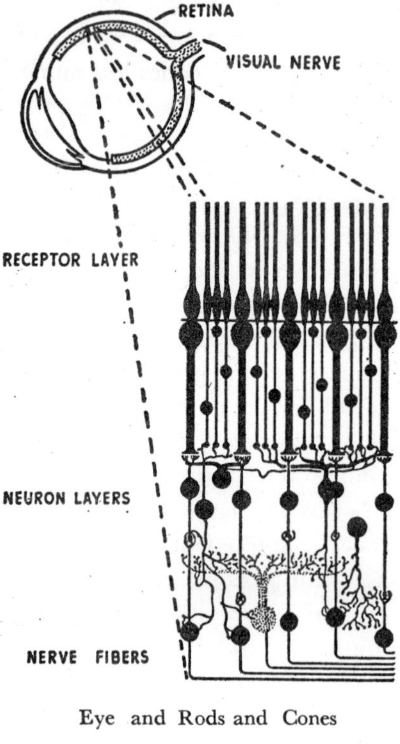

Eye and Rods and Cones

vitreous humour. It fills the cavity between the lens and the retina. Behind it there is the retina. The point of the retina at which the optic nerve enters the eye-ball is called the blind spot, which is insensitive to light. It is devoid of rods and cones. Nearly at the centre of the retina there is the yellow spot, the point of clearest vision. In its centre there is a pit or depression, the *fovea centralis*. In the fovea there are only cones. As one proceeds from the fovea, the rods become more numerous, the cones less numerous, until at the periphery the cones are almost entirely absent.

Light passes through the cornea where it is refracted. Then it passes through the acqueous humour. It is admitted into the inside of the eye-ball through the pupil in the iris. Then it passes through the lens where it is again refracted. Then it passes through the vitreous humour, and finally reaches the retina where it sets up neural changes, which are conducted by the optic nerve to the brain. These sensations of brightness or colours are produced in the mind.

Visual sensations are of two kinds : (1) sensations of brightness, and (2) sensations of colour. Brightness sensations are produced by mixed light waves of various lengths. Pure colour sensations are produced by homogeneous light waves, or waves of practically equal length. The more homogeneous the light waves, the more saturated, the purer, the colour. In fact, we never get colour sensations without brightness sensations also. The intensity of colour sensations depends upon the amplitude of light waves. Light waves are very short vibrations of light. They are waves of electromagnetic energy. They vary in length, in amplitude and in form. Different lengths of waves give us different colour sensations. Variations in the amplitude of waves account for the intensities of the colour sensations. Very often we see several waves of different length or amplitude combined. This combination gives a variation of form of the total wave. The wave form gives us sensations of saturation.

Red, yellow, green, and blue are really elementary colours. Orange is a mixture of red and yellow. Violet is a mixture of blue and red. Purple is a mixture of red and violet.

Peacock is a mixture of blue and green. Two wave lengths are complementary to each other if they act together on the retina and produce a white or grey sensation. Red and blue-green, green and purple, yellow and indigo-blue, orange and green-blue, violet and yellow-green, are complementary colours.

Blue and yellow, red and green, clash with each other. This is called colour contrast. A girl with red hair should not wear a green dress, for the green will make the hair look redder. Yellow and blue appear yellower and bluer respectively, when seen side by side, than when seen apart.

### After-images or After-sensations

There are two kinds of visual after-images, positive and negative. They are due to the prolonged stimulation of the retina after the withdrawal of the stimulus. They should be called after-sensations. If you look at a bright light and quickly look towards a dark surface, you will see a patch of light for some time. This is a positive after-image. The colour of the positive after-image is the same as that of the original sensation, but only weaker in intensity. If you look at a piece of red paper for ten or fifteen seconds and then look at a white wall or paper, you will see a greenish spot of the shape of the red paper. This is a negative after-image. If instead of red paper you use a piece of blue paper, when you look at the white background, you will see a yellow patch. This is also a negative after-image. The colour of a negative after-image is complementary to that of the original sensation. Try looking at a white paper. You will find that the negative after-image will be black.

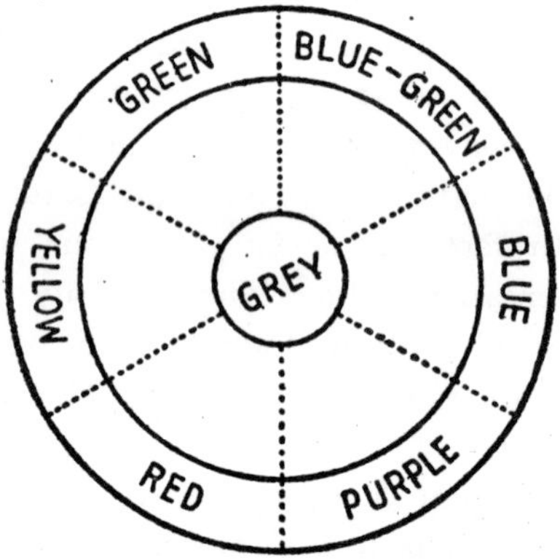

Complementary Colours

## Colour Blindness

Some persons are totally colour blind. They see all colours in terms of their brightness, i.e., as white, grey, or black. They are colour-blind to blue and yellow as well as to red and green. Some persons are partially colour-blind. Most of them fail to see red and green, and combinations of red and green, but can see other colours. Red-green blindness is very uncommon among women. But three or four per cent of men are insensitive to red and green. They have red-green blindness. Blue-yellow blindness is another variety of partial colour-blindness. Some persons are insensitive to blue and yellow.

Different parts of the retina respond to different colours. The central portion of the retina around the fovea is sensitive to all colours. Red and green are only seen accurately for a

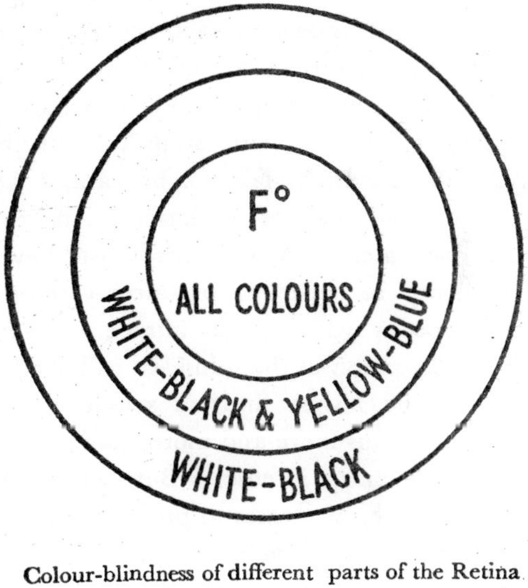


Colour-blindness of different parts of the Retina

short distance outside this region. Yellow and blue are lost next. All colours appear white or grey in the extreme periphery of the retina. These are the different zones of the retina responding to different colours.

## Rod and Cone Vision

Go into a dark room, and at first all seems black to you ; but gradually you begin to see things, because your retina becomes dark-adapted. Come out of the dark room, and your eyes are 'blinded', but gradually your retina becomes light-adapted and you can see distinctly. When your retina becomes dark-adapted in the dark room, you see only light and shade, and no colours. The fovea reacts to all colours. It has only cones. It is devoid of rods. It has the best colour vision. But it cannot become well adapted to dark. It cannot react in very dim light. Vision in very dim light is rod-vision, and not cone vision. The periphery of the retina reacts to very dim light.

## Weber-Fechner Law

Stimuli of various intensities act upon our sense-organs. But we cannot be conscious of all of them. Stimuli of very low degrees of intensity cannot produce sensations in our minds. Similar is the case with stimuli of very high degrees of intensity. An extremely faint light cannot be seen. An extremely faint sound cannot be heard. An extremely faint odour cannot be smelt. A stimulus must have a certain degree of intensity in order to produce a sensation in the mind. The point at which it is intense enough to produce the least intense sensation in the mind is called the limen or threshold. It is the lowest limit of sensation. Increase the intensity of the stimulus more and more, and the sensation will become more and more intense. But when the stimulus becomes very intense, it ceases to produce any sensation, but produces pain. An extremely bright and dazzling light produces acute pain. A very loud sound, extreme heat, and extreme cold produce pain. The point at which a stimulus produces pain is known as the upper limit of sensation. The interval between the limen or threshold and the upper limit or the height of sensibility is called the range of sensibility.

## Weber's Law

Weber, a German physiologist, formulated a law. Between the upper limit and the lower limit or threshold, the greater is the intensity of the stimulus, the greater is the intensity of the corresponding sensation. The intensity of the stimulus must be increased by a constant fraction of it in order to produce an appreciable difference in the intensity of the sensation. The addition to the intensity of the stimulus must be a definite fraction of the original stimulus. In the sensation of pressure 1/20 of the stimulus must be added to the stimulus to produce an appreciable change in the pressure sensation. We must add a whole gram to a weight of 20 grams placed upon the hand, to produce a change in the pressure sensations. We must add 5 grams to a weight of 100 grams to observe a change in intensity of the pressure sensation. In the case of sound sensations, 1/3 of the stimulus must be added to the stimulus to produce a change in the intensity of the sound sensation. In sensation of brightness, 1/100 of the stimulus must be added to the stimulus in order to produce a change in the intensity in the brightness sensation. The same fraction must be added to the stimulus to produce an appreciable change in the intensity of the corresponding sensation. The fractions are constant. They are different in different sensations.

## Fechner's Law

Fechner formulated the law as follows : "To increase the intensity of a sensation in arithmetical progression, the stimulus must be increased in geometrical progression." This is known as Weber-Fechner Law. It means that the stimulus must be multiplied by a constant fraction, in order that the corresponding sensation may increase by the addition of a fixed unit. Suppose $x$ to be the liminal intensity of a sound sensation, 9 to be the intensity of the stimulus (air vibration), 1 to be the least discernible increase of sensation, and 4/3 to be the constant fraction by which the stimulus has to be multiplied in order to increase $x$ by 1. Than in order to produce the intensities of the sensation such as $x+1$, $x+2$, $x+3$, and so on, the intensities of the stimulus must respectively be 12 or $(9 \times 4/3)$, 16 or $(12 \times 4/3)$, and so on. The constant fraction is called the quotient of sensibility.

(1) The law has not been verified in the case of taste and smell sensations. The results are uncertain in the case of temperature. The law has been approximately verified in the case of hearing, sight, pressure, and the muscular sense. (2) The law holds true most accurately in the medium ranges of intensity. The results are quite uncertain towards the upper and lower limits. The sensation increases more rapidly towards the lower limit, and less rapidly towards the upper limit, than is demanded by the law. (3) The law tacitly assumes that the sensation increases by a fixed unit. But this is not true. The addition of 1 gram to 20 grams may not be felt in the same way as the addition of 1 kg. to 20 kg. (4) James and Munsterbeg point out that a strong sensation is not a compound of many weak sensations but an entirely new sensation in quality. In spite of these objections urged by psychologists, the Weber-Fechner law holds good of the relation between stimuli and sensations in their intensities.

## REFERENCE

[1]*Psychological Principles*.
[2]*Brief Text-Book of Psychology*.
[3]*Manual of Psychology*, 1910, pp. 203-04.
[4]*Angell, Psychology*, p. 113.

# CHAPTER VIII

*Perception*

## The Nature of Perception

Perception is the knowledge of objects with their qualities. It consists in the interpretation of sensations. It brings out their meanings. You hear a sound. This is a mere sensation. But when you know that it is a sound as distinguished from colour, taste, smell, etc., and that it is the sound of a bell situated in a particular place in the external world, your sensation becomes perception. Sensation is mere awareness of a quality. Perception is the knowledge of an object with qualities. Sensation is the first impression of something, the meaning of which is not known. Perception is the interpretation of its meaning in the light of past experience.

## Analysis of Perception

(1) Perception consists of sensations and their meanings. It is a combination of many kinds of sensations. Their meanings are known through images of past experiences.

(2) I perceive a mango by combining the sensations of its taste, smell, touch, colour, shape, size, etc., into a unity. I refer them to an object, which occupies a portion of space in the external world, and recall its name. I may perceive some of its qualities, e.g., shape, size, and colour, and remember its other qualities, e.g., smell, taste, touch, etc. I combine these sensations and images into a unity. Thus perception is a combining activity. It gives the knowledge of meaningful objects.

(3) Perception involves association. You look at a white wall. It appears solid to you. You directly perceive its white colour with your eyes. But you cannot perceive its solidity with your eyes. The idea of solidity is suggested to your mind by the perception of white colour by association. You percei-

ved its solidity through touch in the past. You are reminded of it now by association. The visual percept of white colour is associated with the tactual image of solidity. Perception involves implicit memory. Sensation is a presentative process. Its stimulus is present. Memory is a representative process. Its object is absent. Thus perception is a presentative-representative process.

(4) Perception involves recognition. When we perceive an object, we recognize it. We perceive a book and recognize it to be a book. We know it to belong to the class of books. This process is called recognition. Recognition is a fusion of a percept and an image.

(5) When we perceive an object, we perceive it as a whole and react to it as such. When we perceive a chair, we perceive it as a single unit, and not as an aggregate of parts. There is a certain unity of interest in the object, which binds its members into a single whole.

### Sensation and Perception

(1) Sensation is a simple impression produced by a stimulus. It is a presentative process. Perception is the interpretation of sensation. It is a complex mental process. It is a presentative-representative process. Perception is a fusion of sensations and memories or images, which make an indistinguishable whole.

(2) Sensation is an abstraction ; it has a hypothetical existence. We postulate its existence in a small baby. We have no sensations. Our sensations are converted into perceptions. But perception is a concrete experience. Adults have perceptions. A pure sensation is a psychological myth. It is not to be found in adult experience.

(3) Sensations are bare awareness of qualities. The qualities (e.g., tastes, smells, etc.) are not referred to objects by them. Perception is the knowledge of objects. In perception we refer sensations of qualities to external objects. We refer a sound to a bell.

(4) Perception involves apperception. Apperception is assimilation of a new experience to an old experience. In

perception there is fusion of a present experience with a past experience. We perceive an object as belonging to a class. Perception involves recognition. It involves apperception.

(5) In perception the mind is more active than in sensation. In sensation it is not entirely passive. It requires a minimum mental activity in the form of receptivity. In perception the mind is more active, because it has to interpret its meaning.

(6) Both sensation and perception are produced by nerve-currents coming from the periphery produced by external stimuli. In sensation only sensory areas of the brain are stimulated. But in perception sensory areas and association areas are stimulated. Woodworth calls sensation the first response of the brain to a stimulus, and perception, its second response.

## Perception and Attention

Perception is the knowledge of objects in the environment. It is obtained by interpreting the meanings of sensations and referring them to external objects. It compares an object with similar objects and dissimilar objects, and refers it to a particular class. It recognizes an object as belonging to a particular class. These processes involve attention. Without attention perception is not possible.

Attention is preparatory to perception. Attention brings an obsever into the presence of a fact. Perception is grasping or knowing the fact. Grasping presupposes attention. Attention preadjusts a sense-organ to an object. Perception observes and recognizes it. A cat lies in wait for a mouse. She watches it from a distance, adjusts its sense-organs to it and springs upon it. Thus perception involves attention[1].

## Perception and Illusion

Perception is the right interpretation of sensations. Illusion is wrong interpretation of sensations. When we perceive a post as a post, we have perception. But when we perceive a post as a man, we have an illusion. When we mistake one thing for another, e.g., a rope for a snake, a bush for a bear, a patch of moon-light for a ghost, a shell for silver, we have illusions. They are wrong perceptions.

Both perception and illusion are produced by external stimuli. They produce sensations in the mind. They are correctly interpreted by perception, while they are wrongly interpreted by illusion. The fault does not lie in the senses, but in the reaction of the mind.

In both perception and illusion there are sensations produced by external stimuli. Perception is the correct interpretation of them. But illusion is the wrong interpretation of them. There is a wrong reaction of the mind in illusion.

### Causes of Illusion

(1) Some illusions are due to peripheral factors. A vertical line appears to be longer than a horizontal line of equal length, because more muscles of the eye are involved in vertical movements. (Fig. 1.)

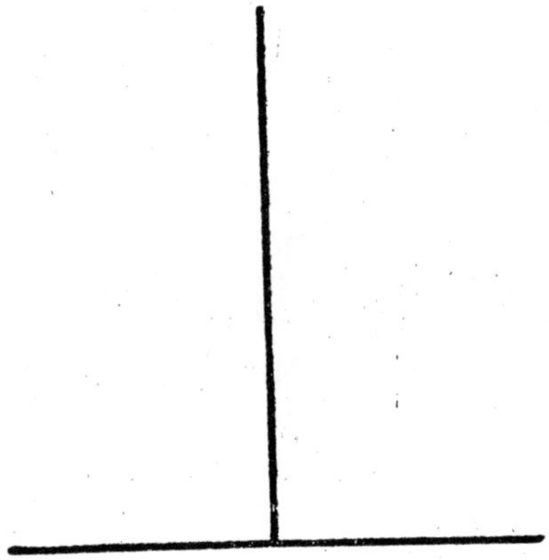

*Fig. 1.*

(2) Contrast is the cause of many illusions. A tall man appears taller by the side of a short man. A dark person appears darker by the side of a white man. Red beside blue appears different from red beside yellow. A sound appears to be much louder in the midst of perfect calm.

(3) Some illusions are due to the defects of the sense-

organs. A white object appears yellow to a person whose eyes are affected by jaundice. Sugar appears bitter to a person who suffers from fever.

(4) Some illusions are due to the central interpretative factors. Habit is the cause of some illusions. We are apt to read the word 'mispirnt' as 'misprint' owing to habit. Proof-reader's illusions are due to habit. Expectation is the cause of some illusions. You eagerly expect a friend to join a dinner in your house. You are apt to mistake any man who comes for your friend. Anxiety or fear is the cause of some illusions. At night a timid householder hears the sound of house-breaking and hears the burglars pass from room to room. Other sounds are wrongly interpreted by the anxious householder. Illusions of this sort are readily induced by recency of similar experience. If a theft has recently been committed in the house, the nervous householder will easily be a victim of illusions. If a terrible earthquake has happened recently, any kind of tremor produced by a moving bus will be mistaken for an earthquake. Imperfect isolation of the fact to be perceived is a source of some illusions. Many optical illusions are of this type. A figure is so drawn as to make it difficult to isolate the fact from other irrelevant facts. Of two equal straight lines, the one ending in feather-heads appears greater than the other ending in arrow-heads. (Fig. 2). Two parallel lines

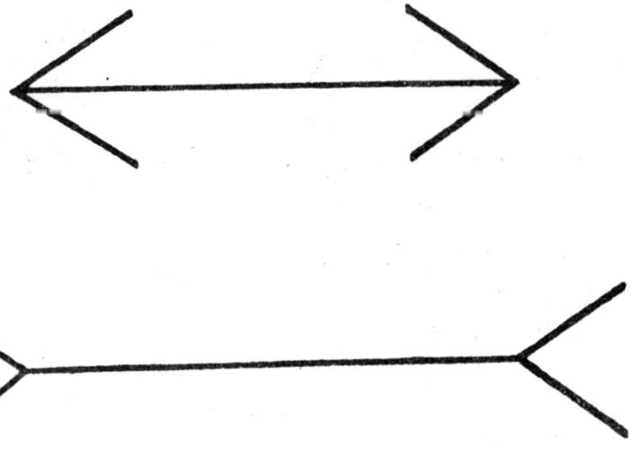

*Fig. 2.*

appear to bulge in the presence of the other irrelevant lines. (Fig. 3). The lower figure appears shorter and thicker, though

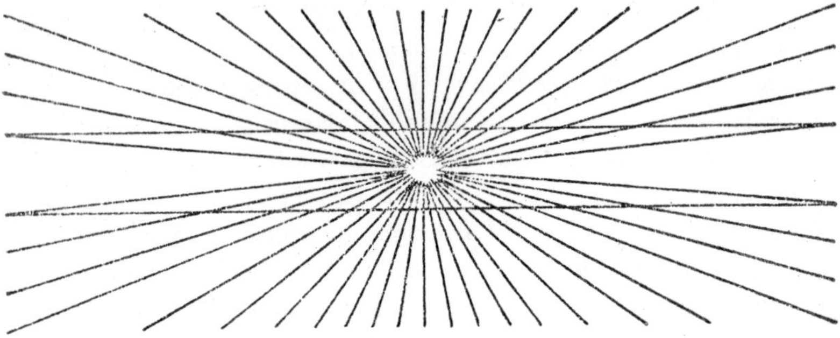

*Fig. 3.*

they are equal. (Fig. 4). The lower figure appears to be smaller than the upper one, though they are equal. (Fig. 5).

The two oblique lines appear to be parts of the same

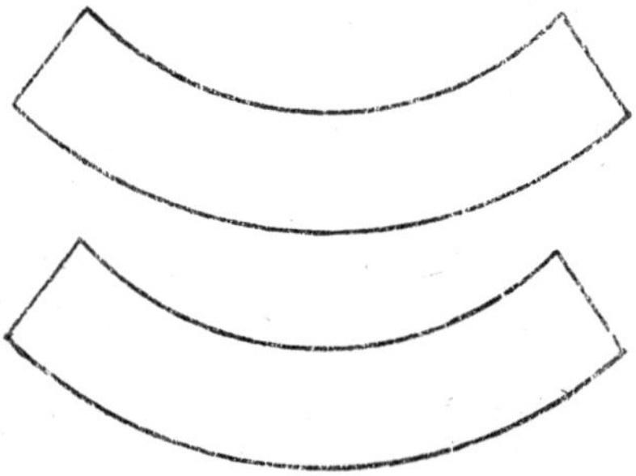

*Fig. 4.*

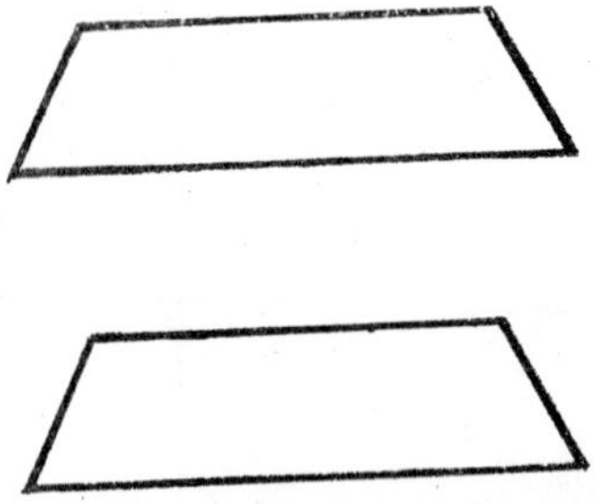

*Fig. 5.*

straight line. (Fig. 6). The long lines are really parallel. But they appear not to be so in the presence of the irrelevant lines.

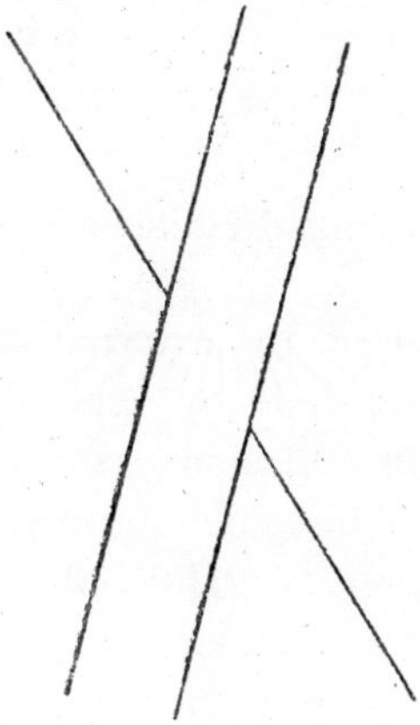

*Fig. 6.*

(Fig. 7). Here illusions are due to total impressions which are not analysed. These optical illusions are common to all persons. But illusions due to central factors are not common to all.

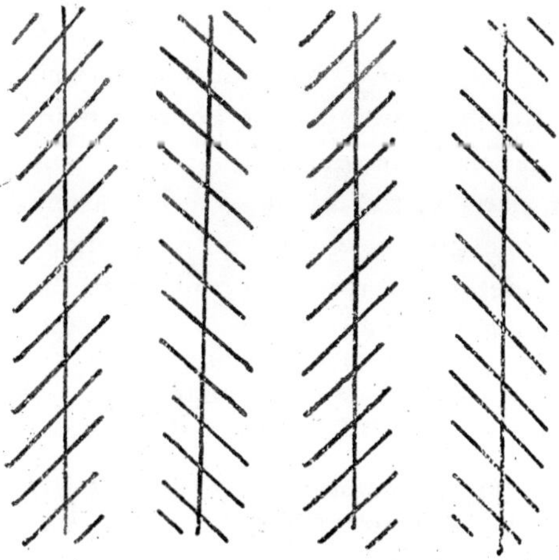

*Fig. 7.*

The size-weight illusion also is of this type. Take two round wooden boxes, one several times as the other, and load them so that both weigh the same. Then lift them. You will feel the smaller box as the heavier one, much heavier than the other.

## Illusion and Hallucination

Illusions are produced by external stimuli, while hallucinations are not produced by them. Hallucinations are centrally excited, while illusions are peripherally excited. Hallucinations are called by some subjective perceptions without any basis in external objects. Hallucinations are vivid images which are projected upon the external world, and appear to be external objects actually perceived. Hallucinations do not occur in the normal condition of the mind. In high fever or delirium the highly excited brain produces hallucinations of non-existent things and persons. A murderer is sometimes a victim of an hallucination. He sees the ghost of the murdered person pursue him. Or, he hears his voice threatening to murder him. Hallucinations are common phenomena in mental disorders.

## Perception of Figure and Ground

The Gestalt psychology has made an important contribution to perception by distinguishing between figure and ground. In visual perception we perceive an object as a figure in a ground. We perceive the moon as a whole object, a figure, a gestalt, in the background of the sky. The indefinite sky is the ground. The definite form of the moon is the figure. The figure is a compact whole. It has a definite form. It attracts attention. It is prominent in consciousness. The group is vague, indefinite, devoid of a regular form. We perceive a white figure in a blackboard, which is its ground.

The white portion appears to be a lamp in a black background. The black portions appear to be two human faces in a white background. (Fig. 8).

In tactual perception also we distinguish between figure and ground. We perceive an ant creeping on the skin as a figure in the background of a mass of indistinct tactual sensations.

In auditory perception also we distinguish between figure and ground. We perceive the beat of a drum as a figure in the background of a mass of indistinct sounds.

When a baby is born, his mind is not a chaos of confused sensations. He feels certain sensations distinctly in the background of a mass of indistinct sensations. He sees a patch of light on the wall. He perceives light as a figure in the background of the wall.

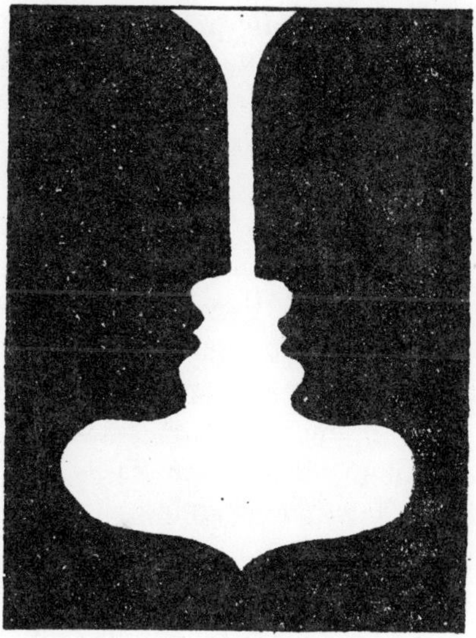

*Fig. 8.*

The Gestaltists do not regard perception as a complex of sensations associated with one another. That was the doctrine of the Associationists. The Gestalt psychologists regard perception as experience of a whole, a gestalt, a figure, or a pattern. Perception of an object is not experience of an aggregate of its parts. A tree is perceived as a whole. A person is perceived as a unit. A chair is perceived as one thing. It is not perceived as legs+back+arms+seat. Perception is a whole experience. It is experience of a whole object.

### Laws of Perception : Factors of Advantage in Perception

Perception involves attention. Attentive perception is called observation. Observation is selective. Perception is subject to the law of selection. It is subject to the law of combination.

We see groups more easily that isolated units. At night when we look at the sky, we group together certain stars into certain patterns. It is easier to perceive them in groups than as separate units. Perception is subject to the law of advantage. We perceive some objects more easily than others. Some factors of advantage in perception are the following :

(1) Proximity.—Proximity is favourable to perception. Among irregular dots we really perceive the dots, which are close to one another, and form them into groups.

(2) Similarity.—If dots are of different colours, dots of the same colour are perceived as a group. If triangles, circles, and squares are mixed up together, triangles are perceived as one group, circles as another group, and squares as a different group.

(3) Inclusiveness of a pattern.—If some parts readily fall into a pattern, they are perceived easily as a group. The parts which do not fall into a pattern are left out. Groups are more easily perceived than separate elements.

(4) Familiarity.—A familiar object among a collection of unfamiliar objects can easily be perceived. We easily perceive a familiar face in a crowd of strangers. We easily hear a familiar vice in a confused medley of unknown voices.

(5) Set or Readiness.—If a person is set or prepared to see a particular thing, he will easily perceive it when it comes. If he is set to hear a particular sound, he will easily hear it when it appears. When we are ready to perceive a star at night, we can easily perceive it, though it is very faint.

Thus proximity, similarity, inclusiveness of a pattern, familiarity, and readiness are factors of advantage in perception. It involves selection and combination, which are facilitated by these factors.

### Perception of Space or Extension

Space means extension. It consists of two factors, material and formal. Plurality of co-existent, resisting points constitute its material factor. The order and arrangement among them constitute its formal factor. We perceive extension through the co-operation of three factors: (1). extensity, (2) local signs, and (3) movement. The extensity of visual or tactual sensations gives us a presentation of a plurality of co-existing, resisting points together. Local signs of visual or tactual sensations inform us that they are different from one another. Through active movement we perceive the order and arrangement among the different resisting points co-existing with one another. Thus movement converts extensity into extension.

### Tactual Perception of Space or Extension

Let us see how these three factors co-operate with one another in the blind man's tactual perception of space. The blind man touches an extended object, e.g., a table with one or both hands simultaneously. But he does not move his hands. This bare contact is called passive touch, because it does not involve active movement from one part of an object to another. Stout calls it synthetic touch, because it yields a total simultaneous impression of all or many parts of the object. Through the extensity of tactual sensations the blind man perceives all or many parts of the object simultaneously. When his palms are in bare contact with the table, the different parts of his palms are stimulated by different parts of the table, so that the tactual sensations produced by them have different local signs. Thus through the local signs of the tactual sensations he perceives the different parts of the table as different from one another. Then he moves his finger-tips from one part of the table to another in various ways. Through the active movement of his finger-tips he perceives the distance, direction and position of the different parts of the table. This is called active touch, because it essentially consists in active movement. Stout calls it analytic touch, because it analyses an extended whole perceived by synthetic touch into a series of successive impressions. Thus the perception of spatial order is due to the intimate union and co-operation of synthetic and analytic touch with a unity and continuity of interest. Neither passive touch nor active touch alone suffices[2].

### Visual Perception of Space or Extension

Extensity, local signs, and movement co-operate with one another in visual perception of space also. Here passive sight co-operates with active sight. Passive sight corresponds to passive touch, and active sight corresponds to active touch. You look at the stars at night in the sky with fixed eyes. You see many stars together. The extensity of visual sensations informs you that there are many stars co-existing together. When you look at the stars, different stars stimulate different parts of the retina. Through the local signs of the visual sensations you perceive that the stars are different from one another. Then by movement of your eye-balls or active sight you perceive the distance, direction and position of the stars. Thus you perceive the order and arrangement among the stars by active sight. Passive sight in co-operation with active sight, guided by unity of interest, yields the perception of spatial order or extension.

Generally, visual perception of space and tactual perception of space co-operate with each other in normal life. Our actual perception of space or extension is due to the co-operation of sight and touch. Our perception of space is different from a born blind man's perception of space. His perception of space is tactual.

### Tactual Perception of Distance (or Space of the Third Dimension)

By active touch or movement we can perceive distance directly. We can perceive a small distance by stretching out our hands or legs. We can perceive a long distance by walking or running. This is called active touch or movement. It contains two factors, viz., (1) tactual sensations and (2) muscular or motor sensations. Through active touch or tactuo-muscular sensations we can perceive distance directly.

### Visual Perception of Distance (or Space of the Third Dimension)

We can perceive distance by active touch directly. We

cannot perceive it directly by vision. Vision gives us certain visual signs or cues by interpreting which we can perceive distance. Thus we have an acquired visual perception of distance. We cannot directly perceive distance by vision, because the eye-ball cannot run out of its socket to measure distance, and because the objects in the same line of vision placed at different distances affect the same part of the retina.

The Monocular Factors.—The visual signs for longer distances are following :—

(1) Aerial perspective or clearness of outline.—If the outlines of an object are clear and distinct, it is near. But if its outlines are vague and hazy, it is distant. But if the atmosphere is foggy, even a near object appears to be faint and indistinct.

(2) Superposition.—The distant object is partially covered by nearer objects. When we see the outline of a house broken by the interference of another, we see the former to be farther away. Thus superposition is a visual sign of distance.

(3) Shadows and Shading.—The distribution of light and shade is an important visual sign for distance. The lighted portion of a picture appears nearer, and the shaded portion appears farther. If a picture is shaded properly, we actually see the objects as at different distances.

(4) Mathematical perspective.—If the real size of an object is known, we can judge distance from its apparent size or magnitude. When we fly a kite, it appears smaller and smaller as it soars higher and higher into the sky. The nearer an object, the larger it appears ; the more remote it is, the smaller it appears.

(5) Relative motion.—When we move, things which are near us appear to move more rapidly than things which are farther away. Hence we can judge distance from the apparent relative motion of objects when we ourselves are moving. When we move in a running railway train, the things near us appear to move very rapidly in the opposite direction, but the distant objects appear to move slowly.

The Apparent Convergence of lines known to be paralled.—The greater the distance, the greater the apparent convergence of the lines known to be parallel. The straight railway lines appear to converge more and more as the distance becomes greater and greater.

Accommodation.—The lens of the eye-ball is accommodated to different distances by the ciliary muscle and processes within it. The nearer the distance, the greater the convexity of the lens ; and the greater the distance, the less the convexity of the lens. The different degrees of tension of the ciliary muscles and processes suggest different distances.

II. The Binocular Factors :—Binocular Vision.

(1) Convergence.—We can converge our eyes on a single object by means of the six muscles attached to them from the outside. The nearer the object, the greater the convergence of the eyes. The greater the distance (up to a certain limit), the less the convergence of the eyes. Thus different degrees of tension of the external muscles of the eyes involved in convergence suggest different distances.

(2) The Disparity of Retinal Images.—The nearer the object, the greater the disparity of the retinal images and the greater the strain in fusing them into one. The greater the distance, the less the disparity of the retinal images and the less the strain in fusing them into one. These are the visual signs by interpreting which we perceive distance through vision.

## Perception of Time

We perceive events or changes in the framework of time. The perception of time is not possible without that of changes. Changes occur in succession and last for some duration of time. We perceive time as duration or block of time. We do not perceive the present as a mathematical moment but as a span of time with an extension, as it were. William James calls it the "specious present". It contains "an echo of the immediate past and a foretaste of the immediate future."

The Apparent Convergence of lines known to be parallel. (p. 94)

When we perceive an action (e.g., a dinner) taking place, we perceive it to be present. When an action is over, we perceive it to be 'no more' or past. When an action is not yet begun, we perceive it to be 'not yet' or future. Thus we perceive the immediate past and the immediate future.

We know the past by memory and the future by imagination. We cannot perceive the past and the future.

Succession of events or changes helps us perceive time. Time filled with a few events is perceived to be short. Time filled with many events is perceived to be long.

We have a pysiological sense of time. We can perceive the passing of time through rhythmic activities in our bodies. Breathing, hunger, thirst, etc., help us perceive the passage of time.

### Direct Perception and Acquired Perception

Touch a bit of ice. You perceive its coldness. This is direct perception. See it with your eyes. It looks cool. This is acquired perception. You cannot directly perceive coolness with your eyes. You perceived the coolness of ice in the past through touch. Now, when you see a bit of ice, the sight of it suggests to you the idea of coolness which you perceived through touch on previous occasions. The visual percept is complicated by the suggested tactual image. Stout calls it complication. Sully calls it indirect or acquired perception. Here an implicit idea is tied to a percept. Look out of your window in the morning. The ground looks wet. But you cannot directly perceive its wetness through vision. The ground gives you certain visual signs. You interpret their meanings in the light of your past tactual perception of wetness. Thus your visual perception of wetness is acquired.

We have acquired visual perception of distance, solidity, movement and magnitude, which are suggested by vision.

### Perception and Apperception

The term 'apperception' has been taken in different senses by psychologists. We take it in the sense in which Herbart understood it. "Apperception is the process by which a mass of presentations (apperception-mass) assimilates relatively new elements, the whole forming a system (apperception-system)." It means understanding a new experience in the light of old experience or incorporating new material of knowledge in the system of knowledge already acquired. Perception of a new thing is possible when it is assimilated to the stock of ideas already possessed by the mind. Perception involves the synthesis of a new experience with an old experience. Thus perception involves apperception.

## REFERENCE

[1] *Manual of Psychology,* pp. 256-57.
[2] *Ibid, 1932,* pp. 450-64.

# CHAPTER IX

## *Memory*

### Perception and Memory

Perception is the apprehension of a present object. Memory is the apprehension of an object of past experience. You perceive the book you are reading. You remember the school in which you read in the past.

Perception is the interpretation of sensations produced by external stimuli. It is a presentative process. But memory is the process of remembering objects of past experience. Memory or remembering is a representative process. Perception is produced by external objects acting on the sense-organs. But recollection is not produced by external objects. You read a poem a number of times. This process of learning is perception. But when you remember it later, you have memory or recollection of the poem learnt in the past.

### Factors in Memory

Memory is recollection of a thing perceived or learnt in the past and retained in the mind. Recollection is revival of a past experience. It is recall, re-instatement or reproduction of a past experience. Memory consists in reviving past experience, which has been retained in the mind in the form of a subconscious impression.

It is exact reproduction of the contents of our past experiences in the same form and order. It does not consist in the rearrangement of past experiences in a different order, which is called imagination. Remembering depends on retention; retention depends on previous learning.

Remembering involves the following factors :—

(1) Learning.—We learn a lesson a number of times, repeat it for a few days, understand its meaning, relate it to

other lessons, and impress it deeply on the mind. Learning consists in observing, and repeating a thing, understanding its meaning, and forming associations in the mind. The things learned are registered in the brain as physiological dispositions and in the mind as mental dispositions. Their nature is not definitely known.

(2) Retention.—Perception is an event or experience ; its recall is another event or experience ; but what is retained is a disposition, not an experience. When we learn a lesson repeatedly with attention, it leaves a subconscious trace in the mind in the form of a mental disposition, and it also leaves a mark on the plastic brain in the form of a structural modification called physiological disposition. Thus past experiences are retained in the subconscious level of the mind as mental dispositions. Corresponding to them there are structural modifications of the brain also. But the brain cannot be said to be the repository of past experiences. The fact of retention can be proved by recall. We can recall those things which we learned and have retained in the mind. Recall presupposes retention. Past experiences are retained in the mind not as isolated functions but as members of an organised structure. Retention is sometimes called conservation.

Forgetting during sleep is slower than during activity in waking condition. Memory traces settle down when the mind is more inactive during sleep. Or, there are no activities during sleep, which may interfere with memory traces. Hence sleep or rest facilitates retention.

(3) Recall or Reproduction.—Remembering consists in the recall or revival of past experiences. It is re-instatement or reproduction of past experiences in the same order. It consists in bringing to the level of consciousness the subconscious traces of past experiences. You learnt a lesson in the past ; it has been retained in your mind ; now you call it back to the level of consciousness. This process of ideal revival is recall or reproduction. Retention is a prior condition of recall. It is inferred from the fact of recall. If past experiences are not retained in the mind, they cannot be recalled

afterwards. Thus retention and recall are the two important factors in memory.

(4) Recognition.—You see your old class-fellow after a long time. You recognise him to be your class-fellow, who read with you in a Junior High School. Recognition is the feeling of familiarity which accompanies the revival of past experiences. It is a fusion of a percept and an image. The object of recognition is present to the senses. Definite memory must involve definite recognition. And definite recognition involves temporal localisation. It consists in remembering the time and place of the original past experience. Sometimes memory involves indefinite recognition. It is the sense of familiarity not accompanied by the revival of the time and place of the original experience. You see a person; his face appears familiar to you; but you cannot remember where and when you saw him. In indefinite recognition the past associations tremble on the verge of consciousness, but they connot be recalled to the level of consciousness. Recognition distinguishes memory from imagination. It depends upon association and the sense of familiarity. Recognition gives us a feeling of relief which is pleasant.

Complete memory involves definite recognition; it involves temporal localisation. The past experience which is revived is referred to a particular time in the past. Definite recognition involves the recollection of the time and place of the origin of the memory image. This is called temporal localisation. Memory refers to the past time. This mark distinguishes memory from expectation which refers to the future time.

## Methods of Memorising

Experiments have shown that the following methods are economical of time in learning:

(1) The Part and the Whole Learning.—If a long poem of 240 lines has to be memorised, children will show better results by the part method of learning. They are discouraged by the length of the material to be learnt. So they divide

the material into different parts, and learn them one after another. They first learn the first stanza, then the second stanza, then the third stanza, and so on. If some stanzas are difficult, they should be first committed to memory, and then the other stanzas should be memorised one after another. Children do better by this sectional method. This method is good for immediate memory.

But adults show better results by the whole method. They should learn the whole poem a number of times till they master it thoroughly. This entire method is good for permanent memory, because it is favourable to intelligent understanding of the material.

(2) Spaced Learning and Unspaced Learning.—Experiments have shown that spaced learning is better and more economical of time than unspaced learning. Spaced learning is learning with some interval of time. Unspaced learning is learning without any interval of time. Some time is required for ideas to settle down in the mind. Rest is needed for the formation and deepening of associations of ideas. So spaced learning is better than unspaced learning. The rate of forgetting just after learning is more rapid than that after longer intervals. So it is better to revise the lesson learnt for some days continuously for some time, and then at longer intervals. Spaced learning is good for permanent memory. Unspaced learning is good for immediate memory.

(3) Recitation.—Recitation is an economical method of memorising. Learn a lesson a number of times, close your book, and then recite the matter to yourself. If you cannot remember a part of it, look at it, and then recite it again. Recitation is good for permanent memory. It shows what parts of the material have been mastered, and what parts require closer attention to be mastered. Recitation, if it is successful, gives satisfaction to the individual. If it is unsuccessful, it gives dissatisfaction to him. Therefore the Law of Effect, reward and punishment, operates in recitation.

(4) Unintelligent Learning and Intelligent Learning.—Unintelligent learning consists in mechanical repitition of a material without understanding its meaning. It is rote learn-

ing or cramming. Childrn generally learn poems by cramming. Rote learning or cramming is good for immediate memory. It is not good for permanent memory. Many students, who have no interest in education, cram answers to certain selected important questions just before the examination, and forget them entirely after the examination is over. So cramming is not useful. The matter crammed up does not set in the mind. It is not incorporated in the system of knowledge. It remains in the mind for some time only as undigested material of knowledge. But cramming is not entirely useless. Rules of grammar in a foreign language, multiplication tables, and such other material of knowledge can be memorised by cramming only.

Intelligent learning consists in learning a material with the understanding of its meaning. When the meaning of a passage is understood thoroughly, and it is repeatedly learned intelligently, it is deeply impressed in the mind, retained for a long time, and can be recalled easily afterwards. The matter learned intelligently is incorporated in the system of knowledge. So it can be retained in the mind for a long time. Intelligent learning is good for permanent memory.

(5) Intention to Remember.—The individual, who wants to memorise a material, must learn and repeat it with the intention to remember it. Then only he will be able to retain it in the mind, and recall it. If he has no intention to remember it, he will not pay close attention to it, and will therefore fail to retain and recall it effectively. The intention to remember involves greater attention, and therefore it is more effective in memorising. Witnesses in a law suit cannot remember trifling details of a matter of dispute, which happened long ago, because they did not pay attention to them, when they perceived them in the past, with the intention of remembering them long afterwards. The intention to remember is necessary for learning a matter effectively.

## Overlearning

If a material can be learned by reciting it 20 times, it is overlearned by 50 per cent if it is recited 30 times. Overlearned material is forgotten slowly. **Material** learned minimally is quickly forgotten. If a skill is to be performed in public, it should be overlearned to prevent its being blocked by stage fright, anxiety, or distraction. Overlearning is a factor of advantage for easy recall.

### Conditions of memory

Memory involves two main factors :—(1) Retention and (2) Recall or Reproduction. Hence the conditions of memory are the conditions of retention and reproduction.

1. Conditions of Retention and Association.

(A) Physiological Condition.—The plasticity of the brain is a condition of retention. William James holds that the brain is the receptacle of past experiences. He does not believe in subconscious ideation. We do not deny that corresponding to subconscious ideas there are structural modifications of the brain. Some persons have a very plastic brain ; others have a less plastic brain. Plasticity means modifiability. Persons are born with particular types of brain. If their brains are very plastic, they have greater power of retention. If their brains are not plastic, they have less power of retention. Fatigue is unfavourable to retention.

(B) Physical conditions : (1) Intensity of the stimulus.—An audible sound, a bright light, etc., produce deep impressions on the mind, and these can be retained for a long time. A faint light, a faint sound, and the like cannot be retained for a long time.

(2) Clearness and distinctness of the stimulus.—A confused mass of colours cannot produce a distinct impression ; so it cannot be retained in the mind. But clear and distinct pictures produce distinct impressions which can be retained easily.

(3) Duration of the stimulus.—A musical sound which lingers for a few seconds cannot produce a deep impression on the mind and so cannot be retained. But a song which continues for some time produces a deep impression and can be retained.

(4) Frequency.—If a song is repeated many times, it can be retained. We learn a poem a number of times and retain it. The teacher repeats a lesson many times and the students retain it easily. But repitition without attention is not very effective.

(5) Recency.—The impression of a recent experience can be retained. The impression of an experience in the distant past may fade and be wiped off.

(C) Mental Conditions : (1) Attention.—If you pay close attention to your lesson, it will produce a deep impression, which will be retained for a long time, and recalled easily afterwards. The greater the attention paid to the original experience, the greater the power of retention. If you closely attend to your lessons, you can retain them easily. The physical conditions of retention are the conditions of attention as well. Thus attention is a condition of retention.

(2) Interest.—Interest is a condition of attention. So it is a condition of retention also. If you have deep interest in psychology, you can retain the lessons easily. If you do not find any interest in it, you cannot retain your impressions of it for a long time. Therefore interest is a condition of retention.

(3) Intention to remember.—When we learn a lesson with the intention to remember it, we can retain it. Many details of our past experiences cannot be remembered, because we did not intend to remember them. Witnesses cannot remember insignificant details of a past event, because they did not carefully take note of them.

(4) Apperception.—Apperception is a logical understanding of a subject. If you thoroughly understand a subject and the logical connection among its different parts, you can retain it easily. But a subject which is not understood thoroughly cannot be retained for a long time. Therefore cramming is not very useful.

(5) Massive experience.—The more massive an experience is, the more it affects the whole personality, the more it is retained. Everybody remembers his experience which affects his whole personality. For example, nobody can forget his interview with a great man like Mahatma Gandhi.

II. Conditions of Reproduction:—

(1) Conditions of retention.—Recall depends upon retention. So conditions of retention are also conditions of reproduction.

(2) Psycho-physical condition.—A healthy, fresh and vigorous condition of the body and mind is favourable to recall of past experience. The body and mind must be fresh and healthy both at the time of learning and at the time of recall. Fatigue is unfavourable to retention as well as reproduction.

(3) Cue and bonds of association.—Impressions were associated in the past experiences. Bonds of association have been established among the subconscious traces of past experiences. Hence the recall of past experiences depends upon an appropriate percept, idea, or cue with which they were associated in the original experience. The sight of the school in which you read will bring back many delightful recollections of your past experiences to your mind.

(4) Influence of the context.—Associated ideas belong to more or less related trains of ideas. The entire context determines which of several possible ideas will be revived at a particular time. If the idea 7 times 9 bobs into your consciousness, it is promptly followed by the idea 63. If, however, 4 times 9 comes to your mind, it is followed by the idea 36. Which idea will be recalled depends upon the context.

(5) Particular disposition at the time of revival.—An idea reminds us of different ideas under the influence of different contexts. The sight of a photo may remind you of the person whom it represents, or the photographer, or the person who presented it to you according to your dominant interest at the moment. The sight of a book may remind you of its author, its publisher, its price, or its contents according to the dominant trend of your mind.

## Good Memory

Quickness of learning, permanence of retention, promptness and accuracy of recall, and its serviceableness or relevance to purpose are the marks of good memory.

Some persons can learn quickly ; but they quickly forget.

This is not a blessing. Some persons are slow to learn, but can retian things for a long time. This is better. Some persons can remember things when they are not needed. Others can remember accurately when they are needed. Serviceableness is an important mark of good memory. The minds of some persons are packed with all sorts of information, but they cannot call up any of them when needed.

## Kinds of Memory

(1) Personal and Impersonal Memory.

In personal memory the facts learnt in the past are recalled together with many other personal details. When you recall your first visit to a big town, you recall many of your personal experiences in connection with the town. This is personal memory. But in impersonal memory only a fact is remembered but not along with other personal details. When you remember the fifth theorem of Euclid, you do not recall the particular incidents connected with the process of acquiring the knowledge of it. So it is impersonal memory.

(2) Rote Memory and Logical Memory.

Mechanical repetition of an experience without intelligent understanding is called rote memory. It is cramming. It does not involve understanding. A boy mechanically recites a poem again and again, and commits it to memory. This is rote memory. Logical memory depends upon intelligent understanding of the material learned. It does not depend upon mere repetition. This is also called association memory. A boy thoroughly understands a theorem of Geometry and reads it a number of times. He can easily retain this knowledge and reproduce it when needed. This is logical memory.

## Types of Memory Images

Persons differ in the way they remember past experiences. Some remember the visual image of blue water of the sea. Some remember the auditory image of its roar. Some remember the tactual image of the feel of its water. Others remember the motor image of wading through its water or swimming in it. Few can remember tastes or smells. Some have affective images. They remember their emotions.

### Percept and Memory Image

Stout states the following points of difference between percepts or impressions and memory images.

(1) Fragmentariness of Image.—When you perceive a mango, you see its colour, form, size, etc., taste it, smell its flavour, and touch it. These actual sense-experiences form an inseparable whole. But when you remember the mango, you call up its visual image only, and do not remember the images of other sensations. Thus a memory image is fragmentary ; it is cut off from its context in the original experience. Only a part of the original perception is recalled in a memory image.

(2) Intensity.—Percepts are more intense than memory images. Some hold that images are faint copies of original percepts. They differ in intensity or degree. The image of a mango is fainter than the percept of it. But this is wrong. Images differ in kind from percepts. Percepts are aggressive ; they are thrust upon the mind from without. But memory images are not aggressive ; they do not break in upon the mind and disturb the flow of consciousness. They are evolved from within the mind.

(3) Distinctness.—A percept is full and detailed while an image is sketchy and lacking in detail. Percepts are distinct. You perceive a rose ; your percept is clear and distinct. You can distinguish its different parts from one another. But you call up the image of the rose ; it is vague and hazy, because you cannot possibly remember all the parts and qualities of the rose. You cannot distinguish the different parts of a memory image clearly.

(4) Relation to Attention.—Percepts are steady because they are produced and sustained by external stimuli. Images are evolved by the mind from within and are sustained by attention. But attention is by nature flickering ; it is not

steady; it flits from object to object. So images are unsteady. Images require a greater amount of attention than percepts to be sustained in the mind.

(5) Relation to movement.—Percepts are produced by external stimuli acting on the sense-organs. So they are changed by movements of the body. As you cast your eyes on different objects while you walk, they produce different percepts in your mind. But you can carry the same image (e.g., the image of a departed friend) in your mind while you walk along. The memory image is not affected by movements of the body.

## Image and Idea

An idea is the meaning of an image; an image is the sensuous content of an idea. An image is the dress of an idea, which is clothed in it. An image may convey different ideas to different persons. The image of Mahatma Gandhi may excite a train of painful ideas in an Englishman's mind, because he was the leader of the freedom movement in India. But it excites a train of pleasant ideas in an Indian's mind for the same reason.

## Eidetic Image

Many children under fourteen years of age, perhaps half of them, have eidetic images. If they observe any complex object or a picture with great interest for half a minute, and then shut their eyes, or turn them upon a grey background, they can see the object as if it were still before them. This type of primary memory image is quite vivid. It is almost a reproduction of the original object. But sometimes it is not an exact reproduction of the original percept; it is likely to undergo modifications. In memory image the object may appear larger, or in motion, or with a different colour. These changes may be due to the subject's interests. These peculiarly vivid primary memory images are called eidetic images. The individuals having such images are called eidetic individuals. Eidetic images are common to later childhood. But they fade out in adolescence and adulthood.

## Suggestion and Association

Recall or reproduction of past percepts is caused by the forces of suggestion which work according to the Laws of Association. Reproduction is due to suggestion. Suggestion is due to association. A past percept is revived in consciousness, because it is suggested by some present percept or idea. And the present percept or idea suggests the past percept because they were associated in the past experience. Suggestion is the process by which a given percept or idea stirs up the subconscious trace of a past percept and revives it in consciousness as a memory image. Association is the connection between a percept and an idea or between one idea and another by virtue of which one appearing in consciousness tends to revive the other. You perceived a chair and a table always together in the past; an association has been established between the ideas of the two things in your mind. Therefore whenever you perceive or think of one of them, you are reminded of the other. The percept or idea of a chair suggests the idea of a table, because the two ideas are associated in the mind.

Association means bond of connection between subconscious traces or mental dispositions. Corresponding to mental dispositions there are physiological dispositions or structural modifications in the brain. Connections are established among them also. But the nature of mental dispositions and physiological dispositions is not known definitely. These are hypotheses or assumptions made to explain retention and recall. Some deny the existence of mental dispositions or subconscious ideas. We believe in their existence and have given the evidence of it already.

## Laws of Association

Past experiences are revived or brought back to the level of consciousness by suggestive forces. Suggestive forces work according to certain laws. They are the different modes of association among percepts and ideas. There are three Laws of Association : (1) the Law of Contiguity, (2) the Law of Similarity, and (3) the Law of Contrast.

(1) The Law of Contiguity.—The Law of Contiguity

states that when two objects have been perceived in the past always simultaneously or in succession, the percept of one reminds us of the other. If A and B have been perceived in the past several times simultaneously or successively, the percept or idea of A will remind us of the idea of B. The visual perception of a ripe mango suggests the ideas of its sweet taste and flavour, because they were always perceived simultaneously in the past. The percept of an inkpot suggests the idea of ink or a pen, because they were perceived simultaneously several times in the past. The perception of a flash of a forked lightning may suggest the idea of a thunder, because they were always perceived in close succession in the past.

Continuity of attention and interest determines the connections among ideas which went together or in close succession. When percepts and ideas are attended to together, they become connected with one another. Percepts and ideas which do not evoke our interest are dropped out.

(2) The Law of Similarity.—The Law states that similar ideas tend to suggest each other. The percept of an object which resembles another object perceived in the past tends to revive it. For example, a photo reminds us of the person whom it represents. A picture suggests the idea of its original. There is similarity between the photo and the person, the picture and its original. So the photo suggests the person, and the picture suggests the original object.

The Law of Similarity can work only when there is partial difference between two similar things. The photo and the person resemble each other in many respects. But they also differ in some respects. The photo is small and devoid of thickness, life, mind, and voice. The person is large, thick, living, conscious and endowed with the power of speaking.

(3) The Law of Contrast.—The law states that a percept or an idea tends to suggest its opposite. Opposites tend to suggest each other. Pleasant thoughts bring sad thoughts to the mind. Adversity reminds a person of his days of prosperity; his prosperity reminds him of his adversity. The heat of summer suggests the cold of winter. Peace suggests war; war suggests peace.

**Forgetting and its causes**

Some persons forget more rapidly than others. Overlearned material is forgotten more slowly. Meaningful material is much more slowly forgotten.

Forgetfulness is due to (1) the effacement of the subconscious traces of past experiences. If the subconscious traces are wiped off, they cannot be revived in consciousness. (2) Forgetfulness is due to the effacement of the bonds of association among subconscious traces of past experiences. If the connections among the subconscious traces are effaced, then also they cannot be revived. If bonds of association have not been fixed adequately, it will lead to forgetfulness. If a boy has not learnt his lessons well, he cannot repeat them in the class. He forgets them because he never learnt them adequately. (3) If the connecting pathways in the brain also be impaired, past experiences cannot be recalled. The effacement of these pathways due to serious illness, old age, or mental derangement causes forgetfulness. (4) If the memory traces are not used for a long period of time, they cannot be revived. They become inactive owing to disuse. (5) The connection S-R1 is interfered with by S-R2 connection. The name 'Rama' was originally connected with a particular person perceived repeatedly. Later it was connected with another person observed repeatedly. The first connection was interfered with and effaced by the second. (6) Sometimes forgetfulness is brought about by repression or desire to forget. Freud wrongly diagnosed a patient. She was really suffering from an ulcer of the stomach. But Freud treated her for a neurosis. He entirely forget the case, the name and all. His lapse of memory was due to repression or desire to forget. Thus forgetting is motivated or actuated by a desire. A painful experience, which hurts our self-respect, is repressed, and cannot therefore be recalled. Repression is a cause of forgetfulness. (7) Recall may be blocked by emotions. Nervousness or anxiety may interfere with recall. A well-prepared student may fail to recall correct answers owing to fear or nervousness. Self-confidence is necessary for recall. An actor, who has thoroughly learned his part, forgets it on the stage owing to fear[1].

### Forgetfulness is a condition of memory

Forgetfulness relieves the mind of useless details and makes it free to acquire new things. We should forget useless and unimportant things and remember essential and useful things. The mental energy is limited. The mind cannot remember an unlimited number of things. Thus Ribot truly said that forgetfulness is a condition of memory.

### How not to forget

Review the learned material at intervals. Forgetting is rapid after learning. So review for a few days after learning. Recite the learned material as much as possible. Recitation and review consolidate the memory traces and facilitate recall.

### Diseases of Memory

There are certain abnormalities of memory, viz., amnesia, aphasia, and hypermnesia. Amnesia is sudden loss of memory. It is an abnormal form of forgetfulness. Ribot divides amnesia into general amnesia and partial amnesia. General amnesia may be temporary, periodical, progessive, or congenital.

(1) Temporary amnesia is often caused by an accident or overstrain ; there is a loss of memory of the knowledge of events immediately preceding the accident. This is called retroactive amnesia. A person is thrown off from a carriage by its collision with a motor car. He falls unconscious. When he recovers consciousness, he cannot remember anything preceding the accident. (2) Periodic amnesia is found in double personality. A person entirely forgets his past life and begins a new life and continues it for a long time. Then he suddenly recalls his past experience and resumes his former life. A man meets an accident, suddenly forgets his home and his relations and all his antecedents, goes to another place, sets up a shop there, and behaves like an entirely different man. Then after two years he gets up in the morning and suddenly recalls his whole past life. This is periodic

amnesia. (3) Progressive amnesia is found in old age. Old persons first forget their recent experiences. They may not forget earlier experiences for a long time. They forget proper names first, then common nouns, then adjectives, adverbs, prepositions and conjunctions. Those words which are very often used in various contexts are lost last of all, and those which are least frequently used are first lost. It is sometimes found that old persons forget the names of their children, and even their own names. (4) Congenital amnesia is found in idiots and imbeciles. Their forgetfulness is due to the defects of their brains, with which they are born. But sometimes they may have excessive development of memory in one particular direction.

Partial amnesia is loss of memory for particular things. One may lose visual memory, auditory memory of the like, if particular parts of the brain are injured. Temporary failures of memory of a minor kind are common to normal persons. Examinees forget the lessons crammed by them as soon as the examination is over. Lawyers forget the facts of a suit as soon as it is over.

Aphasia covers many kinds of irregularities of speech. Sometimes a person understands what he reads, but not what he hears. Sometimes a person understands what he hears or reads, but cannot express his ideas in words. Sometimes a person cannot read but can write words. These are the different kinds of aphasia.

Hypermnesia is a sudden increase of memory. Sometimes it is found that long-forgotten experiences suddenly flash into the mind in dreams, delirium, etc. A person suddenly remembered the language learnt during infancy. Some rare individuals have prodigious memory. They can, for example, remember pages of a book after reading them only once. Some persons can remember many digits after hearing them once and multiply them mentally.

Paramnesia is false recognition. Sometimes we feel that we have previously been in the place where we are at the moment, though we are quite sure that we could not possibly have been in the place before. Sometimes we feel that we have previously said the words we are now saying, though we are sure that we could not have spoken the words. This is called paramnesia. Many explanations have been advanced for this phenomenon. But still its origin is obscure[2].

## Can Memory be improved by practice ?

Memory mainly involves learning, retention and recall. William James holds that retention is a physiological phenomenon. It is a physiological quality, given once for all to man with his nervous system, which he can never change. It differs no doubt in disease and health ; it is better in health than in illness. But the power of retention is inborn, and cannot, therefore, be improved by practice. But James admits that the power of learning can be improved by increased attention. This is the view of James.

James is right when he says that increased attention is the ultimate cause of the improvement of memory by practice. Well-directed attention fixes an object in the mind and makes its trace more permanent, brings it into relation with other objects, and makes it a permanent unit of the system of knowledge. So it can easily be recalled. Interest is a condition of attention. Hence learning can be improved by increased attention and interest.

But Stout contends that, though memory in general cannot be improved, memory in a particular direction can be improved by practice. Mental dispositions interpenetrate one another. If a man has made a certain amount of progress in learning a foreign language, his further progress is facilitated by his knowledge of certain general characteristics of the language. Actors can quickly learn their parts ; clergymen can quickly learn their sermons ; professors can quickly master their lectures[3]. Experiments have proved that the power of retention cannot be appreciably improved by practice. The power of learning can be improved by practice. But the power of retention, recall and recognition cannot be improved.

## REFERENCE

[1]Woodworth, *Psychology*, 1955, pp. 552-54,
[2]Mellone & Drummond, *Elements of Psychology*, pp. 410-11. Angell, *Psychology*, p. 225.
[3]James, *Brief Text-Book of Psychology*, ; Stout, *Manual of Psychology*, pp. 526-28.

# CHAPTER X

## *Imagination*

### Memory and Imagination

Memory is the exact reproduction of the contents of past experience in the same order in which they were experienced in the past. Imagination consists in reproducing the contents of past experience and rearranging them in a new order different from that in which they were originally experienced. Sometimes memory is called reproductive imagination, because in it the contents of past experience are reproduced in the same form and order. You perceived the rooms of your house many times in the past. You may remember them now exactly in the same order. This is memory. But you arrange the rooms of your house in a new order in your mind and construct a new image. This is imagination. Therefore, imagination is sometimes called productive or constructive imagination.

### Nature of Imagination

Imagination is constructive or productive. It does not create the elements or materials of an image. It reproduces the elements of past experiences and forms them into new combinations. Imagination is not exact reproduction of past experience. The contents of past experiences are reproduced and combined in a new order. Woodworth describes imagination as mental manipulation. When we mentally arrange chairs and tables for a tea party, we employ imagination. We do not actually manipulate the chairs and tables, but manipulate them in imagination.

There is conjunction or combination in a new manner. You perceived roses and blue colour in the past, but never blue roses. But you can reproduce the image of a rose and the image of blue colour, and combine them into the image of a blue rose. Similarly you can picture the image of a golden mountain or a ten-headed monster. Sometimes there is disjunction or separation of the elements of past experiences. You always perceived walking men with heads. But you disjoin the heads from walking men in imagination and picture the images of headless walking men. Sometimes there is substitution. Some elements of past experience are replaced by other elements. We may imagine a person whose hands are made of glass. Sometimes there is increase of the contents of past experience. When we increase the size of men hundred times and picture the images of giants, monsters, Brobdignags, etc., there is increase. Sometimes there is diminution of the contents of past experiences. When we decrease the size of men and picture the images of dwarfs, imps, Lilliputs, etc., there is diminution.

## Difference between Memory and Imagination

Memory is sometimes called reproductive imagination. It is exact reproduction of past experience. Imagination is sometimes called productive imagination. It consists in reproducing the elements of past experiences and rearranging them into a new pattern. It conjoins, disjoins, increases or diminishes them, and forms new images.

Memory involves recognition. In memory we recollect our past experiences and recognise them as our own experiences in the past. There is a feeling of familiarity in it. But in imagination there is no recognition or feeling of familiarity.

Memory has always a reference to the past. There is temporal localisation in definite recollection. But imagination is free; it has no reference to time. Sometimes imagination may refer to the future when, for example, I make a plan of a tour in the summer vacation.

## Relation of Memory to Imagination

Imagination depends upon memory. It consists in reproducing or remembering the elements of past experience and rearranging them into new patterns. If the elements of past experience were not remembered, there would be no imagination of new patterns. Imagination cannot create new materials. A man born blind can never imagine colours. So imagination presupposes memory.

Memory also sometimes involves imagination. Sometimes it is not necessary to remember the details of a past experience. In such cases we remember the general outline and fill in details by imagination. If you perceived the Tajmahal in the past, you remember its general outline and fill in its details by imagination. But sometimes memory may not involve imagination. When a student is asked to quote a poem from memory, he is required to reproduce it exactly with its punctuation. Here memory has no element of imagination. Sometimes we find discrepancy in the testimony of reliable persons as to the same object perceived by them, because they cannot exactly remember their past experiences, but fill up the gaps by imagination.

## Perception, Memory and Imagination

Perception consists in the interpretation of sensations, which are produced in the mind by external stimuli. In perception there are external stimuli acting upon the sense-organs. But in memory and imagination there are no external stimuli acting upon the sense-organs. Perception is largely a presentative process. But memory and imagination are representative processes.

Memory is sometimes called reproductive imagination while imagination is called productive imagination. Memory revives images of past experiences in the same form and order. But imagination revives past experiences and rearranges them into new patterns. Imagination does not create its materials ; it simply puts the materials supplied by memory in a different order. In memory the past experience is recalled in the same order. The contents are revived, and arranged in the same order. In memory the whole experience and the elements are familiar.

## Kinds of Imagination

(1) Passive Imagination and Active Imagination.

The mind is not completely passive at any time. It is partly active when it is conscious. In passive imagination the mind is comparatively passive ; it does not exert itself ; it does not make any effort of the will to picture the images. The images come of themselves to the mind and are combined automatically by the suggestive forces. This easy play of imagination is called passive imagination. When we are in a listless mood and fall into a revery or day-dream and build castless in the air, our imagination is passive.

In active imagination the mind exerts itself to picture an image ; it makes an effort to receive the contents of past experience and combine them into new patterns. The images are not automatically combined by suggestive forces in it. The combination of images is effected by an effort of the will. The mind actively selects certain materials, rejects others and constructs a new image. When we write an essay, we put forth effort of the mind to remember the relevant elements of past knowledge and arrange them in a fresh manner. So we have active imagination here.

(2) Receptive and Creative Imagination.

In receptive imagination the mind makes an effort to picture a scene described. The materials of imagination and the order of their combination are suggested to the mind from without. When we read stories, novels, dramas, poems, history, geography, travels, and the like, we have receptive imagination in which we receive the images from without.

In creative imagination the mind constructs an imaginary situation ; it creates a new image out of the materials which it receives from within itself and arranges them in a fresh order. When an engineer constructs the plan of a building, he employs creative imagination.

(3) Intellective, Practical and Æsthetical Imagination.

Intellective imagination serves the purpose of knowledge. It is also called cognitive imagination. Imagination engaged in intellectual construction is called intellective imagination.

When we write a story or a play we have intellective imagination. When Newton hit upon the hypothesis of gravitation to explain the fall of bodies to the earth by a stroke of imagination, he had intellective imagination. These are examples of creative imagination. But there may be also receptive imagination which serves the purpose of knowledge. When we read history, geography, novels, stories, dramas, etc., we have receptive imagination which adds to our knowledge. Thus intellective imagination may be either creative or receptive.

Practical imagination serves some practical purpose. It is involved in a practical construction. When we devise a plan of a building or a machine, we have practical imagination. When we devise plans for a picnic, or a railway journey, we have practical imagination. It fulfils the practical needs of our life.

Æsthetic imagination satisfies our aesthetic impulse. It is directed towards the gratification of aesthetic sentiments. It does not satisfy any practical need. It does not add to our knowledge. It is neither practical construction nor intellective imagination. It satisfies our craving for beauty. When a painter paints a picture, he has aesthetic imagination. When a musician composes a song, he exercises aesthetic imagination. When a poet composes a poem, he has aesthetic imagination.

## Types of Imagery

There are different types of imagery. We may have images corresponding to every variety of sensation. Hearing a tune in imagination is an example of an auditory image. Seeing a building in imagination is an example of a visual image. Touching a block of ice in imagination is an example of a tactual image. Enjoying the scent of a rose in imagination is an olfactory image. Eating a mango in imagination is a gustatory image. Climbing a hill in imagination is a kinaesthetic or motor image. We may imagine ourselves fatigued and have organic images. It is possible to have any or all of these types of imagery.

Different persons have different kinds of images of imagination. Many persons imagine things and events in terms of visual images. They are called visiles. Others can easily picture auditory images. They imagine a factory in terms of sounds. They are called audiles. Others can easily picture tactual images. They imagine the sea in terms of the coolness of water. They are called tactiles. Images of blind and deaf persons must be almost entirely of the tactual nature. A few persons imagine things in terms of their smells. They are called olfactiles. Zola, a great French novelist, distinguished towns, streets, and even seasons of the year by their smells, and had a rich variety of olfactory images. Thus there are different types of imagery. Different kinds of images are treated as symbols only; we mean by them not only themselves but others associated with them in sense-experience.

### The Role of Images in Mental Life : Values of Imagery

(1) Enjoyment.—Imagination affords pleasure to a person. He can remember past scenes of great enjoyment and imagine himself enjoying them over again. He can anticipate future experiences full of joy and derive pleasure from them. Vivid reminiscences and expectations are sources of great delight.

(2) Social sharing of interest.—It depends upon vividness of imagery. Persons of vivid imagination can easily follow and enjoy descriptions of concrete things. They can appreciate narration of events. They can carry on conversation fluently. They can lend colour to their language on account of their vivid imagery. They can appreciate wit, humour, and even slang. They can enjoy jokes. They can understand delicate shades of meaning, similes, metaphors, fables, parables and the like.

(3) Sympathy.—Sympathy is the ability to share the feelings and emotions of others. This depends upon the ability to put oneself in the place of others, and this involves imagination. Thus sympthy depends upon imagination. We can enjoy a drama by identifying ourselves with the imaginary characters. Children can enjoy stories of the people of other lands and other times by means of their vivid imagery.

(4) Creative work.—Weaving beautiful plots, creating interesting scenes, making grand designs, inventing machinery,

and the like depend on creative imagination. Engineering, architecture, sculpture, painting, music, poetry, drama and novels utilise creative imagination.[1]

## Misuse of Imagination

(1) Lies.—Young children have very vivid images. So they are apt to confound images with percepts. This is the reason why sometimes they tell lies. They cannot distinguish between things perceived and creatures of their imagination. They mix up percepts with images unconsciously. Little children do not deliberately tell lies. They omit those parts of the incidents which are disagreeable to them and insert incidents which are agreeable to them. Sometimes they fail to remember certain minor incidents that happened in the past and fill in the gaps by imagination.

(2) Night Fears.—Many night fears of young children are due to the confusion of images with percepts. They vividly imagine ghosts, giants, demons or hobgoblins in the dark corners of a room when alone at night, and seem to perceive them actually. Their vivid images are hallucinations. They are images projected upon the external world and appear to be real objects or perception.

(3) Imaginary Companions.—Little children three or four years old often experience imaginary companions. They have vivid images of playmates and confuse them with percepts. They are found to play with imaginary companions when they are all alone. Constant indulgence in play with imaginary companions does not develop the qualities of co-operation and fellowship. If it is continued up to adolescence, one may become reserved, morbid and unsocial.

(4) Living in Unreality.—The timid and introvert child flies away from reality and lives in an imaginary world. Excessive day-dreaming is harmful. It makes the child diffident and unable to cope with the world. In adolescence also persons indulge in day-dreams and substitute an imaginary world for a real world. These are the misuse of imagination[2].

**Development of Imagination**

Imagination depends upon memory. Memory depends upon perception. Children under three have only reproductive imagination or memory. They can only revive their past experiences. At a later stage their imagination is largely reproductive and receptive. They can picture images as suggested by other persons or books. They cannot create images. During the third and fourth years children have abundance of creative imagination. They are very fond of fairy tales in disregard of the reality. From four to eight their creative imagination is of the fantastic type. It is divorced from reality. It is due to their lack of knowledge of the external world and its laws. Manual skill, constructiveness, make-believe in play, and story-telling indicate the development of imagination in children. Manual skill depends upon mental manipulation or imagination of objects. The child's constructiveness also is an expression of his power of imagination. He builds a house with damp sand or mud, arranges dolls for a dinner, takes things apart and puts them together. He first sees the ways in which things can be arranged.

The child's imagination is expressed in make-believe which is an important element in play. The little boy rides a rod and treats it as a horse. He knows that it is a mere rod, but imagines it to be a horse for the time being. The child later develops the power of story-telling. In telling stories he mentally manipulates certain objects. The imagination of the children of this age is fantastic, and not controlled by the conditions of the real world.

As they grow older, they acquire knowledge of the external world and become more practical and matter-of-fact. Their creative imagination ceases to be fantastic and becomes more pragmatic or useful. Pragmatic imagination satisfies the demands of the reality. It is more objective than subjective. Constructive imagination should be encouraged at this stage in connection with handwork projects.

During adolescence fantastic imagination again becomes

predominant with a strong element of emotion. But it does not indulge in fairy tales but in the youth's or the maiden's own ambitions and aspirations. The adolescents become the heroes of their own day-dreams. Adolescence is pre-eminently the age of day-dreaming. Excessive day-dreaming is harmful to the individual, because it makes him worthless and unable to cope with the world. He will be apt to live in his own world of imagination.

As the period of adolescence passes, imagination again becomes practical. It ceases to be fantastic and emotional. Pragmatic imagination takes the place of emotional day-dreaming.

At last artistic imagination emerges. It creates ideals of truth, good, and beauty. It rises above the practical needs of life and satisfies the deeper cravings of the mind. This may also be called idealistic imagination. These are the stages in the development of imagination[3].

## Day-dream or Reverie

Day-dreaming is passive imagination. There is free association of ideas in it. Images suggest one another by the force of association. They "come of themselves" to the mind which remains comparatively passive. This was the view of the older psychologists.

The modern psychologists hold that day-dreams are motivated. They gratify some desires. They look forward to the future. They plan a future course of action, though it is not a serious plan. They are mere play of imagination, which gratifies some desires. Day-dreams are expressions of some desires which give an impetus to the imagination.

There are two kinds of day-dreams : (1) conquering hero day-dreams, and (2) suffering hero day-dreams. The dreamer himself is the hero. The conquering hero day-dream in which the dreamer tides over all difficulties in life, defeats his rivals, and carves out a career for himself, satisfies his mastery motive or instinct of self-assertion. It does not require the efforts for real execution of the plan. Such day-dreams are very common.

The suffering hero day-dream seems to be inexplicable at first. But this also may satisfy the mastery motive. A young man severely rebuked by his parents may think of a career for himself. He may imagine himself either a martyr or a desperado or some other kind of suffering hero. The dreamer imagines himself to be persecuted[4].

## Dream

Day-dreaming is passive imagination. Dreaming also is passive imagination during light sleep. It is more free from control and criticism than day-dreaming. Images come of themselves due to suggestive forces and are combined in various ways. They are the work of the subconscious mind. They are apprehended as actual perceptions during dream. But they are not percepts produced by external objects and do not agree with them. They are images produced by the subconscious mind. They are contradicted by waking perceptions. Sometimes dream images are vivid and distinct. They are projected in outer space and appear to be real objects of perception. The critical faculty is mostly suspended. Hence dream-images are often combined in an absurd and incoherent manner owing to the absence of criticism. The critical faculty does not act in dream. Sully recognizes two kinds of dreams : dream-illusions and dream-hallucinations.

(1) Dream-illusions are excited by external stimuli. A man sleeping in a well-lighted room sometimes dreams of a conflagration. A man sleeping with insufficient clothes may dream of swimming in a river, when exposed to a shower of rain. A man sleeping with a hot water bottle at his feet dreamt that he walked on the crater of a volcano. These are dream-illusions.

(2) Dream-hallucinations are excited by a train of thoughts and images. They are excited by central stimuli. A young man enamoured of a girl dreams of his beloved. An examinee constantly thinks of his examination and dreams that his examination has begun, but that he is prevented from entering into the examination hall[5].

(3) Some dreams are actuated by the ungratified sex desire. Freud is an exponent of this theory.

(4) Some are actuated by other desires also, e.g., poetic impulse, musical impulse, artistic impulse, and the like. Some dreams are actuated by the mastery motive, e.g., flight dreams.

(5) Some dreams are a mere fantastic play of imagination. Images are suggested spontaneously by one another with some desire giving impetus to them. These dreams are due to automatic suggestion and association.

## Freud's theory of Dream

Freud holds that dreams are motivated by ungratified sex desire (*libido*). The sex desire is not gratified in conscious life. It is banned by the society. So it is repressed and driven to the unconscious. Freud calls the subconscious desires the unconscious desires. During sleep the Censor or the critical faculty relaxes its vigilance. So the repressed *libido* forces itself into the level of consciousness, and fulfils itself directly or indirectly in dreams. Dreams are direct or indirect wish-fulfilments. Freud holds that dreams always refer to the past repressed *libido*. In children dreams are direct wish-fulfilments. But in adults they are disguised or indirect wish-fulfilments. The repressed *libido* appears in disguise, and assumes symbols to escape the vigilance of the Censor. 'King' stands for 'father,' 'queen' stands for 'mother' and so on. Children's dreams are direct wish fulfilments. They are not allowed to eat sweetmeat during illness. So they dream that they are eating sweetmeat to their heart's content.

Adler holds that dreams fulfil the mastery motive or the instinct of self-assertion. They always refer to the future. They are a rehearsal of the individual's adjustment to the environment in future. They forecast his plan of action. Jung holds that dreams refer to the present conflict in the individual's mind. He is confronted with a complex situation. He cannot adapt himself to it effectively. There appears a conflict in his mind. This conflict is expressed in dreams. Freud, Adler and Jung are exponents of three schools of psychoanalysis[6].

**Criticism of Freud's theory of dream**

(1) First, Freud makes too much of the sex motive or *libido*. All dreams are motivated by it. This view is wrong. The sex is one of the dominant motives. But it is not the only motive. Some dreams in grown up persons are undoubtedly fulfilments of the sex desire or *libido*. But all dreams are not fulfilments of the sex motive. Freud sometimes takes the word 'sex' in the wide sense of 'love' of all kinds—love of father, love of mother, love of animals, pleasure of passing urine or stool, pleasure of sucking the thumb, pleasure of being rubbed, etc. Even then all dreams are not fulfilments of love or desire for pleasure. Freud overdoes the sex motive.

(2) Secondly, Freud overdoes the unconscious. Every ungratified desire is not driven to the unconscious. An ungratified desire may persist in the margin of consciousness and colour the whole field of consciousness. An ungratified desire is not necessarily unconscious. Freud overdoes the unconscious.

(3) Thirdly, Freud passes from the abnormal mind to the normal mind. The dominant part played by the sex motive in the dreams of many neurotics and insane persons is applied by him to normal persons. We should pass from the normal mind to the abnormal mind, but not from the abnormal mind to the normal mind. We should apply the laws of the normal mind to the phenomena of the abnormal mind.

(4) Fourthly, Freud's theory contains an important truth that most dreams are motivated by conative tendencies. They are motivated by all kinds of desires. They are motivated by the sex desire, the mastery motive, the will-to-live, the aesthetic desire, the desire for knowledge, the religious sentiment and the like. They are motivated by all kinds of instincts, emotions and sentiments. Freud does not recognise unmotivated dreams. But many dreams are due to automatic association of ideas in a fantastic manner. They are really innocent, not innocent-looking. It is absurd to probe into the sexual meanings of innocent dreams.

### Hallucination

A hallucination is a vivid image projected upon the external world and mistaken for a real object of perception. It is a subjective perception. It is a vivid image mistaken for a percept. It is excited by the brain. It is not produced by an external stimulus.

Hallucinations are images excited by the brain. They are not excited by external stimuli. They are pure creatures of the imagination. They are entirely subjective creations. They are projected upon the external world and appear to be real objects of perception. A murderer sometimes sees the ghost of the murdered person pursuing him. This is a case of hallucination. The fixed idea of his mind is projected upon the external world and appears to be an actual object. Macbeth saw the ghost of Banquo sitting in the throne. It was a hallucination produced by his excited brain. Insane persons and hysteric patients are often seen to talk to imaginary ghosts. They are victims of hallucinations. Normal persons in the normal condition of the brain cannot have hallucinations.

### Hallucination and Illusion

An illusion is excited by peripheral stimulation, while a hallucination is excited by central stimulation. In an illusion there is wrong interpretation of a sensation produced by an external stimulus. When you mistake a rope for a snake, the rope produces sensation in your mind, but you wrongly interpret it. Your idea of the snake does not tally with the rope. This is an illusion. But in a hallucination there is no external stimulus. It is produced by an abnormal condition of the brain.

### Delusion

A delusion is a persistent false belief. It is not produced by an external stimulus. So it is not an illusion. It is not a vivid image projected upon the external world. So it is not a hallucination. It is a false belief, which persists and cannot be shaken off. An individual, who is a victim of a delusion, wrongly believes that he is an Emperor, or Napoleon, Hitler, Jesus Christ, or any other great person. He is impervious to all arguments. He cannot be shaken out of his false belief. He is open to arguments in all other matters, but not in this particular matter.

There are two kinds of delusions : (1) delusions of grandeur, and (2) delusions of persecution. The victim of delusion may wrongly think himself to be a great hero. This is a delusion of grandeur. Or he may wrongly think himself to be always persecuted by others. This is a delusion of persecution.

A victim of a grandiose delusion may think himself to be a millionnaire, though he is really extremely poor, and cannot meet his expenses. A victim of a persecutory delusion wrongly believes that others are always conspiring against him, and trying to injure his life, wealth, and reputation.

In an abnormal person a delusion may be accompanied by hallucinations. A victim of a grandiose delusion may get messages from great men through spirits. He may have auditory hallucinations. He may hear inner voices. A victim of a persecutory delusion may also have visual and auditory hallucinations. He may see imaginary enemies conspiring against him. He may hear imaginary voices of enemies intending harm to him, or abusing him or his family. Thus delusions may be accompanied by hallucinations. But they are not identical with each other. Hallucinations are subjective perceptions of unreal objects. Delusions are false beliefs.

Delusions are mostly due to thwarted mastery motive. They are due to frustrations in life in mastering the situation. They are imaginary compensations for real inabilities and inefficiencies in life. Those, who cannot face the reality and overcome difficulties in life, become victims of delusions.

Delusions of grandeur correspond to conquering hero day-dreams. Delusions of persecution correspond to suffering hero day-dreams. The conquering hero day-dreams may give rise to grandiose delusions, when they are in excessive degree. The suffering hero day-dreams may give rise to persecutory delusions, when they are in excessive degree. Excessive day-dreaming is dangerous. It may result in flight from reality and indulgence in excessive imagination, which is the cause of delusions[7].

## REFERENCE

[1]*Psychology of Childhood.*
[2]*Ibid.*
[3]*Ibid*, pp. 224-26.
[4]Woodworth, *Psychology.*
[5]Sully, *Illusions.*
[6]Woodworth, *Contemporary Schools of Psychology.*
[7]Hart, *Psychology of Insanity.*

# CHAPTER XI

*Thinking*

## The Nature of Thinking

Thinking is a higher process of cognition than sensation and perception, memory and imagination. It analyses the material supplied by these elementary forms of activity and combines them into new patterns. It involves analysis and synthesis. Woodworth points out that thinking consists of the following elements :—

(1) orientation towards a goal ;

(2) seeking this way and that for realising the goal ;

(3) recall of previously observed facts (memory) ;

(4) grouping these recalled facts into new patterns (imagination) ;

(5) inner speech and gestures.

All these activities may not be present in every act of thinking. In idle thinking there may not be any particular goal. Sometimes there may be thinking without inner speech. But generally when we think in order to solve a practical or theoretical problem, the first four elements are present in thinking. The solution of the problem is the goal or purpose of thinking. We think of this means or that means to solve the problem. We recall facts of past experience bearing on the problem. We group them together into new patterns to solve the particular problem. We may give partial expression to our thinking by inaudible speech movements ; or at best we may assume a particular gesture to facilitate thinking. And at last we may succeed in reaching the solution of the problem. Thinking does not involve free association as in rêverie, but controlled association. Suggestive forces are controlled by a definite purpose in purposive thinking.

Thus thinking involves analysis and synthesis. It analyses the concrete details of perception, selects certain aspects of it, and combines them into a new whole. Thinking involves comparison and discrimination also. In thinking we try to have a key to a novel situation. In order to do so we recall all the facts of past experience, which are similar to the present one, compare the old situations with the new situation, break them up into their elements, discriminate them from one another, and recombine them into a new whole. Thus thinking involves analysis and synthesis, comparison and discrimination.

## The Nature of Reasoning

Reasoning is typical thinking. Woodworth regards it as mental exploration and finding a new relationship among the data perceived or recalled. Reasoning is a substitute for motor exploration. Suppose, you have lost your way in a new place. You may explore the different ways by actual movements. Or, you may sit down and think. You may explore the novel situation mentally, and try to find out a clue. By following one clue after another you may at last find out the right way which will lead you to your destination.

In motor exploration you perceive the clues and act upon them. But in reasoning you follow clues by thinking them through. You recall facts prevously observed and follow them as clues. Reasoning is mental exploration. It is a substitute for motor exploration.

But sometimes reasoning cannot reach a solution; so it yields to actual motor exploration and observation of fresh facts. Thus reasoning is a trial and error process. It is mental exploration. But this must be followed by reaching a solution. An individual recalls the relevant data, groups them together into a new pattern, interrelates them to one another, and finds a new meaning in them. He find a new relationship among the data. This type of seeing a new relation ship is called inference. Thus reasoning consists in mental exploration of the data and grasping a new interrelation of the data. It consists in seeking and finding the solution of a problem.

## Psychology and Logic of Reasoning : Deduction and Induction

Psychology studies the process of reasoning. Logic studies the product of reasoning or argument. Psychology tells us how we actually think, whether correctly or incorrectly. It is not concerned with validity of thought. Psychology deals with the exploratory process. Logic deals with inference, which is the result of mental exploration. Inference consists in drawing a conclusion from the given premises. The two premises and the conclusion, set forth in order, constitute the syllogism. For example :—

All men are mortal ;
Socrates is a man :
∴ Socrates is mortal.

The conclusion is inferred from the data or premises ; it is seen to be implied in the two premises taken together. From the standpoint of Logic, reasoning consists in inferring a new judgment from two or more given judgments or data through the medium of the common factor or the middle term among them. It consists in putting together the data and grasping a new relation among them. The reasoning given above is deduction.

The following reasoning is induction :—

John is mortal ;
Abdul is mortal ;
Mohan is mortal ;
Hari is mortal ;
∴ All men are mortal.

A universal judgment is inferred from many particular judgments in induction. Particular judgments are gathered from perception. A universal judgment is inferred from them with the help of the Uniformity of Nature and the Law of Causation, which are the formal grounds of induction.

## Reasoning or Thinking and Imagination

Woodworth defines imagination as mental manipulation, and reasoning or thinking as mental exploration. In imagination we recall the elements of past experience and group them into a new pattern. In imagination we manipulate things mentally. For example, we arrange tables and chairs mentally for a tea party. Thus imagination is mental manipulation. It is a substitute for motor manipulation.

Reasoning which is typical thinking is mental exploration. You have lost your hammer. Without actually searching for it here and there, you think out the clues and guess where you put it last. This is mental exploration. It is a substitute for motor exploration.

Thinking or reasoning involves controlled association because it is directed towards a goal. Imagination generally involves free association. For example, reverie or day-dream involves free association of ideas. But pragmatic imagination, theoretical or practical, which is directed towards a useful goal, involves controlled association.

Thinking involves memory and imagination. It consists in recalling relevant facts of past experience and combining them into a new pattern in order to realise a goal. But thinking is a higher mental process than imagining. Imagination is carried on through concrete images. But thinking is carried on through verbal images, generic images, or imageless ideas and concepts. Thinking may be imageless. Thus thinking is a higher mental process than imagination.

### Value of Reasoning

(1) Reasoning is mental exploration as distinguished from motor exploration. It consists in mentally surveying a situation and solving a problem. It consists in analysing a complex situation and finding out a new relationship among the data observed or recalled.

(2) Reasoning saves time and energy. It is mental exploration of clues. It consists in following clues after clues mentally until the problem is solved. Motor exploration of a given situation takes more time and requires a greater amount of energy. Finding a way out of a known forest by walking and running here and there is a tedious and arduous task. But thinking it out by recalling relevant facts and

rearranging them into a new pattern is easier, quicker and often more successful.

(3) Reasoning takes fewer trials. It notices only relevant facts and solves the problem by a few trials. But in motor exploration we have to try a large number of possible solutions until by accident we come upon the right solution.

(4) Reasoning makes use of images. Images are more plastic than concrete things. They can be easily evolved from within the mind, and combined and re-combined into any pattern to suit our purpose. But concrete things cannot be so easily managed. Therefore reasoning is more economical of material. It requires much less material than actual motor exploration.

(5) Reasoning is sometimes concerned with abstract and general problems.—Generalisation is the highest type of thinking. It consists in arriving at general principles from the study of concrete situations. General laws are derived from particular facts.

## Thought and Language : Value of Language

Generally, thinking is expressed in language. When we think over a difficult problem, very often we talk to ourselves internally. If we are alone, we may talk aloud with gestures. Man is a thinking animal. He is also a talking animal. Thinking and talking are products of social intercourse.

They develop together. Language is the expression of thought. And thought is aided by language. But thought is not identical with language. Thinking may be carried on without language.

(1) Language is the expression of thought. We can record our thoughts in language and communicate them to others through language. When our thoughts are recorded in language, they may be used by ourselves in future and add to the knowledge of others. Our knowledge is developed by social intercourse which is carried on through language.

(2) Language is an aid to thought. Discussion and argument stimulate thought. Discussion with well-informed

persons provokes thinking and makes our ideas clear. When we speak to children, we stimulate their thinking. When we discuss something with them, they are compelled to think. Even when we think alone, we carry on thinking in an imaginary company of persons.

(3) Language is an aid to recall. Ideas are vague but names are definite. We can easily retain and recall those facts and principles to which we have assigned definite names, and which have, therefore, been deeply impressed on the mind.

(4) Language is a thought-saving instrument. Ideas are vague. Names are symbols ; they are definite and precise. Symbols can more easily be manipulated than mere ideas. We can use words, signs, symbols, formulae, and the like easily. But we cannot manipulate ideas so easily. Progress of mathematical thinking has been made possible by the use of symbols.

(5) Thought and language develop together. Development of thought is greatly aided by development of language. And development of language is greatly aided by development of thought. The more thought is developed, the more language is developed. And the more language is developed, the more thought is developed. They develop side by side.

## Concepts

Concepts are tools of thinking. Reasoning consists in inferring a judgment from other given premises or judgments. A judgment is a combination of ideas or concepts. Ideas are either particular or general. Ideas of particular things are particular. Ideas of classes are general. General ideas are called concepts.

How are concepts formed ? Conception consists of the following steps : (1) Observation of several individuals ; (2) analysis of each of them into its component qualities ; (3) comparison of them with one another in order to find out their points of similarity and their points of difference ; (4) mental unification of the common attributes into a concept after eliminating the points of difference ; (5) assignment of a name to the concept. In order to form the concept of 'man' we first observe several men and resolve them into their qualities. Then we compare them with one another and find out their points of similarity and their points of difference. Then we eliminate their points of difference, fix our attention on their points of similarity (e.g., animality and rationality), and group their ideas into the concept of 'man'. Then we assign the name 'man' to the concept.

Thus conception involves analysis, synthesis, comparison, assimilation, discrimination, and abstraction. It analyses individuals into their constituent qualities, compares them with one another, finds out their points of similarity and their points of difference, eliminates the points of difference, and groups the ideas of the similarities into a concept. At last, a name is assigned to the concept in order to make it definite, and impress it deeply on the mind, so that it may be easily retained and recalled, and communicated to others. Conception consists in abstracting from some particular situations some elements common to them.

## Concept and Image : Imageless Thinking

A concept is different from an image. An image is particular and concrete, while a concept is general and abstract. We have an image of a particular man, or an animal. But we have a concept of 'man' or 'animal'.

(1) A concept is a mental creation ; it is the product of an act of thought which grasps the common element among many particular objects.

(2) A concept is not representable ; it cannot be imagined. We can think of the class 'man', but we cannot have an image of it. Conception is a higher mental process than imagination.

(3) A concept is not a composite photograph. If we take photographs of ten men on the same plate so that they are superposed on one another, we have a composite photograph. It is a blurred image of man representing only the common

features of the different men. The peculiarities of the different men cancel one another. Likewise a generic image is a blurred image resulting from the superposition of many images. It is an image which represents the common features of many individuals. It lies midway between a concept and an image. A concept is not representable, while a generic image can be represented. A concept is the thought of the common element of many individuals. A generic image represents the common element of many individuals. This is the point of similarity between them. A generic image is the intermediate step between an image and a concept.

We carry on higher thinking by means of imageless concepts. We do not pause to picture concrete, visual, auditory, or verbal images of things. Imageless thinking is carried on through concepts and ideas devoid of images.

A concept is a general idea formed by mental activity. Thinking is carried on through concepts. A concept may be attached to an image, visual, auditory, or verbal. Or it may not be attached to any image and be imageless. Thinking is largely carried on without the help of images. It is mostly imageless in its advanced form. Abstract thinking is imageless.

## Perception and Conception

Conception consists in finding out some elements common to particular facts perceived. A child perceives a red house, a red coat, a red rose, or a red flag. He thinks of the quality common to all these objects and calls it redness. Redness is a common quality separated in thought from the red objects. It does not exist apart from the red objects. But it is separated in thought from the objects. Thus the concept of redness is formed by the mind. Concepts of 'man', 'table', 'tree', etc., cannot be formed without perceiving particular objects and situations, analysing them into their component qualities, and finding out those qualities which are common to them. Thus perception of particular objects and concrete situations is the basis of conception. There can be no conception without previous perception.

## Judgment

Judgment is the mental process by which the mind compares two or more ideas or concepts with one another. It is the apprehension of the relation between two things or qualities, or between a thing and a quality. Judgment is the process of consciously combining two or more distinct notions, percepts, ideas, or concepts into a more complex idea. 'The sky is blue'. This is a judgment. Here the mind consciously puts together the percept of the sky with the percept of blue, and combines them into the complex idea of the blue sky and believes in its reality. 'Man is mortal'. In this judgment the mind combines the concepts of 'man' and 'mortality' into the complex idea of 'mortal man' and believes in its reality.

## Conception and Judgment

From the standpoint of Logic, conception is prior to judgment. Judgment is the conscious synthesis of concepts. Thus concepts are the elements of judgments, and are, therefore, simpler than judgments. Judgment is the more complex mental process of combining concepts together.

But from the standpoint of Psychology, judgment is prior to conception. A judgment is the simplest unit of knowledge. A concept is the result of a series of judgments. An orange is a fruit. It is yellow. It is round. It is sweet. These simple judgments are combined together in the concept of 'orange'. Again, complex judgments presuppose the concepts. The judgment 'man is mortal' presupposes the concepts of 'man' and 'mortal', without which it is not possible. Thus conception and judgment are interdependent on each other.

# CHAPTER XII

## *Feeling*

### The Nature of Feeling

Every concrete mental process has three aspects ; cognition, feeling and conation. When cognition is predominant in a mental process, we call it a cognitive state. When feeling is predominant in it, we call it an affective state. And when conation is predominant in it, we call it a conative state. This fact must be borne in mind when we speak of cognition, feeling and conation. In order of experience there is first a cognition ; it affects the mind which feels pleasure or pain ; then the feeling gives rise to conation or mental activity. Thus cognition gives rise to feeling ; and feeling gives rise to conation. Conation or mental activity gives rise to bodily movement.

Thus feeling is the way in which the mind is affected by a cognition. It is a passive state of the mind. It is either agreeable or disagreeable. It is either pleasure or pain. Feeling is sometimes called 'affection'. It arises from a cognition, and gives rise to a mental act or conation. Look at a flower. You have a cognition of it. It affects your mind agreeably. In other words, it gives you pleasure. Then it produces an impulse in your mind to pluck it. Thus feeling arises from a cognition and gives rise to a conation. As contrasted with cognition and conation, feeling is subjective experience *par excellence*. It is an elementary mode of consciousness. It is neither a function of cognition nor of conation. It is a unique mode of consciousness and cannot be derived from cognition or conation. Feeling is also called affection.

### Cognition and Feeling

Cognition informs the mind of the nature of an object. Feeling informs the mind of its own passive state. We are conscious of an object, e.g., a flower. It affects our minds agreeably, and gives us pleasure. Thus cognition tells us the 'whats' of the states of consciousness, while feeling tells us the "hows" of the states of consciousness. Cognition informs us of external objects, while feeling informs us of our own mental condition.

But cognitions can directly revive one another, while feelings cannot directly revive feelings. The idea of an examination may revive the ideas of the examination hall, the examiners, the marks obtained, and the like. But the feeling of pleasure at the sight of a mountain peak cannot directly revive the pain of climbing the peak. The pleasure can indirectly revive the pain through the idea of climbing the peak.

### Sensation and Feeling

Sensation is a simple cognition produced by an external stimulus in the mind. It is objective since it depends upon an external stimulus. Feeling is subjective since it depends upon the mind or subject. It is the way in which the mind is affected. The same stimulus sometimes gives rise to a sensation and a feeling. It produces a sensation ; the sensation affects the mind in a certain way, which feels either pleasure or pain. The stimulus produces a sensation, and the sensation produces a feeling. The same stimulus produces the same sensation ; but the same sensation does not affect the subject in the same way ; it may sometimes affect the mind agreeably ; and sometimes disagreeably. For example, the sensation of sweetness produced by tasting sugar is at one time felt as agreeable, at another time as disagreeable. Thus sensation and feeling are different from each other.

Sometimes feeling is regarded as an attribute of sensation. Look at the moon. You have a sensation of brightness. It has a pleasant tone. This is called the feeling-tone, or hedonic tone of the sensation. But this is wrong. The bright moon produces the sensation of brightness. And this sensation produces a feeling of pleasure. Feeling itself has attributes, *viz.*, quality, intensity and duration. So it cannot be regarded as an attribute of sensation.

Feeling or affection agrees with sensation in possessing quality, intensity and duration. But it has no extensity like sensations. Sensations can be localised. But feelings cannot be localised.

### Kinds of Feeling

Feeling or affection as a passive and subjective state of the mind, is either agreeable, or disagreeable, pleasant or unpleasant. Pleasantness and unpleasantness are the elementary forms of feeling. Pleasure and unpleasure or pain are two kinds of feeling. Some psychologists hold that there is another kind of feeling, e.g., neutral feeling or feeling of indifference. This is not admitted by others.

### Is there any Neutral Feeling ?

Feeling is either agreeable or disagreeable. Pleasure and unpleasure or pain are the only feelings. There is no neutral feeling or feeling of indifference. The so-called neutral states are cognitions ; they are not feelings. Stout rightly holds that if we consider our total consciousness at any moment, we shall always find in it an element of feeling,—pleasure or pain. Thus the so-called 'neutral states considered with the background of total consciousness are not devoid of feeling. Pillsbury holds that a stimulus may be indifferent, but a feeling cannot be indifferent and that an indifferent stimulus does not give rise to feeling. Pure feeling must be either pleasant or unpleasant. It cannot be neutral.

### Wundt's Tridimensional Theory of Feeling

Wundt holds that there are three dimensions of feeling, viz., pleasantness—unpleasantness, excitement—calm, and tension—relaxation. The members of these groups may be combined in various ways.

This view is wrong. Excitement and calm are organic and muscular sensations. They are not feelings. When we are excited, our muscles become tense, our breathing becomes quick, etc. When we are calm, our muscles become inactive and the organs function in harmony. Thus excitement and calm are sensations. They give rise to pleasure or pain. So they should not be regarded as feelings.

Similarly, tension and relaxation are muscular sensations. They are cognitive in nature, and cannot be regarded as kinds of feeling. So pleasure and pain only are the two kinds of feeling.

## Feeling and Conation

A cognition affects the mind and produces a feeling in it. The perception of a flower produces pleasure. The perception of a noise produces pain. A cognition gives rise to a feeling. The feeling gives rise to a conation or mental activity. Thus feeling is the link between cognition and conation. A cognition is the cause of feeling ; and feeling is the cause of conation.

Again, a conation or mental activity tends towards an end. When the end of conation is fulfilled there is pleasure, and when the end of conation is baffled, there is pain. The more easily an active tendency reaches its goal, the more pleasant it is. The more an active tendency is thwarted, the more unpleasant it is. Thus conation also is a cause of feeling. Furthered conation gives rise to pleasure ; thwarted conation gives rise to pain.

Attention is a kind of conation or mental act. Attention also is a cause of feeling. Effective adjustment of attention to an object or an idea gives rise to pleasure. Ineffective adjustment of attention to an object or an idea gives rise to pain. Conation in the form of attention is a cause of feeling. Thus the dependence of feeling and conation is mutual.

## Feeling and Desire

If desire is fulfilled it gives rise to pleasure. If desire is frustrated, it gives rise to pain. Desire is directed towards an object. If the object is attained, it gives rise to pleasure. If the object is not attained, it gives rise to pain. Thus desire is a cause of feeling, pleasure or pain.

Feeling also is a cause of desire. Generally, a painful

feeling of want is a spring of action. Pain gives rise to a desire to relieve it. The pain of hunger produces a desire to seek and eat food. Pleasure is not generally a spring of action. Thus desire depends upon feeling.

Desire itself is partly pleasant and mainly painful. It not only often springs from pain, but it is itself very unpleasant because it contains an intense consciousness of the difference between the actual and the ideal. In the desire for food there is a keen consciousness of the difference between the present state of hunger and the future state of satisfaction; and this consciousness is intensely unpleasant, though it is not devoid of a tinge of pleasure arising from the anticipation of future satisfaction. Thus desire is coloured by an affective tone.

### Pain-Sensation and Pain-Feeling

There is a difference between pain-sensation and pain-feeling. The tactual sensation of pain can be localised and combined with other sensations. Organic pain sensations are not always more or less definitely localised. Tactual pain and organic pain are sensations; they may often be distinguished as shooting, burning, gnawing, etc.; thus they may have different qualities. They cannot be identified with the purely subjective feeling of pain which has no objective qualities. Moreover, pain sensations may sometimes be agreeable. At the root of a tooth there are many pain spots. So toothache gives intense pain sensation. But some persons feel pleasure when a loose tooth is touched. A wound gives pain sensation. But if it is gently touched, some persons feel pleasure. Thus a sensation of pain may be accompanied by a feeling of pleasure. Therefore the feeling of pain is different from the sensation of pain.

# CHAPTER XIII

## *Emotion*

### Feeling and Emotion

Affective states are of two kinds, viz., feeling and emotions. (1) Feelings are simple sense-feelings of pleasure and pain. They arise from sensations. They ars peripherally excited. They are produced by the sense-organs, which are stimulated by stimuli. Look at a patch of yellow colour. It gives you pleasure. You suffer from a toothache. It gives you pain. These are sense-feelings. Emotions are complex affective states arising from perception, memory, or imagination of a situation. They always involve memory and imagination. They are centrally excited. They arise from ideas and thoughts. They are higher and more complex affective states. The pleasantness of a colour is a feeling, while the joy of meeting a friend after a long time is an emotion. The pain produced by a shrill sound is a feeling, while the pain of grief is an emotion. Feelings and emotions differ in mental quality. Their specific differences in quality are due to the attendant circumstances which give rise to them. New factors enter into the structure of an emotion at the higher level of ideation which did not exist in a feeling arising from a sensation.

The organic expressions of emotions are more diffuse than those of sense-feelings. Fear is accompanied with rapid palpitation of the heart, trembling of the limbs, shaking of the body, drying of the palate, paleness of the face, and running for safety. But the pleasure of seeing a flower is not attended with diffuse organic changes. Nervous excitation is restricted in sense-feelings. The organic expression of an emotion is more diffused than that of a feeling.

## Characteristics of Emotion

An emotion is a temporal experience. It consists in a series of connected experiences. It continues for a length of time. It is a suddenly aroused experience. It begins abruptly, rises to a climax, and dies down gradually. It is a highly complex experience. It is excited by a situation, and contains cognitive, affective and conative factors. It becomes highly complex with the development of cognition. Feeling is the predominant factor in it. It is coloured by feeling, because the situation itself is pleasant or painful, and because the organic sensations accompanying it are pleasant or painful. Organic excitement constitutes an important factor of an intense emotion. A strong emotion devoid of general organic excitement is inconceivable. It strongly agitates the mind. The agitation of the mind is expressed in the body. Both mind and body are thrown into excitement in a strong emotion. The more intensely excited we are, the more emotional is our experience. Finally, an emotion depends on instincts or acquired conative dispositions. When they are furthered or thwarted, they give rise to emotions. You take away an article of food from a hungry dog. He gets angry. His anger arises from interference with the instinct of hunger. McDougall holds that primary emotions spring from instincts, and that emotions are affective correlates or instinctive acts excited by specific situations.

## Factors in an Emotion

An emotion is the stirred up condition of an individual. All the factors of an emotion are brought out in the following statement.

Every emotion has two sides, bodily and mental. There are the following factors on the mental side :—

(1) The perception of a situation which affects the well-being of an individual ;

(2) an affective quality tending towards pleasure or towards pain ;

(3) a tendency to activity ; and

(4) organic sensations.

There are the following factors on the bodily side :—

(1) diffused changes in the internal organs ; and

(2) muscular movements.

The bodily factors are called the expression[1].

We should attend to the following characteristics in describing an emotion :—

(1) An emotion is excited by the perception, memory or imagination of a situation. An isolated object does not arouse an emotion. But a situation which has a bearing on an individual subject arouses an emotion. For example, the perception of a tiger at large threatens the life of a person, and arouses fear in him. But a tiger confined in an iron cage does not excite terror. A situation often evokes an instinctive act which is felt as an emotion. The perception of a tiger at large evokes the instinctive act of flying away, and this is felt as the emotion of fear.

(2) An emotion has an affective quality ; it is pleasant or painful. Pleasure or pain is an important constituent of an emotion. The perception of a situation produces pleasure or pain. Therefore, it is not cold, neutral, or feelingless. There is the feeling of pain in anger and fear. There is the feeling of pleasure in love and joy.

(3) An emotion affects conation ; it generates an impulse to act ; it involves a tendency to activity. An emotion is a response of the subject to a situation. This response consists in a more or less diffuse excitement, which changes the physiological processes of breathing, circulation of blood, etc., and braces or relaxes many voluntary muscles[2].

(4) An emotion thus produces diffused "organic reverberation" in the internal organs in the language of William James. These are reported to the brain through the sensory nerves and produce organic sensations. These organic sensations are an important factor of an emotion.

(5) An emotion produces movements in various muscles also. These muscular movements are reported to the brain by sensory nerves and produce muscular sensations. These motor sensations also are an important constituent of an emotion.

Thus an emotion contains perception, memory, or imagination of a situation (cognition), pleasure or pain (affection), a tendency to act (conation), organic sensations (cognition), and motor sensations (cognition). An emotion, therefore, contains elements of cognition, feeling, and conation which constitute its structure.

### Emotion and Mood

A mood is a tendency to feel an emotion. It is an after-effect of an actual emotion, which persists in the mind. You were scolded by your father for misbehaviour. It aroused anger in your mind. It has passed away but left an irritable mood behind. A mood is a hang over from an emotion. It is less intense but more lasting in duration than an emotion. It is a persisting after-effect of an emotion. An emotion is a cause of a mood.

An emotion is felt in relation to a definite object ; to be angry we must be angry about something. You pull the tail of a cat, and it becomes angry. You are abused by a person, and you get angry. An emotion is excited by a definite situation. A mood, on the other hand, has no definite object. It is the lingering effect of an emotion. It tends to persist in the mind and colour the whole field of consciousness. It tends to create an object for itself. If you get angry once, you will feel an irritable mood for some time after the outburst of anger. You will be apt to get angry at the slightest provocation. For example, your brother removes your pen or pencil by way of fun, and you get angry with him and box his ears. A mood is a persisting after-effect of an emotion. And sometimes it is the pre-disposing cause of an emotion.

A mood is sometimes produced by organic conditions. A person constantly suffers from indigestion. These organic conditions produce an irritable mood in his mind. Similarly, if a person suffers from insomnia, he acquires an irritable mood. On the other hand, the constant use of drugs (e.g., wine) may produce a mood of hilarity. Thus moods are not always after-effects of active emotional outbursts. They are sometimes produced by organic conditions which cannot directly produce emotions.

## Emotion and Sentiment

A sentiment is not an actual outburst of an emotion. It is a permanent emotional disposition. It is a permanent tendency to feel an emotion. An emotion is a function or an experience. A sentiment is a structure or mental disposition. An emotion is actually felt in consciousness ; it is a conscious process. But a sentiment persists in the subconscious level as a permanent disposition to feel a specific emotion. It is not felt in consciousness. It is a permanent emotional disposition. An emotion is conscious. But a sentiment is subconscious.

An emotion is a temporary outburst, whereas a sentiment is a permanent emotional disposition. An emotion is felt in the focus of consciousness. A sentiment, on the other hand, persists as a comparatively permanent disposition in the sub-conscious. The mother has love for her child. She does not always feel the emotion of love. But she has a permanent emotional disposition to love the child on appropriate occasions. She has sentiment of love for the child. For example, when the child feels hungry and cries, the mother feels love and hastens to feed him. On some occasions only the mother feels the emotion of love. You have hate for your enemy. Your hatred for the enemy is a permanent emotional disposition. It is awakened and passes over into an actual emotion of hate, when you see your enemy or brood over the injury done to you by him. Thus love, hatred, friendship, patriotism, etc., are sentiments or emotional dispositions.

A sentiment is a permanent emotional disposition. It is the result of experiencing a particular kind of emotion frequently. It is an emotional habit. It is a disposition to feel a specific emotion. A sentiment is an organised system of emotional tendencies centred about some object. A simple sentiment is the result of the same kind of emotion. A complex sentiment is the result of many kinds of emotions.

A sentiment is a pre-disposing cause of an emotion. A simple sentiment produces only one kind of emotion. A complex sentiment produces many kinds of emotions. Friendship is a complex and developed sentiment. It produces sorrow on parting from one's friend, joy on meeting with him after separation for a long time, hope for his success, anger against his foes, and fear when he is in danger. A simple sentiment is manifested in one emotion. A complex sentiment is expressed in a variety of emotions.

### Sentiment and Mood

A sentiment is a permanent emotional disposition. But a mood is a temporary after-effect of an emotional outburst. A sentiment persists in the subconscious level. But an emotional mood is felt in the field of consciousness. It is actually felt in consciousness. A sentiment cannot be felt unless it is manifested as an emotion. But an emotion is not the same thing as a sentiment. A sentiment is the predisposing cause of an emotion. It is a permanent emotional disposition. A mood is an actual affection of consciousness. But a sentiment is not an actual experience. It is a subconscious tendency to feel an emotion. It persists as a mental structure when neither the emotion nor the mood is being felt.

When you are in an irritable mood, you feel it in consciousness ; the state of irritability is a conscious feeling. But you cannot feel the sentiment of love or hatred. Sentiments are permanent emotional dispositions which persist in the subconscious level[3].

The nature of complexes will be explained in the last chapter.

### Emotion and Temperament

A mood is a temporary after-effect of an emotion. A sentiment is a permanent emotional disposition persisting in the subconscious level. Temperament is deeper and more permenent than a mood or a sentiment. It enters into the composition of character. It determines the whole attitude of a person's life. It gives a permanent bent to his thoughts, emotions, and volitions.

Intellectual, emotional and volitional attributes are included in temperament. The emotional factor is the most significant of them[4]. It is the innate tendency of an individual to react to emotive situations in a characteristic manner. Temperament is said to be determined by the secretions of ductless glands called hormones.

Four principal temperaments are recognised, sanguine, choleric, melancholic, and phlegmatic. The sanguine individual has a pleasant and hopeful outlook ; he is alert and easily stirred. The choleric individual is strong, alert and quick in response, and predisposed to anger. He displays a more intense interest than a sanguine individual. The melancholic individual is slow in response and predisposed to grief, but he has a strong character and displays a strong and vivid interest when once aroused. He is pessimistic and takes a dark view of things, whereas the sanguine individual is optimistic and takes a bright view of things. The phlegmatic individual is slow in response and displays a persistent but weak interest.

## Emotion and Organic Expression

An emotion arises from the perception, memory, or imagination of a situation, and is expressed in organic changes. Thus according to the common view, first there is perception, memory, or imagination of a situation ; then an emotion arises out of it, and then the emotion is expressed in organic changes. Thus an emotion is followed by its organic expression. For example, you perceive a tiger at large ; it excites fear in your mind ; then you tremble and run away ; the emotion of fear is expressed in trembling and running away. Emotions are prior to organic expressions. They are expressed in diffuse organic changes in the internal organs and muscles, which produce organic and motor sensations. These are important factors of emotions. But they do not constitute emotions.

## James-Lange Theory of Emotion

James and Lange hold that emotions are constituted by organic sensations. Organic expressions are prior to emotions. They do not follow upon emotions. Trembling and running away take place before fear is felt. Frowning, howling, beating, etc., occur before anger is felt. Shedding tears occurs before sorrow is felt. An emotion is a mass of organic and muscular sensations. An object is perceived. The perception of it reflexly excites changes in the internal organs and muscles. They produce organic and muscular sensations. The perception of the object and the organic and muscular sensations constitute an emotion.

James says, "Common sense says, we lose our fortune, are sorry and weep ; we meet a bear, are frightened and run ; we are insulted by a rival, are angry and strike. The more rational statement is that we feel sorry because we cry, angry because we strike, afraid because we tremble, and not that we cry, strike, or tremble because we are sorry, angry or fearful, as the case may be.[5]"

The theory of James is not tenable. First, emotions are affective states, while organic sensations are cognitive states. Emotions tend to vanish if they are attended to. But organic states (e.g., hunger) do not vanish if they are attended to. Secondly, different emotions have the same organic expression. There are tears of joy, tears of sorrow, and tears of rage. Thirdly, the same emotion may have different organic expressions. A savage expresses anger by biting, tearing with nails, kicking, striking, etc. A cultured person expresses anger by frowning, clenching the fist, etc. Fourthly, no emotions are felt sometimes when there are organic expressions which resemble expressions of emotions. When we are afraid, we shiver. Shivering is an expression of fear. But when we shiver from cold, we feel no emotion of fear. Therefore organic sensations do not constitute an emotion[6].

## Organic States in Emotions

Emotions are attended with changes in the internal organs. They are expressed in changes in respiration, circulation and digestion. These are connected with the nerves of the autonomic nervous system. In fear and anger digestion is stopped or arrested ; the gastric juice does not flow into the stomach, and the stomach movements and the churning movements of the intestines cease. So we should not get afraid or angry at the time of and after taking food. Strong emotions produce excitement. Excitement increases blood pressure. The sweat glands are aroused in some emotions, e.g., fear, surprise, etc., and perspiration follows. The tear glands are stimulated in some emotions, e.g., joy, sorrow, rage, and tears are shed. The organic states in emotions prepare the organism for overt actions. They prepare it to escape in fear, and to fight in anger. Emotions are closely connected with the nerves of the autonomic nervous system and the ductless glands[7].

**Biological significance of Expressions of Emotions**

Why do particular emotions have particular expressions? How can we explain their connection? What are the laws of the expression of emotions? Darwin has laid down three principles to account for emotional expressions.

(1) The principle of Serviceable Associated Habits.—Many expressions are survivals of biologically useful actions. They are partial survivals of actions which proved useful to the subject himself or to his ancestors in situations exciting similar emotions. For example, clenching the fist, showing and grinding the teeth, frowning, howling, scratching, biting and the like in anger are survivals of those actions which were useful to our ancestors. They actually used their teeth in anger in fighting the enemies; our showing and grinding the teeth are a mere survival of that useful action. Crouching and hiding in fear are survivals of our ancestors' concealment in bushes, caves, etc., from the source of danger.

(2) Another principle to which Darwin perhaps hardly does sufficient justice may be called the principle of reacting similarly to analogous-feeling stimuli. When a child tastes a sweet thing, he nods his head. Later when he expresses his approval of something he also nods. Both the feelings are agreeable and are expressed in a similar way. When a child tastes a bitter thing, he shakes his head. Later when he expresses his disapproval of something, he also shakes his

head. Both the feelings are disagreeable and are expressed in a similar way. Thus similar emotions are expressed in similar ways.

(3) Darwin accounts for many emotional expressions by what he calls the principle of antithesis. Contrary emotions are expressed in contrary ways. If a certain situation evoking a particular emotion excites a certain set of reactions, then a contrary situation evoking a contrary emotion will excite the opposite set of reactions, though they might otherwise have neither utility nor significance. Anger is expressed by clenching the fists, attempt to strike, tensenesses of muscles, and the like, while fear is expressed by open palms, dropped arms, drooping limbs, relaxation of muscles and the like. Expressions of opposite emotions are opposite to each other. Many emotional expressions can be accounted for by this principle.

## Emotion and Instinct

William James points out that an instinct refers primarily to a physical process, while an emotion refers to a physical process. "An emotion," says James, "is a tendency to feel and an instinct is a tendency to act, characteristically when in the presence of a certain object in the environment.[8]"

Woodworth points out that an emotion consists of internal responses while the instinct is directed outwards, or, at least, involves actions on external objects. He also points out that the emotional response is of the nature of a preparatory reaction, while the instinct is directed towards the end-reaction. The emotional response prepares an individual to realise an end. The instinctive act is directed to the realisation of an end[9].

The close connection of emotion and instinct is as important to notice as the distinction between them. Emotions are based on instincts. McDougall holds that an emotion is a conscious correlate of an instinctive action. He defines instinct as "an inherited or innate psycho-physical disposition which determines its possessor to perceive, and to pay attention to, objects of a certain class, to experience an emotional excitement of a particular quality upon perceiving such an object, and to act in regard to it in a particular manner, or, at least, to experience an impulse to such an action.[10]" He defines a primary emotion as "the affective aspect of the operation of any one of the principal instincts." According to him, primary emotions are based on instincts. No primary emotions are possible without instincts. Emotions and instincts go together.

### McDougall's theory of Emotion : Basic Emotions

McDougall holds that an emotion is the affective aspect of the operation of an instinct. Primary emotions are the conscious correlates of instincts. "Each of the principal instincts conditions some one kind of emotional excitement, whose quality is specific or peculiar to it." McDougall gives the following pairs of instincts and emotions correlated to each other :—

| | *Instincts.* | *Emotions.* |
|---|---|---|
| (1) | Instinct of flight. | Fear. |
| (2) | Instinct of combat. | Anger. |
| (3) | Instinct of repulsion. | Disgust. |
| (4) | Instinct of curiosity. | Wonder |
| (5) | Instinct of sex. | Lust. |
| (6) | Parental instinct. | Tender Emotion. |
| (7) | Instinct of self-abasement. | Subjection. |
| (8) | Instinct of self-assertion. | Elation. |
| (9) | Gregarious instinct. | Loneliness. |
| (10) | Instinct of acquisition. | Ownership. |
| (11) | Instinct of construction. | Creativeness. |
| (12) | Instinct of laughter. | Amusement or Mirth. |

McDougall regards all the emotions based on instincts as primary or basic emotions. He is right when he states the principle that every emotive situation appeals to instinctive tendencies. There is no doubt that emotions are intimately connected with instincts. But Titchener rightly urges that the simple instincts of 'sitting', 'standing', 'walking,' 'running', etc., are not connected exclusively with any particular emotion.

The same emotion may include a variety of instincts in its system. The instincts of concealment and flight both operate in the emotion of fear. But McDougall's theory demands that each of these instincts have a different emotion. Again, the same instinct may be connected with different emotions. The instinct of flight may be excited in birds through fear as well as anger. There are some instincts, e.g., gregarious instinct, constructive instinct, acquisitive instinct, etc. which have no well—defined specific emotions. So emotion is not an integral factor of an instinct[11].

Drever and Woodworth contend that there can be an instinctive act without an emotion. No emotion appears so long as the instinctive act runs smoothly. But emotion appears as soon as there is a hindrance to the instinctive act. When we face a sudden danger, and calmly and resolutely run and escape from the dangerous situation, we do not feel the emotion of fear. We may also fight without the emotion of anger. But if the act of fighting is obstructed, we may feel the emotion of anger. Therefore we usually feel the emotion before the instinctive behaviour takes place, rather than along with it[12]. McDougall's theory may be regarded as a working hypothesis. But it has not yet been established beyond doubt by accumulation of facts. Still it contains a core of truth. Emotions are closely connected with instincts.

McDougall sometimes recognizes eight primary or basic emotions, viz., fear, anger, disgust, parental emotion, wonder, elation, subjection, and sex emotion. J. B. Watson regards fear, anger and love as primary emotions.

## Primary and Derivative Emotions

Some divide emotions into primary and derivative emotions according to their nature. Primary emotions are elementary in their character. They do not presuppose other emotional experiences as their conditions or components. They do not depend upon any preceding emotional experiences. Fear, anger, joy, sorrow, and love, in their elementary forms, seem to be primary emotions. Derivative emotions presuppose some preceding emotional experiences. They depend upon primary emotions as their conditions or components. Jealousy, admiration, pity, gratitude, remorse, wounded vanity, and the like are derivative emotions. Jealousy is a combination of love with fear and anger. Awe is a combination of wonder and fear. Loathing is a combination of fear and disgust.

Primary emotions become refined in three ways. First, they are refined by modifications of the motor response by which socially acceptable reactions are substituted for the primitive emotional expressions such as crying, kicking, scratching, biting and the like. The emotional expressions of a cultured man are different from those of a child or a savage.

Secondly, primary emotions are modified by new attachments on the side of the stimulus. The primary emotion of fear is originally excited by the perception of a loud sound. But if a rat or a kitten is presented along with the sound a number of times, it evokes the fear response. Fear is thus conditioned to a substitute stimulus. Perhaps phobias originate in conditioned emotions.

Thirdly, primary emotions are modified by combination of one emotion with another. Hate is a compound of anger, fear, and disgust. Pity is a compound of grief and tenderness.

### Analysis of Emotions

(1) Fear.—Fear is an emotion excited by the perception or imagination of danger. McDougall holds that the emotion of fear is the affective aspect of the instinct to escape. Fear is excited by a deafening noise, a blinding flash of lightning, a sudden peal of thunder, and other dangerous objects. It arises from the perception of an object which caused pain or injury in the past. A dangerous object or situation is the cause of fear. An object must be aggressive to excite fear. It must break in upon consciousness and disturb its smooth flow of ideas. It must be obtrusive. A sudden and intense impression is sufficient to excite fear. A loud sound or a dazzling flash of light is the cause of fear. Fear is expressed in quick palpitation of the heart, trembling, drooping of the limbs, running away, and the like. Extreme terror is expressed in motionlessness of the body.

(2) Anger.—Anger is excited by thwarting of conation. It arises from obstruction of any instinctive or acquired tendency. McDougall holds that the emotion of anger is the affective aspect of the instinct of combat. Any kind of opposition may arouse anger. Any thwarting of mental activity may excite it. A cow will get angry if you interfere with her new-born calf. A boy will become angry if you snatch away his kite. An author will get angry if his book is criticised unfavourably. Anger is expressed in breaking down opposition, active resistance and fighting. It is expressed in a violent motor discharge. It is expressed in frowning, howling, grinding the teeth, closing the fists, kicking, striking, and the like.

(3) Joy.—Joy arises from the attainment of a cherished object. When the object of desire is attained, it gives rise to joy. It is expressed in "a general heightened tension of the entire body." Erect posture, throwing out the chest, brightness of the eyes, smiling face, shouting, laughing, jumping and the like are the expressions of joy.

(4) Sorrow.—Sorrow or grief arises from the loss of a cherished object. It is excited by the failure to fulfil our desires. When a person is deprived of his cherished objects, he feels sorrow. Sorrow is an emotion of loss or deprivation. It is the opposite of joy, which is an emotion of achievement. When a desired object is attained, we feel joy. When we are deprived of a desired object, we feel sorrow. Joy and sorrow are the opposite emotions. The expressions of sorrow are the opposite of those of joy. Shedding tears, drooping posture, retracting the chest, general relaxation of the bodily tension, and the like are the expressions of sorrow. Deep grief has a prostrating effect. It makes the body motionless.

(5) Love.—The word 'love' is ambiguous. It is used in three senses. First, it means sexual emotion. It is the emotion arising from the sex instinct. McDougall calls it the emotion of lust. Secondly, it means tender emotion or affection arising from the maternal instinct. Thirdly, it means a sentiment or permanent emotional disposition, which is manifested in tender emotion. Selfish love seeks to satisfy itself, regardless of the welfare of the loved object. But when it is excited, not merely

by the presence of the loved object, but also by considerations for the welfare of the object, it is the true emotion of love. It contains the bare emotion of attachment and the emotion of sympathy. Attachment is expressed in fondling or caressing.

Love contains two elements, viz., attachment and sympathy. Attachment consists in fondling and caressing. Sympathy consists in sharing or entering into the emotions of others. Sully holds that attachment or selfish love is the egoistic element, and sympathy, the altruistic element in love. Bain holds that attachment is a tender emotion which is expressed in bodily contact of some sort—touching, caressing, embracing and the like. In fact, the natural outlet of love, in all its forms, is delight in the society of, or in the presence of, the loved object.

(6) Hate.—The word 'hate' is ambiguous. It is used in the sense of a sentiment and an emotion both. According to McDougall, hate is a compound emotion. It consists of anger, fear, and disgust. The object of hatred excites our anger, frightens us, and appears disgusting. A powerful person who insults you excites anger in you. But anger cannot be expressed in fighting him. He is too powerful for you. So he excites fear in you. This impotent anger mingled with fear is further complicated by disgust or loathing for the person. Hate is opposed to love. Love makes a person approach the beloved. Hate makes a person withdraw from the presence of the hated person. Love is an expanding emotion. Hate is a contracting emotion. It is an emotion which is expressed in self-defence and withdrawal.

## The Conditioning of Emotions

Emotions are aroused by particular objects or situations. But they can be conditioned to substitute stimuli. Fear is excited by a loud sound in a baby. But it is not excited by a rat, a cat, or a dog. But if a rat is presented to a baby with the loud sound of a steel bar a number of times, his fear is conditioned to it. Similarly if a cat is presented to a baby with the loud sound of a steel bar a number of times, his fear is conditioned to it. Later a cat excites his anger. Similarly his fear is conditioned to a dog. Fear may be conditioned to a closed space, an open space, a dark room, and imaginary objects, e.g., ghosts, giants, hobgoblins, etc. The elders associate the infants' fear with them repeatedly and thus condition it. Conditioned fear may be deconditioned by extinction of the association. Phobia originates in conditioned fear due to association in childhood. It can be cured by unearthing the conditioned fear of childhood and convincing the patient of the irrationality of the association.

Anger is roused by interference with one's course of action. A dull boy gets angry with his teacher who scolds him often for negligence in his studies. Later his anger may be conditioned to his school, other teachers, etc. A child gets angry with his step-mother who often ill-treats him. Then his anger may be conditioned to any pet of his step-mother. Thus anger is conditioned to improper objects. Similarly, love, disgust, and other emotions may be conditioned[13].

## Concrete and Abstract Sentiments

Sentiments are permanent emotional dispositions. They are the results of many emotional experiences. They are mental dispositions persisting in the subconscious level. They are manifested as actual emotions on appropriate occasions.

Sentiments centre round certain objects or persons, or ideals. They are either concrete or abstract. Concrete sentiments are excited by objects, persons, or groups of persons. Love, hate, friendship, sympathy, patriotism, humanitarianism, and the like are concrete sentiments. Abstract sentiments are inspired by the contemplation of the Ideals of Truth, Good, Beauty and the Holy. They are calm and quiet. They may not have well-defined somatic resonance or physiological correlates. They are contemplative in attitude. They are excited by the contemplation of abstract Ideals. They are neither egoistic, nor altruistic, but wholly disinterested and impersonal.

Abstract sentiments are of three kinds: intellectual sentiments, moral sentiments, aesthetic sentiments, and religious sentiments. They are inspired by the contemplation of the Ideals of Truth, Good, Beauty and the Holy respectively. When intellectual, moral, aesthetic, and religious sentiments are manifested as actual emotions, being evoked by their appropriate objects, we have intellectual, moral, aesthetic and religious emotions. Some psychologists used the term 'sentiment' in the sense of these ideal emotions or emotions excited by contemplation of ideals. But the modern psychologists use it in the sense of permanent emotional dispositions which may be either concrete or abstract.

## Development of Sentiments

First, concrete sentiments are developed. They are directed towards concrete objects or individuals. Gradually they are directed towards wider and wider circles or groups of individuals. Then, gradually abstract sentiments are developed. They are directed towards general principles and abstract ideals.

At first, concrete sentiments are directed towards individuals. The child forms the sentiment of love for his mother. Then he gradually widens the scope of his affection and forms the home sentiment. Then he further widens the circle of his love and develops the school sentiment. In this way he forms the communal sentiment, local patriotism, national patriotism, humanitarianism, etc. Gradually abstract sentiments emerge which centre round general principles, e.g., hatred of injustice or oppression, love of freedom, love of order and progress, hatred of anarchy and revolution. Then abstract sentiments are directed towards abstract ideals, e.g., devotion to truth, love of beauty, love of good, and reverence for God.

Moral sentiments are centred round the ideal of good. The sentiment of self-regard is the master sentiment under which all other concrete and abstract sentiments are developed. It organizes them into a unity.

## Abnormalities of Emotion and their causes

There are the following abnormalities of emotion :—

(1) Apathy.—It is utter lack of emotions. The patient

does not take any interest in the environment. He is neither excited nor depressed, but absolutely indifferent. He seems to be devoid of interest, desires, or ambitions. Emotional dementia is the best example of apathy. The patient sits in a corner with face devoid of expression and head hanging down. He takes no interest in the environment and notices nothing. This is emotional apathy. In the less prominent forms of emotional dementia the patient answers questions and performs routine tasks mechanically without showing any interest. They are devoid of hopes, plans, or ambitions[13]. Emotional apathy is shown by lack of feeling, loss of energy, and absence of the urge of living. It is accompanied by muscular inactivity.

Negativism is the common cause of emotional apathy. It is antagonism to the environment or to the wishes of the persons who are about the patient. Antagonism is expressed in perverse behaviour. Sometimes apathy is due to regression to infantile experience. The patient cannot cope with the complex environment and relapses into the past infantile experience devoid of all emotions. This is called regression. It is due to factors in the environment which produce unhappiness, e.g., father or mather's death.

(2) Involution Melancholia.—There is a marked feeling of unworthiness and sin mixed with sadness. Delusion also may appear in it. Sometimes the patient is haunted by the delusion of death. Delusion is a persistent false belief. The patient wrongly believes that he will be killed, hanged or burnt alive. Sometimes the delusion of death may take the guise of immortality, and the patient believes that he will never die.

Involution melancholia is due to physical degeneration in the declining years of life. It may be due to the imperfect functioning of the endocrine glands. Sometimes it is due to regression. The patient becomes weary of life because he fails to adapt himself to the environment owing to his growing selfishness and egotism. He relapses into the experience of the infant, who is engrossed with his body and indifferent to the world which has little meaning for him.

(3) Depression.—It is the most common form of abnormal

emotions. The patient feels miserable and unhappy. The feeling of sadness is a prominent characteristic of depression. It is due to grief over some loss of friend or property. Sadness springs from hopelessness. The feeling of inferiority is another important element. There is also a feeling of unreality. It is due to the loss of interest. There is sometimes a feeling of inadequacy. It is sometimes expressed in delusions of physical and mental incapacity. Delusions are persistent false beliefs. Depression is due to maladaptation to the environment. Maladaptation is sometimes due to unconscious egotism, which is far in excess of the individual's intellectual endowment. Anxious thoughts and attitudes are expressions of repression. Repeated failures to express the repressed emotions bring about regression to infantile experience and a sense of inferiority.

(4) Mania or Excitement.—In manic excitement the patient displays an abnormal output of energy. He is constantly active. He takes up one occupation, gives it up immediately and commences another. He cannot stick to an occupation for some time. He is never inactive, but displays a constant urge for activity. He is generally abnormally cheerful and contented with himself and his environment. But his mood is mutable like his attention. His cheerfulness suddenly changes into violent anger at the slightest provocation. The manic patient is not amenable to reason and argument. Mania is marked by pleasure, whereas melancholia is marked by unpleasure.

In manic state and depression there is free association of ideas. Ideas are not controlled by a definite purpose. There is a deflection of interest and attention from the environment and from normal pursuits to more primitive interests and fantasies. Thus there is a regression of interest. The patient has delusions and hallucinations which seem real to him. They arouse emotions in him and evoke his actions. Regression involves flight from reality to unreality. It involves flight from the real environment to another imaginary environment or unreality, past as remembered or future as conjured up in fantasy. Thus abnormalities of emotion are due to maladaptation of personality to the environment[14].

## Degrees of Emotional Responsiveness

Normals persons differ in their general emotional responsiveness. There are calm persons who are generally not perturbed by emotions. There are excitable persons who are deeply stirred by emotions. These are two extremes. There are many degrees of emotionality between these two extremes.

(1) Emotional Excess.—Some persons have an excess of emotionality. They are susceptible to all emotions. Their emotions are easily excited by slight stimuli. Joy, fear, anger, sorrow, and other emotions are easily and frequently aroused. They are usually intense. Joy becomes ecstasy, fear becomes terror, anger becomes violent rage, and sorrow becomes intense grief. Emotions are felt in their intensity.

(2) Emotional Instability.—Generally the persons who have an excess of emotionality have also emotional instability. They often shift abruptly from joy to sorrow, from love to hate, from self-confidence to diffidence. This is called emotional instability. It is generally accompanied by emotional sensitivity and excess of response. But excessive emotionality and emotional instability do not invariably go together. Sometimes emotional instability is found along with nervous and mental instability.

(3) Unemotional Nature.—The extremely unemotional individual is not dead to all emotions. But his emotions are not easily aroused. They are less frequently and less intensely aroused. They are by no means unemotional. Unemotional persons do not experience difficulties in adapting themselves to the social environment. But over-emotional persons cannot easily adapt themselves to it.

In the emotional person the sympathetic nervous system is readily excited and brings about visceral changes. Excessive sensitivity of the sympathetic system is the cause of excessive emotionality and emotional instability[15].

## REFERENCE

[1] *The Elements of Psychology*, pp. 225-26.

[2] *Psychological Principles*.

[3]*Manual of Psychology*, pp. 375-76.
[4]Angell, *Psychology*, p. 391.
[5]*Brief Text-Book of Psychology*, pp. 375-76.
[6]Titchener, *Text-Book of Psychology*, p. 482.
[7]J. N. Sinha, *Manual of Psychology*, pp. 278-81.
[8]*A Brief Text-Book of Psychology.*
[9]*Psychology.*
[10]*Introduction to Social Psychology*, p. 29.
[11]*Text-Book of Psychology.*
[12]Drever, *Introduction to Educational Psychology.*
[13]*Foundations of Psychology*, pp. 143-44.
[14]Hart, *Psychology of Insanity*, pp. 27-28.
[15]McCurdy, *Psychology of Emotion.*
[16]Gates, *Elementary Psycology*, pp. 210-13.

## CHAPTER XIV

*Non-Voluntary Actions*

### Non-voluntary Actions

We have discussed the nature of the different kinds of cognition, viz., sensation, perception, memory, imagination, and thinking, and the different kinds of affection, viz., feeling, emotion, and sentiment. Now we shall consider the nature of the different kinds of action, viz., non-voluntary and voluntary. Non-voluntary actions precede voluntary actions. There are several kinds of non-voluntary actions, viz., Automatic Actions, Random Actions, Reflex Actions, Conditioned Reflexes, Ideo-motor Actions, and Instinctive Actions.

### Automatic Acts

The new-born baby does not come into the world in a quite helpless condition. The little stranger can perform some acts at once. Some physiological processes go on within his organism just after birth. Respiration, circulation of blood and digestion are found in the organism from birth. They involve muscular movements, which are called automatic acts. They are evoked by stimuli within the organism. The chemical condition of the blood excites changes in circulation and respiration. The presence of food in the stomach excites digestion. Thus automatic acts are excited by intra-organic stimuli. We are under normal conditions entirely unconscious of these acts. Whenever they are upset, they cause us pain and attract our attention. We become conscious of automatic acts, whenever anything goes wrong with them and they are attended with painful sensations. Thus, we become conscious of hard breathing, indigestion, high blood pressure and the like. Some call automatic acts physiological reflexes.

## Random Actions

Random actions are the spontaneous expressions of energy accumulated in the organism. They are supposed to be due to the automatic excitation of the motor centres. The movements of the chick in the egg and some earlier movements of the infant, as stretching out the arms, the legs, and so forth are random or spontaneous actions. These movements are neither evoked by external stimuli nor actuated by the anticipation of an end.

The aimless and irregular movements of the child in response to external stimuli also are sometimes called random movements. They are the expressions of neural excitement. They are unco-ordinated responses to external stimuli. When a child sees a coloured toy, he makes many aimless and irregular movements. The sensation of colour produces neural excitement which comes out through various motor nerves, and produces many aimless movements in a random manner. These are random actions. Controlled and co-ordinated movements emerge out of these random and aimless diffuse movements. Random movements are the basis of voluntary movements.

Some original random actions, e.g., movements of the baby in the womb are not psychically initiated. They are spontaneous expressions of accumulated energy in the motor centres. Other random actions, e.g., the baby's movements of arms and legs are psychically initiated. They are promted by a feeling of uneasiness due to accumulated energy in the motor centres. Some random actions are not evoked by external stimuli. The random movements mentioned above are not excited by external stimuli. But some random movements are excited by external stimuli. The child's aimless, irregular and diffuse movements at the sight of a coloured toy are called forth by a sensory stimulus. Random movements are adapted to results beneficial to the system. The child's aimless movements of arms and legs serve the purpose of physical exercise. They strengthen the muscles and serve as the basis of controlled and co-ordinated movements. But they are not so adapted deliberately. They are not guided by any idea of an end or purpose. They do not involve anticipation of an end. They are non-voluntary actions. But they are the foundation of voluntary actions.

## Reflex Actions

A reflex action is a prompt muscular or glandular response to a sensory stimulus. It is an immediate response to a stimulus. The response is direct and immediate. It invariably follows upon a stimulus. It is uniform. It is discontinued when the stimulus ceases to operate. When you take a slight whiff of pepper you sneeze. When you cease to take it sneezing ceases.

Reflex actions are always reactions to sensory stimuli. The stimuli may be either external objects or organic disturbances. We close our eyes at the sight of a dazzling object. Here the reflex act is excited by an external stimulus. We sneeze when something (e.g., snuff) obstructs or irritates the nasal membrane. We cough when cold obstructs or irritates the throat. Here the reflex acts are evoked by organic disturbances. All these reflexes are motor or muscular reactions to sensory stimuli, either extra-organic or intra-organic. Some reflexes are glandular reactions to sensory stimuli. If something irritating (e.g., dust) falls into our eyes, we shed tears. If we taste a sour thing, we have salivation. These reflexes are glandular responses to sensory stimuli. A reflex action may be expressed by the formula. S—O—R. S—Natural stimulus ; O—Organism ; R—Response.

There are two kinds of reflex actions, viz., physiological reflexes and sensation reflexes. Reflex acts may be performed with or without consciousness. The reflexes of which we are entirely unconscious are called physiological reflexes. The pupillary reflex is a physiological reflex. When there is bright light, the pupil contracts ; when there is dim light, the pupil expands. We are not conscious of the change in the size of the pupil. The reflexes of which we are conscious are called sensation reflexes. We are conscious of winking, sneezing, coughing, etc. So these are sensation-reflexes. Sometimes consciousness may take cognisance of reflex acts, but does not produce them. We may be conscious that we have winked, but the closing of the eye-lids is a reflex action which is not produced by consciousness. Physiological reflexes are unconscious ; they are independent of conscious control. Sensation reflexes are conscious ; they are preceded and succeeded by consciousness. But generally they cannot be controlled by consciousness. At the approach of a stick to your eyes you are conscious of the stick, and when you have closed your eye-lids, you are conscious of the winking. But you can seldom control the reflex action. Sometiimes sensation reflexes can be suppressed for some time by consciousness. But they come out violently after some time. At the sudden approach of a constable, a thief, concealing himself, can suppress coughing for some time, but after a little time he is compelled to cough violently. Sometimes we may be able to suppress a sensation reflex effectively with a vigorous effort.

There are two important points of difference between physiological reflexes and sensation reflexes. In the first place, the physiological reflexes occur regularly and uniformly, and are excited by intra-organic or extra-organic stimuli, which recur regularly and uniformly. Circulation, respiration, and digestion are regularly and uniformly evoked by intra-organic stimuli. Contraction and expansion of the pupil are excited by bright and faint light. The winks of the eyes, which are generally unconscious, are excited by extra-organic stimuli. The sensation reflexes, on the other hand, occur on a special emergency ; they do not occur regularly and uniformly. Coughing is excited by phlegm, which obstructs or irritates the throat on a particular occasion. Sneezing is excited by phlegm which obstructs or irritates the nose on a special emergency. The eyes are closed at the sight of a flash of lightning. These sensation reflexes do not occur regularly and uniformly because their stimuli do not occur regularly and uniformly.

In the second place, when the mind is pre-occupied with something, we may have a physiological reflex. But when the mind is not pre-occupied by a higher process, we generally have a sensation reflex. When we are intensely absorbed in our study or in the solution of a difficult problem, we may be entirely unconscious of coughing or sneezing, which are then physiological reflexes.

Circulation, digestion, respiration, etc., which are responses to intra-organic stimuli, are called by some physiological reflexes. They take place regularly and uniformly in response to intra-organic stimuli which recur uniformly. They are generally called automatic acts. Coughing is a sensation reflex. It is evoked only now and then, when the throat is irritated by some foreign matter. When the mind is absorbed in an interesting topic, coughing may take place unconsciously and thus become a physiological reflex, though generally it is a sensation reflex in a waking condition.

The reflex arc is the physiological basis of a reflex action. A sense-organ is stimulated by a stimulus. A sensory neuron carries the nerve impulse from the sense-organ to a nerve centre in the spinal cord or the brain stem. There is a synaptic connection there between the sensory neuron and a motor neuron. The motor neuron carries the nerve current from the central switching station to a muscle or a gland. The muscle or gland acts according to the impulse received through the motor neuron. This combination of a sensory neuron with a motor neuron through a synaptic junction in the grey matter of a lower centre is called the reflex arc. It has already been explained.

Reflexes have the following characteristics :—

(1) Reflexes protect the body from possible injury. When an object approaches the eye, it excites the winking reflex. The eye is closed at once when something approaches it. The winking reflex protects the eye from possible injury. Coughing expels the irritating phlegm from the throat. Sneezing expels a harmful substance from the nasal cavity.

(2) Reflexes are beyond the control of consciousness. Physiological reflexes are unconscious. They are independent of conscious control. Sensation reflexes are preceded and succeeded by consciousness. But the motor reactions are not

executed in response to consciousness. Sensation reflexes are preceded by sensations, but not by perceptions or ideas. They are sensation-reflexes as distinguished from perceptual reflexes and ideo-motor actions. They are sometimes called sensori-motor actions.

(3) Reflexes are immediate responses to sensory stimuli, either extra-organic or intra-organic. They are prompt or immediate reactions. They are uniform reactions. The same stimulus causes the same reflex. Bright light causes contraction of the pupil. Dim light causes expansion of the pupil.

(4) Reflexes are not learned. They are innate and inborn. They depend upon pre-organised nervous pathways. No one has to practise to be able to perform the reflexes. When the nervous system develops, the nervous pathways are established in it, which enable the reflex actions to appear. Reflexes are not voluntary acts. They do not involve anticipation of any end or purpose. They are not intentional, deliberate, purposive, or voluntary.

(5) Reflexes are simple responses. They do not involve a complicated series of actions. They are simple responses. They are single reactions to stimuli. Coughing, sneezing, closing the eyes and the like are simple reactions.

(6) They are local responses. A particular part of the body responds to a stimulus in it. Many parts or organs of the body do not respond to a situation. The eyes are closed at the sight of a flash of lightning. The whole body does not react to the stimuli. Only a particular part of it responds to the stimulus.

## Conditioned Reflex : Conditioned Response

Pavlov, a Russian Physiologist, discovered the conditioned reflex about the year 1900. A reflex is an immediate motor or glandular response to a stimulus. There is a natural response to a natural stimulus. If you put meat in the mouth of a hungry dog, there will be secretion of saliva. This is a natural or unconditioned reflex.

(1) But it is found that other stimuli connected with the original stimulus, such as the sight or the smell of food, the

sight of the dish in which the food is usually served, the sight of the person who customarily gives food, or even the hearing of his footsteps in the next room causes rapid flow of saliva in a hungry dog. When the stimulus of food is actually present in the mouth, the salivary response is a natural reflex, but the same response aroused by such a stimulus as the sight of a dish or the sound of footsteps of the person who usually serves food, depends upon the conditions under which the dog has been fed previously. Pavlov called it a conditioned reflex. Here the same response is made to conditions normally connected with the natural stimulus.

Pavlov found that any substitute stimulus, such as the ringing of a bell, the application of heat or cold to the skin, the shining of an electric light, connected with the natural stimulus such as giving food to a hungry dog a number of times,—thirty, forty, or fifty,—evoked the same response, e.g., the excretion of saliva. A substitute stimulus is also called a conditioned stimulus. This kind of reflex action may be expressed by the formula $S^1$—O—R. $S^1$—Substitute stimulus. O—Organism. R—Response. A substitute stimulus acts on the organism and evokes the natural response.

(2) There is a kind of conditioned reflex in which the same stimulus evokes a different response. If a child sees a beautiful dog for the first time, he puts out his hand and pats it. If the dog is gentle, the sight of it will evoke the same patting reaction. But if the dog is vicious and bites the child, the sight of it will cause him to withdraw and run away from it. Here there is the same stimulus (the dog), but the response has been changed completely as a result of experience. It evokes running away in place of approaching and patting. Here the same stimulus evokes a different response. The stimulus remains the same. But the reaction becomes different. This kind of reflex action may be expressed by the formula S—O—$R^1$. S—Natural stimulus. O—Organism. $R^1$—Conditioned response. The natural stimulus acts on the organism, and evokes a conditioned response.

Thus there are two kinds of conditioned reflexes. In the first place, a reflex action (e.g., salivation) is evoked by a

Collection of Saliva : Conditioned Reflex (p. 170)

substitute stimulus (e.g., the ringing of a bell). In the second place, the same stimulus (e.g., a dog) evokes a different response (e.g., withdrawing and running). In the former, a reflex is attached to a substitute stimulus. In the latter, the same stimulus is attached to a substitute response.

### Ideo-motor Actions

They are movements which immediately follow upon the ideas of movements. In an ideo-motor action first there is the idea of a movement ; then this idea is converted at once into a movement. The idea of the movement is so impulsive that it carries itself out into the actual movement at once. Here the movement is not under the guidance of will. It is not a voluntary action. It is an impulsive act. In an ideo-motor action an idea is immediately followed by an action without the co-operation of will. It is non-voluntary in nature. It is not voluntary. It is different from a sensation reflex, in which a sensation (e.g., irritation of the nasal membrane) is immediately followed by a response (e.g., sneezing). In an ideo-motor action an idea,—not a sensation,—of an action is directly followed by the action. While reading, a fly settles on my cheek and I find myself waving my hand and removing it. Sometimes a person who climbs the top of a hill is so obsessed with the idea of jumping into the abyss below that he jumps at once. When we watch a ball game with rapt attention, we make movements of legs to kick the ball. Here the ideas of movements are converted at once into movements. All these are ideo-motor actions. In children an idea of a movement is at once turned into the movement. As soon as the idea of running occurs to a child, he begins to run. He cannot check the movement of running. His idea of running is converted at once into running. But in adults ideo-motor actions are generally replaced by voluntary actions, in which a particular action is chosen and executed in preference to many other possible courses of action.

### Reaction Time

The reaction time is the interval between the perception of

a stimulus and the reaction. The stimulus may be a light, a sound, or a touch. The response may be pressing a button or releasing a key. The subject is asked to get ready before a signal is given. Then a signal is given. Then a response is made. This is a simple reaction time experiment. It helps us learn the mental processes involved in a simple action.

**Instincts : Instinctive Actions**

An instinct may be defined as the innate tendency to perform a complex action pattern adapted to the biological end of self-preservation or race-preservation, prompted probably by a core of emotional excitement, but without any explicit idea of the ultimate end, in response to a total situation. An instinctive act is not a purely biological act. It is a psychical act. It is not simply an inherited arrangement of nervous arcs, but it is a mental process with its threefold aspect. McDougall defines it as "an inherited or innate psycho-physical disposition which determines its possessor to perceive, and to pay attention to objects of a certain class, to experience an emotional excitement of a particular quality upon perceiving such an object, and to act in regard to it in a particular manner, or, at least, to experience an impulse to such action.[1]" According to him, an instinct is a complete mental process—cognitive, affective, and conative. Spiders spin their cobwebs, birds build their nests, and bees build their hives instinctively. A young chick is hatched in an incubator. As soon as it is born, it begins to walk about, pecks at particles of food, and soon is able to take care of itself without any care or training from the mother. The female wasp of a certain species constructs a certain type of nest and lays eggs in it. It dies before its young ones are hatched from the eggs. And yet this specific type of nest is handed down from generation to generation. All these complex action patterns are neither learned by the individuals nor imitated from the elders. They are instinctive.

Instinctive actions have the following characteristics :—

(1) Instinctive acts are native behaviour. They are not

acquired by the individual. They are not learned actions. They are neither voluntary actions, nor automatic imitations of others' behaviour, nor habitual acts. They are not based on the individual's experience, but only on his pre-organised pathways in the nervous system.

(2) Instinctive acts involve an inherited disposition to attend to and perceive a specific class of objects. A bird has an inherited tendency to perceive dry leaves, grass, feathers, sticks, etc., to build its nest before laying eggs. A cat has an innate tendency to run after mice to satisfy its food-seeking instinct.

(3) Instinctive acts have a core of emotional excitement. The instinct to fly at the sight of a dangerous object has the emotion of fear as its affective aspect. The instinct of combat has the emotion of anger in its core.

(4) Instinctive acts are complex action patterns. They are a long and complicated series of acts adapted to one another as means and ends. A reflex is a simple response. But an instinct is a complex response.

(5) A reflex is a local response of a part of the organism to a simple stimulus. But an instinct is a response of the whole organism or a large part of it to complex stimuli or a total situation. Migratory birds migrate instinctively from a cold country to a warm region. Their instinctive act is a response of the whole organism to a total situation. The bird's wooing, mating, building a nest, laying eggs, hatching them, searching for food, taking care of the brood, etc., are complex responses of the whole organism to a total situation.

(6) Instinctive acts involve activities lasting over a prolonged period of time. A reflex act, e.g., pupillary reflex, is an immediate response. It is a single momentary response. But an instinctive act may last for a long period of time. A bird collects material, carries it to the chosen place, assembles it, and builds its nest for a number of days. An instinctive act takes a long period of time, whereas a reflex act is momentary. There is a persisting tendency in an instinctive act, which unifies all its units.

(7) Instinctive acts are adapted to a biological end. Some

instincts are unconsciously adapted to self-preservation. Instinct of flight, instinct of combat, food-seeking instinct, etc., are of this type. Other instincts are unconsciously adapted to race-preservation. The sex instinct, the maternal instinct, etc., are of this type. But the instinctive acts are not consciously adapted to these ends. There is no dim or clear consciousness of these ultimate ends in instinctive acts. But they involve consciousness of proximate ends, though not of the ultimate ends.

(8) Instinctive acts, unlike reflex acts, are marked by persistency with varied effort. A solitary wasp often fails to drag its prey such as a spider or a cockroach into its hole; but it goes on trying various methods such as squeezing, twisting and turning the prey till it succeeds at last. An instinctive act is modified by experience. But a reflex act is not modified by experience[2].

## Instinctive Actions and Reflexes

(1) Both are non-voluntary and do not involve an act of will or volition. (2) Both are innate or hereditary. They are not learned reactions. These are similarities between them. But they differ from each other in important respects:

(1) The typical reflex is a simple response, while an instinctive act is a complicated series of responses adapted to one another as means and ends. (2) A reflex action is a momentary response. But an instinctive act lasts for a long period of time. (3) A reflex is a single response, while an instinctive act is a complex series of many responses of the whole organism or a large part of it. (4) A reflex act is evoked by a single stimulus. But an instinctive act is evoked by a total situation. It is a response of the whole organism. A reflex is a response to a single stimulus, while an instinctive act is a motor response to complex stimuli. (5) A reflex act is adapted to an end near at end, while an instinctive act is adapted to a distant end, viz., self-preservation or race-preservation. (6) A sensation reflex is preceded by the sensation produced by a sensory stimulation and succeeded

by the consciousness of the act. But it is not consciously adapted to the end. It is not guided by the prevision of the end. An instinctive act does not involve consciousness of the ultimate end ; but it does involve consciousness of proximate ends and particular acts performed. Physiological reflexes are essentially unconscious. Some reflexes are unconscious reactions, while instinctive acts are conscious reactions. (7) Typically, a reflex is a prompt reaction. It occurs at once, on the occurrence of its stimulus, and is done with. An instinctive act, on the other hand, is marked by the persisting tendency and directed towards a result which cannot be instantly accomplished. (8) Instinctive acts, unlike reflex acts, are marked by persistency with varied effort. They are not characterised by rigid uniformity as they were supposed to be. A beetle carries a dung-ball and comes across a pit. It makes a slope to carry it across the pit. (9) Instinctive acts, unlike reflexes, are modified by experience. If they lead to agreeable results, they are repeated and ingrained as a habit. If they lead to painful consequences, they are inhibited. But reflex acts are not modified by experience.

**Instinctive acts are modified by Experience**

Experience modifies instinctive acts in two opposite directions :

(1) If an instinctive act proves to be painful, it is suppressed temporarily or permanently. Chicks have an instinctive tendency to peck at food, But if bad-tasting food is given to them, they will inhibit the instinctive tendency to peck. A duck has instinctive tendency to follow the person who gives it food. But if he covers it with a basket and frightens it, it will no longer follow him.

(2) On the other hand, if the instinctive act proves to be pleasant, it will be repeated and turned into a habit. If good food is given to chicks, they will repeat the instinctive act of pecking at food, and turn it into a habit. Instinctive acts are affected by even elementary forms of conscious memory. They no longer remain blind and uniform. Thus instinctive acts are modified by experience.

(3) Instinctive acts are restricted by habit. When a particular object evokes an instinctive act, the same object will evoke the same response later. The animal becomes partial to the first object. The rabbit deposits its dung in the same corner ; the bird makes its nest in the same tree ; the mouse lives in the same hole. Thus an instinctive act is repeated several times and is converted into a habit. Habit restricts the scope of an instinctive action.

(4) Instinctive acts are modified also by the new environment. Instinctive acts are so modified as to cope with the new conditions in the environment. Bees modify the structure of their hives to overcome obstacles in the environment. Birds modify their nests to meet new conditions in the environment. If the nests are partly blown away by the wind, they are rebuilt by the birds. Wasps also modify their cells to overcome obstacles in the environment. An instinctive act admits of variations to meet new emergencies. Many instinctive acts reach the final end by various ways[3].

Instincts were formerly supposed to be blind, fixed, and invariable. But the modern psychologists look upon instincts as modifiable and variable. The characteristics of instinctive acts considered above clearly shew that instincts are not blind. We call attention to their following characteristics again :—

An instinctive act is a concrete mental process involving cognition, emotion, and conation. It involves an instinctive tendency to attend to and perceive a specific class of objects, an emotional excitement, and a tendency to act in a particular manner. It is a psychical act. It is not a merely biological act.

(1) An instinctive act is conscious. It involves dim consciousness of the proximate end and clear consciousness of the means. It does not involve consciousness of the ultimate end, e.g., self-preservation or race-preservation. There is a certain amount of foresight in an instinctive act. It is not blind.

(2) There is a persisting tendency in an instinctive act. This depends upon continuity of interest. The persisting tendency continues till the end is realised.

(3) There is persistence with varied effort in an instinctive action. Various efforts are made to realise the end. This shows that there is consciousness of success and failure in an instinctive act. It involves attention to the future, consciousness of success and failure, and satisfaction and dissatisfaction.

(4) Instinctive acts are modified by experience, habit, and the environment. They are modified to meet new conditions in the environment. They are not uniform and unchanging. They are varied and modified. Therefore instincts are not blind.

## Animal Instincts

The biological or organic needs were formerly called instincts. Hunger and thirst are organic needs. Hunger is organic need for food. Thirst is organic need for water. Our organism should be supplied with those materials at intervals, which constitute its stuff. Need for air or oxygen is imperative, which sustains our life. Needs for elimination, or urination and defecation, are satisfied in a mechanical way. The need for activity and the need for rest are expressed early in an individual's life because his bodily mechanism is fatigued. The need for warmth is satisfied in birds and animals by feathers and thin skin covered with hair respectively. It is satisfied in men by clothing and shelter.

The need for sex or sex instinct is first satisfied by manipulation of the sex organ. This is the autosexual stage of its manifestation. It becomes heterosexual at adolescence, when sexual interest is fixed on the opposite sex only. The sex need is determined by heredity. But the way of seeking a mate, courtship, and the sexual act are acquired by learning.

The maternal need of nourishing and protecting the child is biological and partly determined by hormones. The parental need of helping and protecting the child seems to be biological. The birds have nest-building instinct, hatching instinct, parental instinct in addition to the mating instinct.

The animals have gregarious instinct, defensive instinct, fighting instinct, instinct for self-assertion, instinct for submission, instinct to escape, instincts for acquisition, hoarding, manipulation, exploration, etc. The crows flock together. The monkeys, the sheep, the deer, etc., live in herds. They feel lonely when they are separated from their herds. They have gregarious instinct. They have instinct for fighting or pugnacious instinct. They fight their enemies. They have instinct for aggression and domination. When they are defeated by the stronger enemies, they become submissive. They have instinct for submission to stronger individuals. They have instinct to escape from dangerous objects or situations. They are frightened by the sight of dangerous animals which threaten their life. They are afraid of gun-shots, fire, sounds of drums, crowds of men armed with weapons. They have instinct for pursuit and acquisition. They pursue their prey with persistent efforts and acquire it. They keep some of their food for future consumption. Ants store their food against the rainy day. They have instinct for collection and hoarding. Bees collect honey in their hive for future use. They have hoarding instinct. When squirrels get nuts, they explore and manipulate them in various ways, and then eat them. The birds and animals express various instincts in their play. Their instinctive acts are more fixed and stereotyped than those of human beings. They are less modifiable by experience, intelligence and habit than human instincts.

## Human Instincts

Men also have organic needs such as hunger, thirst, respiratory needs, elimination needs, needs for activity and rest including sleep, and sex need. Hormones secreted by the gonads stimulate the sex motive. They are supplied by the testes in men and the ovaries in women. If they are removed before puberty, the sex motive is weakened. Human beings have strong maternal and paternal instincts. Human childhood is prolonged. So human children require their parents' care and protection for a longer period.

Men have emergency motives which depend upon the environment. They have the instinct for escape from a dangerous object or situation. The perception of it rouses the instinct to fly, and excites the emotion of fear. Men have the instinct for combat when their activity is thwarted. The pugnacious instinct is aroused by interference with one's activity. It is attended with the emotion of anger. The instinct to combat seeks the goal of removing the obstacle by breaking down opposition. Men have the instinct for mastery. When a person encounters an obstacle while engaged in an activity, he strengthens his effort to overcome the obstacle and reach his goal. This motive is called the mastery motive. When the primitive man found a prey, he pursued and caught it by various efforts. When boys play football, they compete with one another to push it to the opposite party's goal. They display the pursuit motive.

Men also have the instincts of exploration, manipulation and curiosity to acquire the knowledge of objects and control over them.

They have instincts for self-assertion, self-abasement, freedom, domination, aggression and the like. They have gregarious instinct and social instincts of co-operation, love, fellowship, etc.

Human instincts are more pastic and modifiable by experience, intelligence and new environment than animal instincts. Men are more intelligent than animals. So they can control and regulate their instinctive behaviour. The major part of their instinctive behaviour is acquired[4].

## Impulse and Movement

When we are about to sneeze, the impulse to seize is clearly conscious. When we are hungry, we feel an impulse to get and eat food. When we are sad, we feel an impulse to weep. Thus an impulse is a conscious tendency to an action. It is the awareness of the state of readiness for some response[5]. Appetites, instincts, and emotions generate impulses to action. Impulse is the consciousness of tendency to movement. In the impulse we are not only conscious of the tendency to movement, but sometimes also of the result to be anticipated from our reaction. An impulse gives rise to an impulsive movement.

## Play

Playful activity is instinctive in the beginning. Play is an expression of many instincts rather than of a single one. The general tendency to play is a result of the general tendency to motor discharge. In little children it is practically identical with the impulse to use the voluntary muscles. It is the free, pleasurable, and spontaneous activity of the voluntary muscles. The child takes playing seriously. Play involves imagination, imitation and 'make-believe'. The child constructs houses with damp sand, clay, or wooden blocks. Here he gives play to his constructive instinct. Play, imitation, and constructiveness interlace with one another in almost inextricable ways. Conscious 'make-believe' of many plays is seldom found in the earlier plays of little children. It is found in plays of later years. Imitation and constructiveness are found together in many plays. The boy plays at teaching, fighting, hunting, and the like. The girl plays at cooking, feeding, fondling a doll, and the like. These involve imitation, construction, and 'make-believe'. The instincts of self-assertion, submission, fighting, escape, exploration, manipulation, laughter, gregarious instinct, social instincts, etc., are satisfied in many kinds of play. Playing with a doll is partly an expression of the maternal instinct and partly an imitation of the mother. Football, hockey, etc., are expressions of the fighting instinct, instinct of pursuit, etc. Dancing is an expression of the sex instinct. Different kinds of play are the expressions of the different kinds of instincts under make-believe conditions[6].

Play is different from work. Work is a voluntary action which realizes a definite end. A child does his home task. It is his work. But play does not aim at a definite end. It is agreeable in itself. A child plays hide and seek. It does not serve any definite end. It gives pleasure to him.

## Impulse and Desire

Impulse is a conscious tendency to movement. We are conscious of it. But it is not enlightened by the distinct idea of its object. But desire is an impulse controlled by distinct ideas. Desire for food is controlled by the idea of food. Thus impulse is not enlightened by the idea of its end, while desire is always excited by the distinct idea of its end.

### Appetite and Impulse

Appetites are the periodic cravings of the organism, which generally press for activity, e.g., hunger, thirst, sleep, and the like. They are generally accompanied by unrest or disquiet, which disappears when they are gratified.

Appetites give rise to impulses. Both of them are conscious but blind. They are not enlightened by the idea of any end. When they are enlightened by distinct ideas of ends, they are converted into desires. Both of them are attended with a feeling of uneasiness, which disappears when they are gratified. But appetites are periodic, while impulses are not. Besides, appetites are organic wants, while impulses arise from appetites, instincts, feelings, and emotions.

### Impulse and Volition

In impulse action follows an isolated conative tendency. But in voluntary action many impulses and their ends are considered in their relation to the total system of tendencies included in the conception of the self. Thus an impulsive action is quite different in nature from a voluntary action[7].

The function of volition is to regulate and organise these impulsive tendencies to action. The function of will is not to repress the impulses but to direct and control them. As volition develops, it reduces the impulses to order. Volition cannot uproot the impulses altogether.

## REFERENCE

[1]*Introduction to Social Psychology*.
[2]Stout, *Manual of Psychology*. Woodworth, *Psychology*.
[3]Angell, *Psychology*. James, *Brief Text-Book of Psychology*.
[4]Woodworth, *Psychology*, pp, 307-18; Bridges, *Psychology, Normal and Abnormal*, 129-34; Munn, *Psychology*, pp. 86-95.
[5]Gates, *Elementary Psychology*, 1933, p. 135.
[6]Pillsbury, *Fundamentals of Psychology*, p. 237.
[7]Stout, *Manual of Psychology*, p. 601.

# CHAPTER XV

## *Voluntary Action*

### Appetite and Desire

Appetites are periodically recurring organic wants which manifest themselves as cravings, e.g., hunger, thirst, sexual cravings, craving for sleep, etc. Animals are conscious but not self-conscious. So their appetites are blind but conscious tendencies. They can feel pleasure and pain. So their appetites are conscious but blind tendencies towards particular ends, in which the element of unpleasant feeling is predominant. But in the higher animals there is a dim consciousness of the object. But in lower animals the consciousness of the object is somewhat dim and vague. In children also appetites are at first conscious but blind tendencies. They are not enlightened by distinct ideas of objects. But gradually the satisfaction of their appetites by particular objects, e.g., milk, food, etc., connects them with those objects in the course of experience. Thus their appetites are converted into desires.

Appetites are different from desires. Appetites are periodically recurring conscious organic cravings unenlightened by distinct ideas of their objects. But desires are conscious cravings enlightened by distinct ideas of their objects. Moreover, appetites are organic, while desires are intellectual, moral, aesthetic, and religious cravings.

Appetites are converted into desires by self-consciousness, distinct ideas of objects, and recognition of them as good. There is the appetite of hunger in animals and babies. But in grown-up men it is converted into a desire for food. There are a distinct idea of food and a definite recognition of it as good. Thus desires can belong to grown-up, selfconscious human beings.

## Analysis of Desire

Desire is a craving of an agent for the attainment of an object to relieve some want. It is a complex mental state consisting of cognitive, affective, and conative elements.

(1) The cognitive elements are the following: (i) the idea of the end or motive which will remove the feeling of want; (ii) the idea of the means, either pleasant, or unpleasant, or partly pleasant and partly unpleasant, which will lead to the attainment of the end; (iii) the consciousness of the distinction between the present state of want with the anticipated state of satisfaction. The greater is the consciousness of disparity between the present state of dissatisfaction and the future state of satisfaction, the more intense is the desire. These are the elements of cognition in desire.

(2) The affective elements are the following: (i) a painful feeling of want which is the spring of action; (ii) an agreeable feeling arising from the anticipation of satisfaction. These are the elements of feeling in desire. The feeling of pain predominates over the feeling of pleasure in desire.

(3) The conative elements are the following: (i) a craving for the attainment of the end or motive to remove the feeling of want; (ii) an active tendency to action to realise the end. These are the elements of conation in desire.

## Levels of Conative Development

Development of conation is intimately connected with development of cognition. On the plane of sensation we have sensation reflexes. On the plane of perception we have the perceptual impulses including instinctive impulses. They find immediate expressions in bodily movements guided by the perception of external stimuli. Perceptual impulses may involve a certain amount of ideal anticipation. On the level of memory and imagination we have desires; they are excited by the anticipation of ends. With the development of ideal thought higher forms of desire and voluntary actions arise. Voluntary actions are excited by the thought of ends. Thus sensation-reflexes, perceptual impulses, desires, and voluntary actions are the different levels of conative development.

## Analysis of Voluntary Action

Voluntary actions are actions performed by an agent deliberately and intentionally in order to realise some foreseen ends. They are actions performed by the mind with a volition. A voluntary action has three stages, e.g., the mental stage, the bodily stage, and the extra-organic or external stage of consequences.

### I. The Mental Stage

(1) The Spring of Action.—Every voluntary action is actuated by a spring of action. It is a feeling of want. It is either an instinct or appetite, or an intellectual, moral, aesthetic, or religious craving. A feeling of want is always painful. But it is usually mixed with a pleasant feeling, which arises from the anticipation of satisfaction of the want in future. Thus the painful feeling of want is mixed with an agreeable feeling of anticipated satisfaction. But the disagreeable feeling predominates over the agreeable feeling.

(2) Desire.—The spring of action or the feeling of want (e.g., an appetite) is converted into a desire. Self-consciousness converts a feeling of want into a desire. It is not blind like an appetite. It is enlightened by self-consciousness. Desire is a craving to satisfy an appetite or a feeling of want by attaining its proper object. In desire there is the idea of the object, end or motive which will satisfy the feeling of want together with the recognition of it as good. There is also the idea of the means for realising the end, whether the means is desirable or undesirable. And there is a yarning for the attainment of the object.

In the case of a simple action in which there is no conflict of motives, choice is made at once and it is followed by action. But in the case of a complex action the desire is not immediately followed by choice.

(3) Conflict of Motives or Desires.—In a complex action sometimes the mind is confronted with different motives competing with one another. Many wants demand satisfaction. They

suggest many ends, motives, or objects of desire simultaneously to the mind. Thus many desires pull the mind in opposite directions. All ends or objects of desire cannot be attained at the same time ; all desires cannot be satisfied simultaneously. Sometimes they are incompatible with one another. If one is satisfied, the other has to be rejected altogether. You are invited to a dinner and a lecture at 8 p. m. to-day in different places. You are inclined to attend both the functions. But you cannot satisfy both the desires. There is a conflict of desires in your mind. Thus there arises in the mind a competition, rivalry, or conflict of motives or desires.

In this state the mind arrests action and is pulled this way and that way by different motives, which are its own states and depend for their existence on it. Some hold that a motive is a chosen desire. So we cannot speak of a 'conflict of motives', but only of a 'conflict of desires'.

(4) Deliberation.—When there is a conflict of desires, the mind arrests action and deliberates upon the merits and demerits of the different courses of action suggested by different motives. The self weighs them in the balance, as it were, and considers the pros and cons. This process of mind is called deliberation.

(5) Decision or Choice.—After deliberation the mind chooses a particular motive and identifies itself with it. It chooses a particular course of action and rejects the rest. This act of selection of one motive to the exclusion of others is called choice or decision. In this state the mind decides to carry out a definite course of action in order to realise a definite end or motive through the chosen means. While the process of deliberation is going on, the motives are motives for deciding ; when the decision is made, the motive chosen by the mind after deliberation becomes the motive for action. During the process of deliberation, the conflicting motives are regarded as possible motives for action ; when the decision is formed, the chosen motive becomes the actual motive for action.

Decision does not mean the triumph of the strongest motive over weaker motives apart from the mind. The motive chosen by the mind becomes the actual motive for action. The chosen motive becomes the strongest motive. The rejected motives are driven out of the field of consciousness and sink into the subconscious level. They may emerge into consciousness at some other time in some form or other. The state of decision consists in the choice of a particular end or motive and a particular means or course of action.

(6) Resolution.—Sometimes decision is at once carried out. In that case there is no scope for resolution. But sometimes the action is postponed and consequently there is a scope for resolution. Resolution means the power of sticking to the decision already made. A person with a vacillating mind may give up the decision made by him after deliberation if there is a sufficient interval of time between decision and action. So resolution or determination is necessary to carry out a decision in some cases.

II. The Bodily Stage.—When choice or decision is made and kept up by resolution, it is converted into a bodily action. What is the relation between volition or choice and bodily action ? In volition we have a clear idea of the nature of the bodily movement which will execute the volition. This clear idea of the movement which dominates the field of consciousness is automatically followed by muscular action. The idea of movement is in itself impulsive, and when it is chosen by the mind and attended to by it, it becomes predominant in consciousness and acquires greater strength and impulsiveness, so that it easily passes over into action. The muscular action is due to the impulsive nature of the chosen idea of movement. This explanation has been offered by William James.

III. The External Stage of Consequences.—The bodily action produces changes in the external world. These are called consequences. The consequences include (i) realisation of the chosen end or motive; (ii) realisation of the chosen means, desirable, undesirable, or partly both; (iii) certain foreseen consequences; and (iv) certain unforeseen or accidental consequences.

## Volition and Bodily Action

Normally, volition is followed by the corresponding bodily action. How does this take place ?

The explanation offered by William James has been stated above. According to him, attention to the idea of a movement makes it impulsive and compels the movement to follow.

Stout pushes the analysis further and points out that the belief of the self that one course of action is to be carried out to the exclusion of others makes the idea of the action so predominant that it is carried out. Thus attention and belief on the part of the self make the idea of the action chosen by it so dominant in consciousness that it passes over into action[1].

## Attention and Volition

William James holds that attention is responsible for the passage from volition to bodily action. Attention is also involved in deliberation or consideration of the merits and demerits of the different courses of action, when there is a conflict of motives. It is involved in decision or identification of the mind with one motive to the exclusion of others. It is involved also in resolution or sticking to the decision already made. So attention is an important element in volition.

Attention converts a volition into a bodily movement. Attention to the idea of a movement makes it dominant. It excludes the ideas of other actions. The dominant idea of a particular action becomes so impulsive that it carries itself out into the action. Attention converts the chosen idea of a movement into the actual bodily movement.

## Voluntary Action and Instinctive Action

Both voluntary action and instinctive action are complex actions. Both consist of a series of simple acts adapted to one another in order to realise an end. Both are accompanied by consciousness, attention and interest.

But there is an important difference between them. Instinctive action is native and unlearned behaviour. But voluntary action is learned behaviour. The former is native while the latter is acquired. Instinctive action is purposive without consciousness of purpose. It involves consciousness of proximate ends or means only. It lacks consciousness of the ultimate biological end served by it. But voluntary action involves consciousness of the ultimate end and the proximate ends. Instinctive action is not intentional, but voluntary action is deliberate.

## REFERENCE

[1]James, *Brief Text-Book of Psychology*; Stout, *Manual of Psychology*, pp. 618-19.

# CHAPTER XVI

*Learning*

## Learned and Unlearned Actions

Learned acts are acquired in the course of experience. Unlearned acts are native behaviour. Automatic acts, random acts, reflexes, instincts and spontaneous expressions of feelings and emotions are native tendencies. These are the basis of learned acts. In the lower animals the native behaviour is more fixed than in the higher animals. In the higher animals, especially in man, the native behaviour is more plastic and modifiable by experience. The power of retention and modifiability of the nervous pathways are the fundamental conditions of learning. Thus unlearned acts are native, while learned acts are acquired. They are acquired by the trial and error method, or by imitation, or by insight.

## Methods of Learning

(1) Learning is a way of doing.—Animals and men learn by reacting. Learning is never a passive process of reception of some thing from the environment. It is an active process of reacting to the environment. Observation, memorizing, acquiring skill, and the like, involve reactions. What one learns are reactions. The reactions are strengthened by practice. Thus learning is never merely passive, but active reaction.

(2) Learning reactions are strengthened by practice.—There is a native nervous pathway ready to function. An adequate stimulus brings out the response through the native nervous pathway. The response is made quicker, easier, and more exact by practice. Practice does not make new pathways in the nervous system. It strengthens native nervous

pathways. Chicks have an instinctive tendency to peck at food. Their native nervous pathway is ready to function. The sight of grains will evoke the response. Practice will strengthen it. Children learn to walk by this method.

(3) Learning is a conditioned response evoked by a substitute stimulus.—We have discussed it already under conditioned reflex. A certain stimulus evokes a native response. But the same response may be evoked by a substitute stimulus. The native response is attached to a substitute stimulus. Food in contact with the tongue is the natural stimulus for salivation. But if it is associated with the sound of a bell forty or fifty times, the sound, the substitute stimulus, will bring on salivation. Thus learning is conditioning a response by attaching it to a substitute stimulus.

A conditioned reflex or response is a kind of associative learning. It consists in forming associations between responses and the stimuli which happen to be present when the responses are made. Pavlop associated salivation with substitute stimuli, e.g., the sound of a bell, electric light, etc. Conditioned responses are examples of associative learning.

(4) Learning is a conditioned response evoked by a natural stimulus.—A certain stimulus evokes a native response. But this response may be replaced by a substitute response. This is another kind of conditioned reflex. Here the motor response is modified by experience. The original native reaction has not been successful. Other methods of reaction have been tried, until by chance the successful response has been found, and this has been repeated and fixed through practice. The 'trial and error', method of learning illustrates this method. A hungry cat fails to come out of a cage by the native response of crawling between the bars. By chance it presses a button and comes out. This successful action will gradually be stamped in by practice. Thus the cat learns to come out of the cage by the substitute response of pressing a button.

(5) Learning is by negative adaptation. When bullocks come to a town for the first time, they run away at the sight of running motor cars, buses, etc. But when they come there repeatedly, they are accustomed to the sight of them,

and no longer run away. When a person buys a dog and a cat and keeps them as pets near each other, they at first fight with each other. But gradually they are accustomed to the sight of each other, and desist from fighting with each other. These are examples of learning by negative adaptation.

(6) Learning is a combination of simple acts into complex acts.—The different simple acts are combined into more complex acts. The simple acts are parts of complex acts. They are either native or acquired. They may be acquired as the result of learning through substitute stimulus or substitute response. The complex acts are results of combining these simpler actions into more complex actions. Walking, running, dancing, swimming, wrestling, type-writing, etc., are learned by this method.

(7) A learned action comes out of random responses.—A stimulus sometimes produces a nervous current which goes to the spinal cord or brain centre, and comes out through many pathways. The movements produced in this way are called random movements. Of these random movements some are found useful and agreeable. They are repeated on similar occasions, and converted into habits. Afterwards they are evoked as immediate responses to the stimulus, which at first evoked them as random responses. Thus controlled and voluntary movements emerge out of random and aimless movements. The different methods of learning overlap one another. They tend to merge into one another.

## The Laws of Learning

(1) The Law of Use.—Native reactions are strengthened by use. Other things being equal, exercise of any reaction, walking, grasping, or swimming, tends to make the reaction more prompt, more certain, more easy. A situation evokes a particular response. Use or exercise of the response strengthens it. Other conditions being equal, the greater the use of the response, the greater the strength of the connection between the situation and the response. Use or exercise strengthens the connection.

(2) The Law of Frequency.—This law is a necessary correlate of the Law of use. If one response strengthens the situation—response connection, two responses will strengthen it further, three still further, and so on. Thus, other conditions being equal, the more frequently the situation—response is exercised, the stronger the connection becomes. This is called the Law of Frequency.

(3) The Law of Disuse.—Any learning process that is not practised for some time, gradually decays. Use strengthens a situation—response connection. Disuse weakens the connection. When a situation does not evoke a specific response for a long period of time, the strength of the situation—response is weakened. The material without any meaning like nonsense syllables, is quickly forgotten. The material with a meaning, like poetry, is not so quickly forgotten. Motor acts, like typing, skating, etc., are forgotten more slowly.

(4) The Law of Recency.—The Law of Disuse is correlated to the Law of Recency. The connection between a situation and a specific response is weakened gradually through disuse. It becomes weaker and weaker day by day. Other things being equal, the more recent is the exercise, the stronger is the connection between the situation and the specific response.

(5) The Law of Primacy.—Other conditions remaining the same, first experiences and first acts are favoured. They are novel and apt to attract attention. They are easily impressed on the mind. The first day at school, the first day in climbing a hill, the first day in flying are easily impressed and learned.

(6) The Law of Effect.—A successful response gives satisfaction to the individual, tends to be repeated and stamped in as a habit. An unsuccessful reaction gives dissatisfaction to the individual, tends to be inhibited and stamped out. The successful response gradually acquires a balance of greater frequency over the unsuccessful. Many experiments have been performed with animals in running a maze with two runaways. The experiment is so arranged that in one runaway the animal gets an electric shock and in the other he gets food. The

Learning by Trial and Error ; Maze Learning (p. 193)

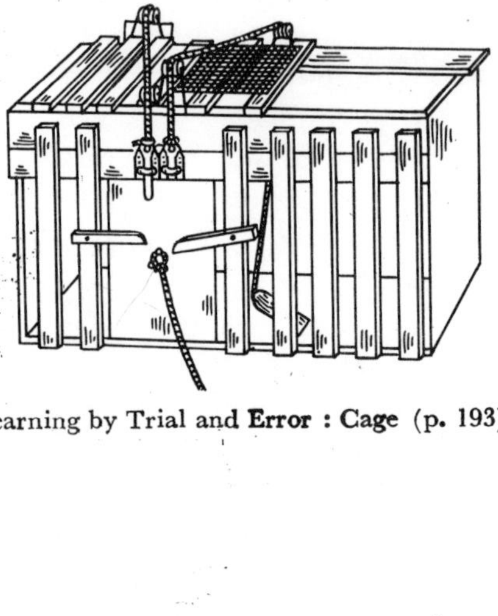

Learning by Trial and Error : Cage (p. 193)

animal is found to learn to go to the runaway that leads to the food, and gives him pleasure. Thus pleasures and pains have their effects on learning reactions.

(7) The Law of Readinesss.—The nervous system is at one time ready to act. At another time it is not ready to act. In the former case it gives pleasure to act. In the latter case it gives pain to act. Readiness of a nervous pathway to react is a condition of learning.

## The Law of Contiguity

Some psychologists regard the law of contiguity as a basic law of learning. It states that, when two mental processes occur together in time or in close succession, they are associated with each other. We have discussed this law in connection with memory. We perceive a pen and an inkpot together. We see a flash of lightning and hear the roar of a thunder in close succession. So they are associated with eaeh other, so that the perception of the one reminds us of the other.

## Learning by Trial and Error

Thorndike made experiments on animals like cats, dogs, and monkeys with the help of cages, in order to observe their method of learning. He confined a hungry cat in a cage closed by a door which could be opened by turning a latch or by pressing a button, and food was put near by where it could be seen by her. She made a large number of random movements. She tried to crawl through the bars. She clawed, bit, and scratched at the walls. Sooner or later by pure chance, she pushed the latch or pressed the button, opened the door, and escaped. But one successful movement did not teach her the method of opening the door. When put in the cage again, she went through a series of random movements a second time, again hit upon the correct response by chance. Each trial, on the average, required less time than the preceding one. After a number of repetitions, varying from a small number to a large member, the cat would perform the successful movement at once every time that she was put into the cage. She could not derive any advantage from having the trick performed for her by an animal that had already mastered it. She could not learn by imitation.

The animal's learning was gradual. She did not pass suddenly from not knowing the answer to knowing it. She did not learn by reasoning. Had she reasoned out the problem, she would have reached the solution at a particular time, and afterwards always made the correct movement. But she did not do so. So she did not learn by reasoning. Another animal who mastered the trick performed the correct movement before her. But she could not perform the correct movement by imitation. She did not learn a movement by watching or imitating, but by doing. She learned it by trial and error. She performed many unsuccessfull movements at first, gradually eliminated them, and finally learned the correct movement[1].

The animal is clearly conscious of the goal or end. It is not unconscious of the end. But it has no knowledge of the means. The animal is aware of the food. Its efforts are directed to the goal. But it is not able to see the path which will lead to the goal. Thus the trial and error method of learning is blind as to the means but not to the end.

## Learning by Insight

Kohler, a German psychologist, performed experiments with higher animals. Chimpanzees do uot learn by trial and error but by insight if the path is clearly visible.

In a cage a bunch of bananas was hung at a great height much beyond the reach of a chimpanzee in it. Three empty wooden boxes were placed on the floor. The chimpanzee played with the boxes for some time. Then suddenly he placed one box upon another, and stood upon the second box, and tried to reach the bananas. They were yet beyond his reach. Again he came down and played with the other box for some time. Then suddenly he placed the third box upon the second one, stood upon it, and reached the bananas and ate them. The chimpanzee learned by insight. His learning was sudden. He learned the trick and repeated it afterwards without any error.

Learning by Insight : Chimpanzee joining a stick to reach food (p. 195)

Another chimpanzee learned the use of a stick to reach a banana on the floor outside a cage. Two hollow sticks were given to him, and a number of bananas were placed too far away outside the cage. They could not be reached with the help of one stick. The chimpanzee made many fruitless attempts to reach the bananas with the help of one stick for over an hour. He went to the rear of the cage, and began to play with the sticks. He pushed the end of one stick into the hollow end of the other stick by chance, and made a bigger stick. Then he jumped up, ran to the front of the cage, and pulled in some bananas one by one with the joint stick. The joint stick fell apart into pieces because they were joined together loosely. He promptly put them together again, and pulled in the remaining bananas one by one with the joint stick and ate them. When the next day the same experiment was repeated, he made a few useless random movements, and then in a few seconds joined the two sticks together, and pulled in the bananas with the joint srick as before. These experiments clearly show that the chimpanzee learned a new movement by insight. He suddenly passed from non-learning to learning. Learning by insight is not gradual but sudden. The higher animals learn by insight[2].

Insight depends upon intelligence. Rats, cats and dogs learn by trial and error, because they have less intelligence. They have hindsight or faint memory of their past experience. But chimpanzees have greater intelligence and therefore can learn by insight. They have insight into a complex situation, and know the key to the solution of a problem. They have a foresight as to how a complex situation will be overcome.

## Human Learning

Young children also learn by insight. They also abruptly shift from uncertain movements to a certain successful movement. They observe a significant fact or see a relationship from insight. But they learn motor skill by trial and error. Riding on a bicycle, playing on a violin, type-writing, swimming, skating, etc., are learnt by trial and error. Young children partly learn by trial and error, and partly by insight. As they grow older and older, they progress from the trial and error method to the rational or intelligent method. They also learn partly by imitation. They imitate the actions of their elders. When the elders hold a meeting, the children also will hold a meeting of their own.

But adult human beings learn mainly by insight. They form hypotheses as to the solution of a puzzle, on the basis of their previous knowledge, and trying them one by one, perform the right movement. Their method of learning is mainly rational or intelligent. Human beings learn more by insight than by trial and error. They learn motor skill by trial and error.

Human learning is superior to animal learning for the following reasons.—(1) Man has greater power of observation than an animal. He observes many characteristics of the environment, which an animal cannot. (2) Man uses memory and imagination, which an animal cannot. (3) Man uses reasoning in solving a problem. (4) Man makes use of language,—names, numbers and symbols—in learning[3].

## Plateau of Learning

Learning curves indicate a flat stretch which shows that for some time there is no progress in learning. It is followed by rapid improvement. This flat stretch indicating no progress is called a plateau.

The same amount of effort is made under similar conditions, but no progress is made for a long interval. The plateau is the physiological limit of progress of the particular act. Further progress is the result of improved methods. During this period old associations or partial habits are more firmly implanted, and this is essential for any further advance.


## REFERENCE

[1]Woodworth, *Contemporary Schools of Psychology*, p. 55.
[2]Woodworth, *Psychology*, pp. 504-05.
[3]*Ibid*, p. 510
[4]*Foundations of Psychology* pp. 152-53. Bridges, *Psychology Normal and Abnormal*, 1951, pp. 182-83.

# CHAPTER XVII

*Fatigue*

## Fatigue

Psychologists divide fatigue into three kinds : (1) muscular fatigue, (2) sensory fatigue, and (3) mental fatigue. Muscular fatigue is due to the exhaustion of the muscles. Sensory fatigue is due to the exhaustion of the sense-organs. Mental fatigue is due to the exhaustion of the brain and the nervous system. Others divide fatigue into two kinds—bodily and mental. Bodily fatigue is muscular fatigue. Mental fatigue is fatigue of the brain ; it may be called brain fatigue or cerebral fatigue. It is due to changes in the tissue of the brain. Bodily fatigue is largely due to changes in the muscles. Muscular fatigue is closely associated with mental fatigue. It produces waste products in the muscles which affect the brain and the nervous system. Thus muscular fatigue may pass over into mental fatigue. A black-smith, after the day's strenuous work, feels not only muscular fatigue but also mental fatigue. Prolonged mental work may bring about muscular fatigue. Fatigue of the brain affects the muscles and produces muscular fatigue. Sensory fatigue is closely connected with muscular fatigue because sense-organs are connected with muscles. Synaptic connections in the central nervous system are the chief seat of fatigue. The sense-organs and the muscles are the secondary seats of fatigue.

## Continuous Muscular Work

Muscular work uses up glycogen which produces energy in the muscles, and develops waste products such as carbon dioxide and lactic acid. These together reduce the capacity to work and bring on feelings of fatigue. Thus continuous muscular work decreases its efficiency.

## Continuous Mental Work

Mental work generally involves the activity of muscles as well as neurons of the central nervous system. For example, in reading, the muscles of the eyes are exercised ; in writing, the muscles of the eyes, arms, and hands are exercised ; the position of the body is maintained by muscular adjustments of all kinds of mental work. Thus mental fatigue is partly the result of muscular fatigue. It is also due to the fatigue of the brain and the nervous system. Thus mental fatigue is due to neural fatigue as well as muscular fatigue.

Continuous mental work is less fatiguing than continuous muscular work. We may carry on mental work for ten or twelve hours without much decreasing its efficiency. But we cannot carry on muscular work for such a long period without much loss of efficiency. Continuous muscular work for two or three hours at maximum effort produces a temporary decrease in the output by ten per cent. Thus the effect of mental fatigue is in sharp contrast with the effect of muscular fatigue.

## Feelings or Fatigue

They are largly sensations from muscles, tendons and joints. They include sensations of numbness, aches, and pain from the eyes, head, and other parts of the body. These are blended with other organic sensations. These constitute the feeling of fatigue which is accompanied by the impulse to stop work. If the work is continued it becomes tedious. Feelings of fatigue and loss of interest for the work commonly indicate decrease of efficiency.

## Symptoms of Fatigue

Mental effects of fatigue are the lack of power of sustained attention, failure of memory, decrease of the power of accurate thinking, general feeling of unrest and uneasiness, loss of vocabulary, and unco-ordinated movements.

The amount of energy passing from the nerve centres to the muscles is decreased. So fatigue brings on weak muscular movements. There is often lack of symmetry in posture and movements. There is often irritability. Much movement follows upon the slightest touch. Jerky movements, at intervals, are perfomed by a fatigued person. Random actions are brought about by fatigue because the nerve centres are exhausted. Slight noises may evoke movements. Unco-ordinated movements are the results of fatigue.

Moral effects of fatigue are greater liability to outburst of passion, general loss of mental control, and loss of power to resist temptation.

## Causes of Muscular Fatigue

There are three main causes of bodily or muscular fatigue.

(1) The exhaustion of the energy-producing compounds in the muscles and the cell bodies of the neuron.—Such compounds are stored up in the muscle fibres. Their chemical composition is not known. But they are known to be exceedingly complex and easily decomposable. They partly break up and produce energy when a nervous impulse passes into the muscles.

(2) The presence of toxic waste products.—The exercise of the muscles produces toxins or waste products. They are poisonous. They are mixed with blood and the tissues are charged with them. The presence of a large quantity of toxins causes the symptoms of fatigue.

(3) Lack of oxygen.—The red corpuscles of the blood carry oxygen to the muscles. It helps the decomposition of the energy-producing compounds in them. Nervous impulses are conducted through nerves with the help of oxygen. So lack of oxygen brings about fatigue. Fatigue, therefore ;, can be removed partly by oxidation.

## Causes of Mental Fatigue

Continuous muscular work, we have already seen, affects the brain, and brings on mental or cerebral fatigue. The toxins produced by the exercise of muscles affect the cells of the nervous system,—especially those of the cortex of the brain which is the seat of consciousness. The blood circulates throughout the body. Therefore toxins produced in any part of the body very soon affect the nervous system. Thus muscular fatigue cannot be separated from cerebral or mental fatigue. It impairs the energies of will and intelligence, and decreases the efficiency of the activity of mind as well as body. Continuous activity of the brain directly produces cerebral or mental fatigue.

### Remedy for Mental Fatigue

(1) The best way for curing mental fatigue is change of occupation. Give a person affiicted with mental fatigue some mental occupation which will make him forget that he is tried. (2) Rest is the sovereign remedy for mental fatigue. Change of occupation is of no use if fatigue is already excessive. Fatigue is removed by rest. (3) Sleep removes fatigue entirely in healthy persons. It is complete rest. But rest througout the day removes fatigue partially and helps recovery of body and mind.

### The Fatigue Curve

The following characteristics are noticed in the fatigue curves. (1) An initial spurt.—An individual starts the task with zest and vigour. So there is a rapid initial rise in the curve. The initial spurt is due to will power and interest. (2) A warming up.—The initial spurt does not carry the person far; he has still to get into the real swing of the task. He has to warm up to the task; during the process there is a steadily increasing efficiency. (3) Adaptation.—This characteristic is psychical rather than physiological. The individual adapts himself to the task, begins to see through it, and to become familiar with its intricacies. The curve shows a fairly constant output of work and tends to remain fairly steady. (4) Spurts after fatigue and disturbance.—The fatigue curve is never steady. There are frequent drops and rises. Sudden drops are due to a temporary loss of interest or to distractions of some kinds. The drops are immediately followed by rises due to spurts. The person realises that his work is wanting, and makes renewed efforts to gain efficiency. (5) End spurt.—In spite of spurts due to repeated vigorous efforts there is decrease in efficiency. There is a rapid rate of decline in efficiency when the limit of endurance is approached. But as the end draws near, the person makes the last desperate effort which results in a rise in the curve just before the end. The end-spurt is always followed by complete fatigue. Fatigue is measured by ergograph.

# CHAPTER XVIII

## *Habit*

### The Nature of Habit

A habit is the product of repeated voluntary actions. When a voluntary action is repeated very often, it is turned into a habit. Voluntary actions involve an effort of the will. But when they become habitual, they dispense with the guidance of attention and volition, and become automatic. Habitual actions are acquired. They are uniform and mechanical, and are performed with ease and facility. Talking, reading, writing, type-writing, swimming, etc., are habitual actions. They are the results of repeated voluntary actions. They are learned actions as distinguished from unlearned actions. They are acquired by an individual through practice of voluntary actions.

Habits have the following characteristics.—(1) Uniformity.—Habitual actions are uniform actions. Voluntary actions vary in their nature in order to adjust the organism to new situations. But habitual actions are performed in the same way. A person walks or writes in the same way. (2) Promptness.—Habitual actions are performed promptly. The stronger is the habit the quicker is the motor response to the situation. (3) Accuracy.—Habitual actions are performed not only promptly, but also accurately. The stronger is the habit, the more precise is the motor response. (4) Absence of attention.—Habitual actions are performed automatically without the guidance of attention. If they are attended to, they are hindered. When we attend to buttoning our coats or tying the laces of shoes, the normally habitual actions are thwarted and lose their automatic nature. But habitual actions are started by attention, and carried on automatically without attention. (5) Ease and facility.—Habitual actions are performed with ease and facility. As habits are firmly established, they diminish fatigue. The miners do not feel fatigue when they get accustomed to their work. The chief difference between the skilled and the unskilled workman is that the former trains his brain, while the latter trains or develops his muscles. (6) Resistance to modification.—The stronger is the habit, the greater is the difficulty of breaking it. An inveterate drunkard finds it extremely difficult to shake off the habit of drinking. Habits leave mental dispositions and physiological dispositions which compel the individual to perform them. A habitual opium-eater or drunkard feels an irresistible impulse to take doses of opium or wine regularly. Even habits of thought resist modification.

### Habit and Instinct

Habits and instincts are alike marked by uniformity, accuracy and facility. They are both mechanical and accurate. They both give rise to periodic cravings, as in taking tea, smoking, drinking, and the like. They both do not require the guidance of volition.

But there is an important difference between them. Instincts are innate, while habits are acquired. Instincts are unlearned or native, while habits are learned by repeated voluntary actions. Sometimes instincts are said to be racial habits, while habits are said to be individual habits.

### Habit and Reflex Action

A habit and a reflex action are alike prompt and uniform in character. Both are automatic and mechanical. Both are without the guidance of attention and volition. But the reflex action is native, while the habitual action is acquired. The former is simple, while the latter is complex. For example, swimming is a very complex action, while sneezing is a simple action.

### Habit and Voluntary Action

A habit is the product of repeated voluntary actions. They are the basis of a habit. They are a stage in the formation of a habit. It is mechanical and uniform in nature. But, a voluntary action is the new response to a novel situation. The new response is exploratory and tentative, while habit is fixed and definite. The new response is slow and uncertain, while habit is fairly quick and accurate. The new response is variable, while habit is uniform. The new response is attended by effort and strained attention, while habit is easy and often only half-conscious. The new response is apt to be unsatisfying to the one who makes it, while habit is comfortable and a source of satisfaction. To break a habit is most uncomfortable. To break a habit we must form a counter-habit[1]. A habit is also formed by the repetition of non-voluntary actions, e.g., instinctive actions.

### Formation of Habit : Laws of Habit

William James gives four laws of formation of habits. They are the following :—

(1) Begin a new habit with a firm resolution. If you make a start with a firm determination, it often carries you along and fixes the habit. If you want to rise early in the morning first make a firm resolve to do it.

(2) Seize the first opportunity to put the new resolve into practice. When you have made a firm resolve to rise early, begin it the very next day. Do not wait for the first day of the next month or the New Year's Day to start the work. If you do so, your resolution will become weak and inspiration will vanish.

(3) Never allow an exception to occur till the new habit is well-learned. Once you have started rising early, continue the action from day to day and never allow an exception on any pretext. If you break it once, the pathway that is formed in the nervous system will become faint, your resolve will become weak, and you may revert to your old habit. But do not permit an exception to occur, and the new habit will be formed.

(4) Cultivate strength of mind by a little free practice of a difficult action every day. In order to cultivate the strength of mind, you should perform a difficult action every day which

requires a great effort of the will. Habits make us conservative. We move in fixed grooves of thought and action. But we must be open to new ideas, to new methods. We can best do this, according to James, by a little practice of something new and difficult every day[2].

## Rules of Breaking Bad Habits

Habits may be either good or bad. Good habits should be cultivated. Bad habits should be broken. We should observe the following rules to break bad habits :—

(1) Begin the new action at once, do not wait for a convenient opportunity. Stop the bad habit wholly ; do not discontinue it gradually. If you want to break the habit of rising late in the morning, rise early the next day and continue the action every day. There is a danger in breaking a habit gradually. It does not wear out the nervous pathway quickly.

(2) Cultivate a positive counter-habit. An opposite habit must be formed in order to break an old habit. An old habit is broken easily if a substitute is formed. Old habits die out from disuse. New habits are formed by repetition. If you are in the habit of going to the cinema every evening, try to form the habit of listening to radio music at the time. A drunkard may form the habit of talking strong coffee instead of wine at stated times. He should continue the habit until he feels sure that the grip of the old habit is loosened.

(3) Live in a congenial environment. Give up the company of the habitual cinema-goers if you want to break the habit of cinema-going. A drunkard must give up the company of drunkards and keep the company of sober pople.

(4) Make your body an ally, instead of your enemy. The nervous system is the physiological basis of habits. Nervous pathways are formed in the nervous system by habitual actions. These must be effaced by steady, persistent, and continuous formation of positive counter-habits. Mere penitent mood will not be enough to break old habits[3].

## Function of Habits

Many bodily habits, e.g., habits of personal cleanliness,

eating, sleeping, evacuation, etc., are fixed during childhood. Habits of dressing, behaving with others, moral and religious habits are fixed during adolescence. Social etiquette and manners are social habits. Moral habits are truthfulness or untruthfulness, kindness or cruelty, generosity or miserliness, obedience or disobedience, which are performed in relation to others. Professional habits are naturally acquired later. The people belonging to different professions have their characteristic gestures, attitudes and habits of action. In a wide sense, habits include habits of thought and emotional habits. These habits help mental development.

Habits play an important role in mental development. They set the mind free to acquire knowledge of new things and perform new actions in new situations. The mind can pass from victory to victory on account of habits which are handed over to the body. There can be no mental development without habits.

But habits are also a drag to mental progress. They keep the mind within fixed grooves of thought and action. They make the mind conservative. So the mind should be on the alert to respond to new ideas and new ways of life in novel situations. The mind should be alive to broader and truer ideals of life and cultivate wider and wider interests. It should not be a slave of habits.

### Habit, Character, and Conduct

Habits are results of repeated voluntary actions. They are the foundation of character. Good habits build good character. Bad habits build bad character. Character is the permanent bent of the mind, constituted by habits of thought, emotional habits or sentiments, and settled habits of will. It is a system of permanent tendencies or dispositions to thoughts, emotions, and actions voluntarily acquired. McDougall lays stress on sentiments, especially the sentiment of self-regard in the formation of character. Novalis defined character as "a completely fashioned will".

Character is different from nature. Character is acquired by a person by his voluntary actions. Nature is innate, but character is acquired. Character is built up by a person out of his natural impulses by controlling and regulating them by reason and will. Natural impulses are converted into desires by self-consciousness. The desires are turned by the mind into volitions. These volitions are converted into habits by repetition. Habits produce permanent dispositions which we call character. Natural impulses are the given elements. which supply raw materials for the formation of character. They are controlled and reduced to an order by reason.

Character is expressed in conduct. Conduct is the outer expression of character. Conduct includes voluntary and habitual actions. They are overt actions. They are determined by character of the self. Character is not absolutely fixed and permanent. It grows and develops. Free acts of will alter the character already formed. These volitions are partly determined by past character. But they are free volitions of the Self, though they are influenced by past character. Thus neither character nor conduct is fixed and unalterable. They are plastic and modifiable. They are modified by each other.

## REFERENCE

[1]Woodworth, *Psychology*.
[2]*Brief Text-Book of Psychology*.
[3]Angell, *Psychology*.

# CHAPTER XIX

## *The Self*

### The Subject or Pure Self

Consciousness is always personal. It belongs to a person or self. The self is the Subject which is conscious. The Subject Self is called the Pure Self or 'I'. It is the presupposition of consciousness. Consciousness is the reaction of the Subject to the object. No consciousness is possible without the Subject or Pure Self. Personality is the organisation of the experiences of the Subject or Pure Self. No organisation of experiences is possible without the unity of the self. It is the thinking, feeling, and willing Self that organises and harmonises its experiences and reactions according to its dominant interests and trends.

The Subject or Pure Self is immanent in experience. But it cannot be made an object of experience. It can be intuited as Subject, but not as object. The Pure Self or 'I' cannot be identified with the empirical self or 'Me'.

David Hume wrongly identified the Pure Self with a rapid succession of feelings and ideas. J. S. Mill wrongly identified it with a series of conscious states, aware of itself as a series. William James wrongly identified it with the stream of consciousness. According to him, "passing thoughts themselves are thinkers". Each thought appropriates the past thoughts in the stream of thought as its own, and plays the role of a thinker in relation to them. But Ward rightly points out that the 'I' cannot be identified with the 'Me'. "The present judging, remembering and appropriating thought" cannot serve as the Pure Self or Ego, as James wrongly maintains.

### The Empirical Self or Me

All the contents of consciousness which are regarded as mine constitute the 'Me'. A person's 'Me' is the sum total of all that he can tell his, his body, his clothes, his house, his wife and children, his friends and relations, his wealth, his mental powers, knowledge, reputation, and works. He identifies himself with them. If they prosper, he feels elated. If they dwindle, he feels cast down[1]. Thus the Empirical Self includes the material self, the social self, and the spiritual self.

### The Material Self or Me

The body is the innermost part of the material self; certain parts of the body form an essential part of the bodily self. The clothes come next. They form an important part of our material self. Good and neat clothes increase our self-esteem. Squalor and rags decrease our self-respect. Our home comes next. A person identifies himself with his home. It forms a part of his life. He lives and grows here. His dear ones live here. It evokes his affections. Property comes next. A person identifies himself with his property. He feels his property as his. The parts of it whicn are saturated with his labour are regarded by him as most intimately his. All his possessions are valuable to him, only because they give him scope for self-assertion.

### The Social Self or Me

Our father and mother, wife and children, are "bone of our bone, and flesh of our flesh. When they die, a part of our very selves is gone". If they prsoper, we feel elated. If they do anything wrong, we feel ashamed. If they are insulted, we get angry. Our friends and admirers come next. They form an essential part of our social self. We have an innate propensity to be noticed, praised and admired by our kind. Our friends admire us and carry our images in their minds. So we cannot offend them. One's dear wife or husband with whom a person most intimately identifies himself in good fortune and misfortune, in prosperity and adversity, is the most peculiar social self. One's intense elation and dejection are caused by good or bad fortunes of this part of the social self. A man's honour or dishonour, and fame, good or bad, are part of his social self. A layman may desert a city infected with cholera. But a priest can never abandon it because such an act he thinks incompatible with his honour. Even a thief or a gambler has his code of honour. A thief must not steal from other thieves. A gambler must pay his gambling debts, although he never pay his other debts.

### The Spiritual Self or Me

The spiritual self or 'Me' is the central part of the empirical self or 'Me'. All cognitive, affective and conative states constitute the empirical self. Our emotions and desires are more intimate than our sensations. Our volitions and decisions are more intimate than our intellectual processes. The affective-active states are more intimate than other processes. They form the central core of our spiritual self or 'Me'. This is the view of Willian James.

REFERENCE

[1]*Brief Text-Book of Psychology*, p. 177-81.

# CHAPTER XX

*Development of the Individual*

## Mental Development

Mental development is allied to organic growth. It is of the nature of unfoldment of innate potentialities. It is not of the nature of accretion or addition from without. It is not mechanical aggregation. It is a transformation of the homogeneous mind into a heterogenous condition from within by adjusting itself to the physical and social environment.

Mental development involves certain powers, viz., discrimination, assimilation, association, retention, recall, recognition, analysis, synthesis, abstraction, etc. Development of knowledge involves all these processes. Development of emotions also involves differentiation and integration. Development of volition presupposes development of cognition and affection and emotion.

Development of cognition passes through different stages, viz., sensation, perception, memory, imagination, judgment, conception, reasoning, and belief. Development of affection passes through different stages, viz., feeling, emotion and sentiment. Development of conation passes through different stages, viz., attention, sensation-reflex, conditioned reflex, instinctive acts, random acts, ideo-motor acts, voluntary actions and habits.

## Conditions of Mental Development

Conditions of mental development are mainly heredity and environment. Physical organism and mental capacities are inherited from parents and ancestors. They are developed under the influence of the physical and social environment. Physical conditions, such as the climate, diet, position and natural scenery of the land have a direct effect upon mental development. Facilities of agriculture, industry and commerce also affect mental development. Social conditions, customs and manners, legal and moral institutions, ethical and religious codes, laws of the State, form of government, and the like exert a paramount influence upon mental development. Parents, relatives, teachers, playmates and companions mould and fashion the mind in a vital manner. Language has a powerful influence upon the power of thinking. Self-consciousness is developed through social intercourse. Physical and social environment are the external conditions of mental development. Heredity gives capacities or potentialities. The environment gives facilities to realise them. It gives us opportunities for realizing the innate capacities. They are potential abilities. They are inferred from the unequal achievements of individuals, although they undergo equal training. Achievements are actual abilies of an individual, which can be measured by the different kinds of tests. The school examinations are the achievement tests. Aptitudes are the capacities of an individual which can be developed through learning and experience. They can be predicted and measured by special tests. Intelligence and mental capacities are inherited.

Imitation, temperament and disposition, and certain mental powers, e.g., attention, discrimination, assimilation, abstraction, and the like are the internal conditions of mental development.

### The Influence of Heredity and Environment on Mental Development

Heredity provides the capacities, and the environment provides the facilities for the full expression of the capacities. The innate capacities are brought into play by right education in a favourable physical and social environment.

(1) Biological Heredity.—Biological heredity has been defined as the sum total of the traits potentially present in the fertilized ovum, which grows into the child. The individual's heredity is derived in equal measure from the maternal and paternal sides. Heredity is the sum total of the inborn individual traits. Likeness and variation both are due to herdity.

We inherit a nervous system from the parents, by which we receive messages from the environment and react to it. The nervous system is plastic and modified by the new conditions of the environment. Man's reactions to the environment are partly fixed and partly modifiable under novel conditions. His mental development is largely due to his adaptability to the environment.

We inherit a large number of instincts which supply the fundamental motives of actions. They are modified by experience, habit, and novel conditions of the environment.

An individual develops his organism through maturation and learning. His hands, legs, teeth, larynx, and brain gradually develop and mature to their full size and in differentiation of parts. This growth of the organism and its organs from an immature to a mature state is called maturation. The lower animals, birds and insects mature early. Human beings take a long period of time to attain to the state of maturity. Their infancy, childhood and adolescence are much longer than those of the other species. An individual develops through maturation and learning. Learning plays a more important part in a human individual.

(2) Social Heredity.—It is a figurative expression. We do not inherit any trait from the society. But we imbibe many traits from the social environment. Our soeial heritage consists of all that is handed down to us by the past generations. Our customs, manners, mother tongue, social etiquettes, laws, traditions, culture, outlook on life, and the like constitute the social heredity. The young child imbibes them from the social environment by unconscious imitation. Each generation receives a social heritage from the past generations. It is the sum total of the past achievements. The child is born with a biological heritage. But he is not born with a social heritage. He is born into it. He imbibes it by unconscious imitation or acquires it by learning.

Social development begins early when the infant responds to the parents' and others' behaviour at home. The child learns from his playmates in the school and takes part in social activities. His social development continues througout in school, college, social groups, factories, business organisations, etc. Development of personality is affected by social intercourse. Love, sympathy, co-operation, competition, rivalry, defeat and success are learned by an individual in his social environment. But changes of personality during adolescence are due to maturation of the organism.

(3) Environmental factors in Mental Development.—The fertilized ovum contains all the biological heritage necessary for the development of the individual. It can develop under favourable conditions of the environment. The environment supplies food, warmth, shelter, oxygen, and the like. It provides facility for the elimination of waste products. The material from the environment is not simply added to the organism ; it is incorporated in it in accordance with its hereditary characteristics.

Woodworth rightly remarks, "Development is the product, not the sum of heredity and environment. The relation of heredity and environment is not like addition but more like multiplication. The individual is not equal to heredity and environment, but to heredity multiplied by environment"[1] Every trait of an individual depends on both heredity and environment. Two individuals born with the same biological heritage differ because of differing environments. And two individuals living in the same environment differ because of differing heredity.

## Sensory Development and Mental Development

All the inner mental life is based upon sense perception. Thinking depends upon memory and imagination. Imagination depends upon memory. Memory depends upon perception. Perception depends upon sensations. Therefore all the inner mental life is based upou sense perception. Herein lies the true significance of sense training.

The normal child is born with sense-organs acute and powerful enough to react to the environment. The powers of the sense-organs are not generally developed by training. Through sensory experience sensory discrimination is devoloped. Through sensory experience the child can discriminate different kinds of colours, sounds, tastes, smells, temperatures, and the like. The stimulation of the sense-organs by well-chosen objects having a meaning for the children of different ages develops their power of sensory discrimination. And this power of discrimination is a condition of intelligent understanding and comprehension. Thus mental development depends on sensory development. For example, thinking is carried on and developed through language. Knowledge of language is devoloped through auditory discrimination of sounds. Musical gift depends upon fine discrimination of different kinds of tones. The gift of painting depends upon fine discrimination of delicate shades of colour. Mechanical skill, maniplation, and construction depend upon discrimination of fine movements. Defects of the sense-organs, such as blindness, short-sightedness, colour-blindness, deafness, and the like have an adverse effect on mental development. Thus mental development dedends largely on sensory development. Intellectual development continues during childhood. It levels off during adolescence. Intettectual alterness gradually declines after adolescence, although greater knowledge may be acquired.

## REFERENCE

[2]Woodworth, *Psychology*, 11th. edition, p. 139.

# CHAPTER XXI

*Intelligence*

## Nature of Intelligence

Intelligence is akin to intellect, but is not identical with it. Intellect is the faculty of observing, remembering, and thinking, as distinguished from feeling and willing. Intelligence is a way of acting. It helps the individual in reaching a goal. It is not an acquired ability. It is a native abilty. It is a shorthand symbol for the fact of behaving intelligently. Woodworth mentions the following marks of intelligence :—

(1) Use of past experience.—Man is more intelligent than the dog. It means that man makes more use of his past experience. An intelligent man makes more use of his past experience to seek a goal. Utilizing past experience is a mark of intelligence.

(2) Adaptation to a novel situation.—Man can adapt himself to a novel situation more easily than the dog. An intelligent person can master a complex situation easily. But a less intelligent person breaks down in a new situation. Capacity to master a novel situation is a mark of intelligence.

(3) "Seeing the point"—Intelligence consists in "seeing the point" or finding out the essentials of a problem, or insight into the key of the situation. Insight into the key of a situation is a mark of intelligence.

(4) Viewing actions from a broader point of view.—Man takes account of a broader situation in his action than the dog can fathom. A stupid person cannot take a broad view of a situation. His perspective is narrow. He follows a fixed routine in his actions. But an intelligent person takes a broad view of a situation and adapts his actions to it. Foresight is a sign of breadth of view which consists in seeing the whole situation as a pattern of interrelated parts.

Intelligence consists in acting in a given situation with use of past experience, with due regard to what is novel in a situation and to the whole situation rather than to some striking part of it. It contains insight into the key to the whole situation.

## Mental Age

As the child grows older, his intelligence gradually increases. The rate of such growth is fairly constant in childhood under normal conditions. It goes on increasing with the increase of age upto the fourteenth or fifteenth year. It does not increase beyond that age.

Intelligence tests have been devised to measure the intelligence of children of different ages. There is a separate test suited to each age level. When a child of 10 years passes a test not higher than that suited to a child of 8 years, his mental age is said to be 8, though his actual or chronological age is 10. Similarly, a child of 8 years may pass a test suited to a child of 10 years. In this case, his mental age is said to be 10, though his real age is 8. The first child is comparatively dull. The second is comparatively bright. The mental age of a normal child is the same as his actual or chronological age. For example, the normal eight year old child has the mental age of eight years.

## Intelligence Quotient

The intelligence of a child is described in terms of his intelligence quotient. It is determined by dividing his mental age by his chronological age. When the child has a mental age that corresponds with his actual age, his Intelligence Quotient, or, in brief, *I.Q.* or *IQ.* is 1·00. If his mental age is 8, and actual age is 10, his IQ is 8/10=·80. If his mental age is 10, and actual age 8, his IQ is 10/8=1·25. Generally, the decimal point is omitted in expressing IQ's and 1·00 is expressed as 100 and ·80 expressed as 80, and 1.25 expressed 125. Thus, the IQ is determined by dividing the mental age by the chronological age and multiplying it by 100. Thus—

$$IQ = \frac{\text{mental age}}{\text{chronological age}} \times 100.$$

Intelligence cannot be determined by mental age alone. The mental age has to be related to the actual age. Intelligence is measured by IQ which is the ratio between the mental age and the actual age. The ratio remains fairly constant throughout life. The IQ of the average individual is 100. It may be asserted definitely that intelligence rcmains the same from twenty to sixty.

## The Binet-Simon Intelligence Tests

During the first decade of this century Alfred Binet devised certain mental tests with the assistance of Theodore Simon, for measuring the intelligence of shool-going children, to determine the classes for which they were fit. These tests were revised by Terman, Kuhlmann and others. The following tests are suited to different ages :—

6-month level : reaching for a small bright object hung before the child within his reach.

12-month level : imitating an action such as shaking a rattle or ringing a small bell.

2-year level : removing the paper wrapping from a piece of candy before putting the candy in the month.

3-year level : stringing at least 4 beads within 2 minutes.

6-year level : finding omissions in pictures of faces from which pictures of some organs are left out. Fcur pictures are shown. Three responses must be correct.

9-year level : both similarity and difference between each of 4 pairs of things (e.g., wood and coal) must be stated.

12-year level : rough definitions of 40 words out of a standard list of 100 must be given ; or a picture of an incident must be corectly interpreted.

14-year level : explaining the absurdity in a given picture.[1]

These tests are intended to measure general intelligence. They cannot measure special ablilities. They suffer from the handicap of language. Hence other tests have been devised to test intelligence.

## Performance Tests

Performance tests measure capacity to perceive and manipulate objects. They test capacity to do things. They do not make use of language. They measure general intelligence.

(1) Form Board Test.—Various performance tests are devised, which use 'form boards'. Blocks of different shapes are to be fitted into corresponding holes in a board. The time of performance is measured, and the number of errors committed is counted.

(2) Picture Drawing Test.—It is suited to children of younger ages, from four to ten. The child is simply asked to draw a man with pencil on paper. The test is scored not for its beauty but for the completeness and coherence of the drawing.

(3) Picture Completion Test.—A picture is shown with square holes cut out; the cut-out pieces also are presented mixed with the squares of the same size, which have irrelevant objects pictured on them. The child has to select, from the whole lot, the proper square pieces and fit them into the holes in the picture. The better his understanding of the picture, the better is his selection.

(4) Maze.—A maze is drawn on paper with many blind alleys. The shortest path has to be traced with a pencil without straying into a promising blind alley. The maze has to be examined as a whole. It should not be attacked with an imperfect understanding of it.

In schools the pupils having IQ's between 70 and 85 are considered as very dull and very slow. Most of them are retarded in their school progress. Children with IQ's between 70 and 85 drop out early in their school career. The IQ's of average children range from 95 to 105. Children of superior intelligence have IQ's ranging between 120 and 145. The IQ's of geniuses range between 180 and 190.

Intelligence grows continuously throughout childhood to age 13 or 15. It grows more slowly to age 18. It does not increase further after age 18. It remains constant after adolescence. Adult intelligence cannot be measured with accuracy. Though IQ is constant in adulthood, it undergoes fluctuation. The better environment gives greater opportunities for the expression of intelligence.

## Group Tests

These intelligence tests are given to a number of individuals at the same time. They economise time. Some persons do better in a group than alone under the direct eye of the examiner. School examinations are group achievement tests. During the Great War group intelligence tests were devised to measure the intelligence of recruits in America in order to select soldiers and officers from among them. The Army Alpha was a test for those who could read English. The Army Beta was intended for illiterates and foreigners. The Army Alpha contained arithmetical problems ranging in complexity from extremely simple to more complex ones, synonyms and antonyms to be distinguished, and the items of information. These tests depended on the subject's stock of knowledge previously acquired. The sub-tests called for alertness and mental flexibility. In the Army Beta there was practically no use of speech. There were picture competition tests among other tests. Group tests measure general intelligence.

## Education of Superior and Dull Children

Superior children possess a high degree of intelligence. They quickly learn the lessons intended for the average pupils and spend their time idly. So they should be taught a higher curriculum and allowed to advance at their proper rate. Then only their intellectual progress will be in harmony with their superior intelligence. Otherwise their intellectual progress will be retarded, and they may become mischief-makers.

Dull or backward children possess a low degree of intelligence. They cannot learn their lessons quickly especially in abstract subjects. They should be taught these subjects with the lower class or in a special class. They are detained in some classes. They are not equally deficient in all subjects. Special arrangements should be made to remove their deficiency in particular subjects. In higher classes in which the pupils are taught elective subjects, they should be helped to elect proper subjects.

Superior children should be allowed to read certain subjects in which they are very proficient with the pupils of a higher class. Backward children should be allowed to read certain subjects in which they are deficient with the pupils of a lower class. Or, special arrangements should be made to meet the special needs of the superior children and the backward children.

## Vocational Guidance

Besides intelligence, abilities and aptitudes can be measured by special devices. Abilities, e.g., verbal ability, number ability, spatial ability, etc., can be measured. Verbal ability is the ability to deal with the use of words. Number ability is the ability to deal with numbers. Spatial ability is the ability to grasp spatial relations. Abilities possessed by an individual can be measured. Aptitudes are measured in terms of individual differences. Certain persons can learn a given type of work quickly and achieve efficiency. Others can learn it slowly and cannot achieve efficiency. The former have aptitude for the work, while the latter have no aptitude for it. Aptitudes are specific. Some have aptitudes for book-keeping, or for accouncy, but have none for mechanical work. Others have aptitudes for carpentry, smithy, cycle-repairing, watch-repairing, book-binding, or printing, but have none for book-keeping, or for accounting. Aptitudes are both inborn and acquired. The present abilities may predict future achievement in a certain work with training. A person has no present ability to fly an aeroplane. But his present abilities may predict that he will achieve success in flying a plane. They may show his aptitude for the work. Aptitude tests help vocational guidance and vocational selection. In a particular vocation or occupation particular abilities are required. Aptitudes for these abilities can be measured by special tests. If an individual has no aptitude for certain abilities, he should never try to learn those abilities. His scope of choice of a vocation is thus limited. Aptitude tests help an expert give cousel in choosing a vocation. They help an individual choose a particular vocation for which he has aptitude. The individual must choose a proper vocation for himself with the counsel of a vocational guide. The aptitude tests help him in vocational selection.[2]

## REFERENCE

[1]Woodworth, *Psychology*, 1955, p. 38.
[2]Woodworth, *Psychology*, pp.82-86. Munn, *Psychology*, pp. 419-20.

# CHAPTER XXII

*Personality*

## Personality

Personality is the synthetic unity of all the characteristics and reaction tendencies of a person in their intimate interplay. The factors of personality can be distinguished by analysis. They form an organic whole of interdependent parts. Personality is not the mere sum of distinguishable parts. It refers to a pattern of traits rather than to a mere collection of characteristics. Personality traits tell us how the individual behaves. They show his characteristic style of action. Personality is the style of life. It is the total quality of a person's behaviour. A personality trait is some particular quality of his behaviour. Personality is not the mechanical aggregate of personality traits. It is their synthetic unity. It is a unique pattern of a person's traits and behaviour. Aggressiveness or submissiveness, cheerfulness or sadness, intelligence or foolishness, persistence or fickleness, emotional stability oı instability, etc., are personality traits.

In appraising a person, we should consider his appearance and other pysical traits ; vocational and recreational interests, aptitudes and abilities ; intelligence, attention, observation, memory, imagination, reasoning and other mental traits : character and moral traits ; sociality or social traits ; temperament or emotional traits ; and will or volitional traits.

## Personality Traits

(1) Physical Traits. Personal appearance, as indicated by height, weight, build, facial expression, and complexion together with voice, dress and other personal characteristics, is an important factor of personality. Physical traits are important aspects of the total personality. They affect other persons powerfully.

(2) Intelligence.—Mental traits such as intelligence, attention, observation, memory, imagination, judgment, and reasoning are important traits of personality. Intelligence means the ability to master novel situations and solve the problems of life. It is allied with the ability to learn. Mental alertness must go along with intelligence. Acquired abilities and special aptitudes, e.g., vocational interests also affect personality.

(3) Temperament.—Emotional traits and tendencies are important factors of personality. We ask whether a person is calm or excitable, cheerful or gloomy, courageous or timid. Temperaments are said to be due to the hormones secreted by the endocrine glands. Emotionality has much to do with personality.

(4) Volition and Character.—Volitional traits or will power and moral character are important factors of personality. Volition is the control of voluntary actions. We ask whether a person is active or lethargic, strong-minded or vacillating. By character we mean a person's moral traits. It includes those reactions which are related to our moral and religious codes and to our personally approved standards of conduct.

(5) Sociability.—Social traits constitute the most important aspect of personality. Sympathy, co-operation, fellowship, comradeship, aggressiveness, self-assertion, humility, modesty, and the like are important social traits. We ask whether a person is social or unsocial, aggressive or retiring, boastful or modest. Different persons have different degrees of sociability.

(6) Forcefulness or Persistence.—This is the most important factor of personality. This personality trait is essential to success. Very bright persons are often found to fail in life owing to lack of forcefulness or persistence. Their failure is due to lack of tenacity of purpose and effort. Many persons with mediocre ability outstrip such persons by dint of dogged persistence. Ability and persistence are essential to personal success. All these traits are integrated in a person. Complete integration or unification is the ideal of personality.

## Development of Personality

Personality is the unity and organization of an individual's innate mental tendencies or dispositinos. Intelligence is the innate power of attention, observation, learning, memory, imagination, and thinking. Instincts are the innate propensities. They are impulses to action, and give rise to emotions. Instincts are the basis of primary emotions. Derived or complex emotions are the blends or complex forms of primary emotions. Complex emotions organise several instincts in their structure. Sentiments are permanent emotional dispositions centred round certain objects, which may organise in their strncture many instincts and emotions. Sentiments are acquired dispositions. Instincts are native dispositions. Both constitute mental structure. They are not functions or actual experiences. Sentiments arise out of the organisation of instincts and emotions. The will is the power of inhibiting impulses and performing a chosen action in order to realise a purpose. Characrer is achieved by the will. Repeated acts of volition lead to the formation of character. It is the settled habit of willing. It has also a cognitive aspect and an affective aspect. Character also includes in its structure permanent habits of thought and permanent emotional dispositions or sentiments. McDougall holds that self-sentiment or the sentiment of self-regard is the dominant factor of character. Personality is achieved by the integration of intellect, the organisation of instincts, emotions and sentiments, and the systematisation of impulses by reason and will, and formation of character.

The main factors in the development of personality are heredity and environment. The physiological constitution and mental capacities are inherited. The physical and social environments rouse the capacities and develop them. A tropical climate may foster an easy-going disposition. A cold climate may foster a tough dispositson. Life in a congested town may develop a narrow outlook. Country life may develop a wide outlook. Thus the physical environment has an important influence on personality. The social environment exerts a paramount influence on personality.

## Factors in the Development of Personality

The Social Environment.—(1) The child's rôle in the home develops certain particular traits. If the parents are too anxious for the safety of the child, they allow him little opportunity to develop self-reliance and independence. They make him over-dependent. The unwanted and hated child becomes sullen, reserved and unsocial. Adler makes too much of the birth order of a child in developing particular traits. The only child, the favourite of the parents, tends to be over-dependent and sometimes tyrannical. The eldest child, who gets the entire affection of the parents for a few years and then is ousted from his privileged position by the second child, is apt to develop into a jealous person. He will believe in authority and privilege. The second child is expected to be a rebel against the established order. He will always try to rob the eldest child of his privilege. The youngest child, the perpetual baby of the parents, is apt to become over-dependent.

(2) The child's rôle in the gang. It is another important social factor in the development of personality. The child cannot play an independent part in the home. Among his comrades he escapes from the rôle of a dependent, and finds a scope for adventure and independence. One child becomes the 'brains' of the gang ; he makes plans for adventure. Another child plays the 'dare-devil' ; he is the excutive head of the gang. Another may serve as the funny boy. Another may serve as the 'cat's paw'. Thus different children play different rôles in the gang according to their different aptitudes. They are apt to play similar parts in the wider social life in after-life.

(3) Group codes and rôles.—The child unconsciously imbibes language, customs, manners, etiquette, fashions, morals, and the like from the group of persons among whom he lives. He unconsciously imitates the 'mores' or 'folkways'. It he fails to conform to them, he is criticised, ridiculed, and punished by the group. So ultimately he is compelled to adopt the group modes of behaviour.

(4) Adopting the style of the Group.—Besides the morals

and manners of the group unconsciously imbibed by its members, there is its particular style of behaviour which is consciously and deliberately adopted by them. A particular way of dressing, a particular way of speaking, a particular deportment and such other subtle shades of behaviour constitute the style of the group. These are unconsciously imbibed by an individual member of a group. These factors in the social environment contribute to the development of personality.

II. The Biological and Psychological Factors.

These are the internal biological factors, e.g., the endocrine hormones determining temperament, and psychological factors, e.g., mental capacities and dispositions. And there are the external environmental factors in personality such as the rôle of the child in the home, the rôle of the child in the gang, the 'folkways' or 'mores' and the 'style' of the group. But personality is not a mere sum of these factors inherited from the ancestors and those imbibed from the environment. The environment rouses him to activity. But his personality is developed by his own activity. He can partly overcome the influence of his social environment.[2]

## Types of Personality

According to temperament, there are four types of personality : (1) the elated type, (2) the depressed type, (3) the irritable type, and (4) the unstable type.

(1) The elated type.—Some persons are always elated and happy. They are always optimistic and cheerful. They cannot take things seriously. So they often get into trouble.

(2) The depressed type.—Some persons are always depressed and gloomy. They are moody and pessimistic. They suffer from continued emotional depression.

(3) The irritable type.—Some persons are always irritable. They are hot-headed and given to violent scenes. They are not inclined either to be happy or melancholy. They are always looking for fights and usually find them.

(4) The unstable type.—Some persons are elated at one moment and depressed at another moment, though there is

no seeming cause for the change. They are in fitful moods. They have no balanced temper.[3]

According to sociability, persons are divided by Jung into extroverts and introverts.

(1) Extroverts.—In extroverts mental energy is turned outward to the social environment. They meet every social situation in an objective manner. They are interested in other people more than in their own ideas and emotions. They are usually interested in the social environment. They spontaneously take part in what goes on the social environment. They are dominated by feeling. They participate freely in social doings. Social and political workers, athletes, actors, etc. belong to this objective type.

(2) Introverts.—In introverts mental energy is turned inward to their ideas and feelings. They are withdrawn from the social environment. They are especially concerned with themselves. They are more interested in their own ideas and feelings than in the immediate social environment. They are dominated by thought. They are given to meditation and reflection. They try to influence others by their thoughts. Whenever they encounter a difficulty in the social environment, they withdraw into themselves. They do not usually take part in the social doings. They may take interest in the physical environment, e.g.,, in plants, animals, machines, and the like. Scientists, philosophers, poets, and mystics belong to this subjective type. Jung suggests that persons who are extraverted in their conscious lives are introverted in the unconscious, and *vice versa*. Their unconscious personality is a complement of their conscious personality.

Jung also admits a middle type called ambiverts. They are midway between extroverts and introverts. Their interests are not predominantly either in the self or in the social environment. This shows that extroverts and introverts are the extreme types. Moreover, interest in one's own thought and observation is not necessarily incompatible with interest in other people. Jung also divides persons into a sensing type, a thinking type, a feeling type, and an intuitive type.

Hence his division of persons into extroverts and introverts is only a tentative hypothesis.

### Measurement of Personality

Personality can be measured by measuring the personality traits of an individual and comparing him with other individuals. It can be measured by putting questions to an individual to find out his personality traits and their degrees. It can be measured by putting an individual in particular situations and finding how he behaves. This is the performance test of personality. Personality is also measured by an individual's imaginative responses to ambiguous pictures.

## REFERENCE

[1] Gales, *Elementary Psychology*, p. 498.
[2] Woodworth, *Psychology*, 1955, pp. 133-42.
[3] Morgan & Gilliland, *Introduction to Psychology*

# CHAPTER XVI

## *The Abnormal Mind*

### Integration of Personality

Personality is the synthetic unity of all personality traits. All the mental traits—intelligence, emotions and sentiments, impulses and volitions, native and acquired reactions—must be organised and integrated into a unity. Complete integration of the traits of personality is an ideal. Only in a sound and strong personality they are integrated completely. A sound personality comprises reaction tendencies that are not loosely reorganised and integrated according to more dominant interests and ideals. Although gradually changing during long periods of time, the personality usually possesses a continuity of pattern, which the person himself and others recognise. In every person there is the primary or dominant self constituted by his enduring and dominant interests. His other interests are subordinated to it. Integration of personality consists in integration of intellect and integration of character (McDougall). All the conflicting reaction tendencies should be harmonised and organised gradually aud integrated with the dominant trends. A personality should be well-integrated and flexible. An integrated and inflexible personality cannot adapt itself to the changing environment. An ideal personality should be well-integrated and flexible. It should reveal in some degree the characteristics of unity or integration and flexibility. If a person has no flexibility, he cannot effectively adapt himself to a changing social environment. Therefore he should be flexible also.

### Disintegration of Personality

The conflicting reaction tendencies in a person may not be harmonised and organised into a unity. The disturbances of personality are due to disintegration or dissociation. The term 'dissociation' applies to all forms of disintegration of consciousness into separate parts. It covers practically all mental abnormalities. Dissociated or alternating personalities are interesting phenomena. Insanity is due to mental disintegration. An insane person is torn between conflicting demands of reality and an imaginary unreal world. He cannot adjust himself to the social environment.

## Disease of Personality : Multiple Personality

In the successive form of alternating personalities a person may suddenly lose his memory of his past life, his name, his home, his friends, and relatives, and think himself to be another person with a new name, a new occupation, and the like. He may change in temperament and character. A few months later he suddenly recovers all his memories of his earlier life, but he completely forgets everything which happened during the period of his altered personality. He suddenly recovers his former normal personality. The alternating personalities may be very different; one vivacious, cheerful, competent and kindly, the other stuipid, gloomy, careless and mischievous. The individual seems to be dissociated into two personalities which have been torn apart so that each functions independently. The more lasting state is the primary state; the less lasting state is the secondary state. In the secondary state he generally remembers the primary state, but speakes of it as belonging to another person. But he is unable to remember in the primary state what he has done in his secondary state.

Doris, a girl of three years, was thrown to the floor by her drunken father. After this event she developed double personality. She became an extremely quiet, industrious and conscientious child. Only at intervals she became reckless and mischievous. Doris, in her sober state, had no memory of her pranks done in the mischievous state. But the mischievous Doris knew all about the sober Doris, and spoke of her with scorn.

In the case of simultaneous personalities we have a more complicated condition. Here in addition to the normal consciousness there is a split off consciousness independent of it. The two personalities may differ in temperament and character. The two personalities seem to have distinct memories. Sometimes, as in the successive type of alternating personalities, the secondary personality generally remembers experiences of the primary personality but speaks of them as belonging to another person, but the primary personality appears to have no memory of the secondary personality. The two personalities are separate selves occupying the same body. They are not integrated into one personality. They do not work together. They do not influence each other. They are not integrated into a unity. The two split up parts function independently. This is dual personality.

Beauchamp, a young woman, had a double personality. She had troubles in early life. These compelled her to adopt an extremely religious, conscientious and benevolent attitude. But she lapsed occasionally into mischievous conduct. Later on, in the course of psychiatric treatment, she devoloped a third personality with aggressive, self-seeking tendencies. The primary, benevolent personality had no memory of the experiences of the secondary or the tertiary personality. Thus Beauchamp developed triple personality out of double personality. The doctor tried to integrate these three fragments into a complete person through hypnosis, suggestion, and integration of her memories and her goals[1].

## Hysteria

Hysteria is allied to multiple personality. Hysterical patients show a tendency towards the 'splitting up' of their organisation of ideas into isolated fragments, mainly under the force of suggestion, when they accept ideas uncritically. They fall into a trance and lose control over their bodies. They perform all movements demanded by normal consciousness, but are not conscious of them. Sometimes they are paralysed in some limbs. They cannot move them. But this does not arise from any bodily injury. This is solely due to suggestion. They are extremely suggestible. When they return to their normal state of consciousness, they do not remember anything that happened during trance, but follow their normal routine of tasks.

## Hypnosis : Hypnotic Suggestion and Post-hypnotic Suggestion

Hypnosis is a state of trance induced in a person by suggestion. He is called the 'subject' or the 'medium'. The person who induces trance is called the 'operator'. The 'subject' lies with outstretched limbs and relaxed muscles. Gradually under the force of suggestion he falls into a trance. The operator gives suggestions to him : "Sleep, sleep, deep sleep". He repeats the suggestion a number of times till the subject falls into a trance. He loses all consciousness of external objects except the operator's suggestions. He loses all control over his body. His mind becomes extremely suggestible. He responds to the suggestions of the 'operator'. He accepts uncritically whatever ideas are suggested to him by the 'operator', He carries out his commands automatically without reflection. He is compelled to do so. He assumes the rôle of different persons under thc force of suggestion. It is a clear case of dissociation of consciousness. When the medium wakes up from his trance, he forgets all that he did during hypnosis. During trance the medium loses his normal personality.

Suggestion carried out by the subject during trance is called hypnotic suggestion. Sometimes the medium carries out the suggestion of the 'operator' given during trance, when he wakes up from trance at the appointed time automatically under subconscious compulsion. This is called post-hypnotic suggestion. The 'medium' is commanded by the 'operator' to light a candle on waking from trance at 2 P. M. in his room in the presence of others, and keep it burning for half an hour. Or he is directed to walk up and down in his room with his open umbrella up. Or he is ordered to throw his hat out of the window. He cannot but perform these movements, however awkward they are, under subconscious compulsion. This phenomenon is called post-hypnotic suggestion.

## Insanity

Insanity is mental derangement due to dissociation of consciousness. It takes different forms, such as mania, melancholia, dementia, etc. In mania there is excessive mental excitation followed by acute delirium. In melancholia there is excessive mental depression. In manic-depressive insanity there is alternation of excitement with depression. In dementia there is loss of personality. Insanity was formerly traced to nervous disorders. But Freud and his followers trace it to repressed unconscious wishes. Mental derangement is due to mental conflict, repression and dissociation.

## Types of Insanity, Mania, Depression, and Manic-Depressive Insanity

In mania there is great mental excitement. The patient feels exalted. The slightest stimulus calls forth mental excitement. He can never keep his attention fixed on one thing for a long time. He talks on one thing, then sees another thing, drops the talk on the first thing, and begins to talk on the second thing. His attention is scattered over a large number of objects, that appear before him.He keeps cheerful. He sings, dances, and runs. He is always active. He cannot remain inactive. In the manic state there is continuous mental excitement.

In depression there is constant melancholy. The patient has apathy and indifference to all things and persons. He does not make any emotional response to them. He is always in a depressed state. He is emotionally indifferent, inattentive and inactive. He is immersed in his own imaginings. He is reserved and uncommunicative. He cannot be persuaded to talk. His face is not expressive. It is dull and colourless. He is always gloomy and melancholy. In a lunatic asyslum a patient suffering from depression sits in a corner of a room, hanging down his head, calm and quiet, without talking or making any movement. He remains sitting in this gloomy state of mind for hours together. Depression or melancholia is a state opposed to mania.

In manic-depressive insanity there is alternation of mania with depression. The patient has mental excitement or exaltation for some time. Then he has depression or melancholia for some time. Emotional exaltation is alternated with apathy, indifference, and gloom. There is emotional instability. Now there is emotional excess. Then there is emotional indifference. Exaltation is succeeded by apathy and gloom. Then apathy is sueceeded by emotional excitement. There is no emotional stability. Manic-depressive insanity is characterised by excessive emotional instability. In the manic state the patient is lively, cheerful, and talkative. In the depressed state, he is sad, brooding, and malancholy. Mania, depression, and manic-depressive insanity are dissociative disorders.

### Neurasthenia, Compulsions and Obsessions, and Schizophrenia

A young man feels a strong desire to go into business, acquire wealth, and live in luxury. He has also an intense desire to enter college, and distinguish himself as a great scholar. His intellectual ambition overcomes his desire for wealth. He enters college, and pursues his studies. But he cannot concentrate on his studies, and suffers from headache and insomnia. Psycho-analysis reveals that he has recurrent dreams, which clearly show that he has a repressed desire to go into business and acquire wealth. This repressed desire causes his headache and insomnia. This is a mild case of neurasthenia. The repressed desire for wealth, tinged with a painful emotion, forms a complex in the subconscious mind. The complex finds expression in dreams, day-dreams or phantasies of wealth and luxury. They interfere with the desire for intellectual pursuits. In neuraesthenia there is a lack of energy, or an inability to concentrate energy on the task, with fatigue or excessive liabality to fatigue. There is rationalization. The repressed desire for wealth may distort the patient's judgment.

He may become a rabid socialist or a communist. He may entertain intense animosity against successful businessmen, or even against friends who have gone into business, and acquired wealth. He may defend his unjust hatred for wealthy persons by arguing that they are robbers, sharks, cruel persecutors of the poor. His reasonings are distorted by his animosity against them, generated by his repressed desire for wealth. This process is called rationalization[2]. Thus neurasthenia is due to repression.

Compulsions are uncontrollable impulses to excute particular movements. They are involuntary actions. The uncontrollable impulse is due to repressed sex propensity, anger, or fear. A prisoner was being conducted to the rear by a soldier. The prisoner attacked the soldier. The soldier, in a fit of anger, killed the prisoner. His memory of the incident was repressed by horror and remorse. Still whenever be walked in a solitary place with another man, he had an uncontrollable impulse to kill him. This is called compulsion. He was cured of the compulsion, when he was enabled to bring back the memory of the incident and overcome the repression.[3]

Tics are involuntary movements, which are repeated again and again at brief intervals. But they can be suppressed by the patient with difficulty and by special effort. Twitches of muscles of the face or neck-muscles, and distortions of the movements of walking are examples of tics. They are not due to habit. They cannot be cured by the formation of counter-habits. They are due to repressed memory. They are cured by bringing back the memory of the incident, which was repressed. They are suddenly and completely cured by recall of the repressed incident. A soldier developed the symptom of walking with legs wide apart. He had a recurrent dream that a shell glided behind him almost touching him, but never exploded, as he run madly for life. Psycho-analysis brought back the memory of an incident. When he was standing with his legs wide apart on a trench, a shell fell between his feet. He fled madly from the spot. He ran at top speed for more than a mile, and then returned to his post of duty. He was ashamed of his deed, which was repressed. He forgot the incident. The idea of it was tinged with the painful emotion of fear, and repressed on account of its unpleasantness. It formed a complex. The repressed complex was unearthed by psycho-analysis, and the incident was called back to memory. The ridiculous symptom of walking with legs wide apart abruptly ceased. Thus tics or recurrent involuntary movements are due to repression.[4]

Obstssion is a 'fixed idea' due to repression. A child suffers from excessive fear of a closed room. He does not know the reason why he is afraid of it. He knows that it is irrational and absurd to entertain fear of a closed room. But he cannot cure himself of the irrational fear. Psycho-analysis reveals that while he was stealing fruit in a closed room, he was frightened by a savage dog. He had a sense of guilt. He repented for his conduct. He was ashamed of the unhappy incident. The memory of it was repressed. When the memory of it was called back to the mind by psycho-analysis, he was cured of claustrophobia. All kinds of obsessions are due to repression.[5]

In dementia precox or Schizophrenia the patient is completely withdrawn from the environment. He does not respond to it. He does not take any interest in any thing that happens around him. He is immersed in his own imaginary, hallucinatory world. He loses all touch with the reality. The dementia precox patient is an extreme introvert, while the manic-depressive individual is an extreme extrovert.

## Mental Confliet

Definite symptoms of mental disorder are preceded by a period of mental conflict. A person is torn asunder by a conflict of motives or conative tendencies seeking goals, which are incompatible with one another. A young man has a strong desire to achieve academic distinction and pursue knowledge in a university, and he has also a strong desire to amass wealth and live in luxury. He cannot adopt the one goal with whole-hearted devotion. While he pursues knowledge in university, his intense desire to go to business and acquire vast wealth preys upon his mind. The conflict of motives persists in his mind. It consumes his energy and produces a strain. He cannot overcome the conflict and produce a balance, unity, and integrity of mind. Such a prolonged conflict may lead to dissociation or repression.

A young woman fond of her mother has a strong desire to nurse her during her prolonged ill-ness and restore her to health. She has also an intense desire to marry her young lover, separate from her mother, set up a new home, and enjoy a married life. These two motives are incompatiable and irreconciliable. The prolonged conflict of motives may lead to dissociation or repression. It may result in mental disorders.

Mental conflicts are due to obstructions of the environment to the satisfaction of motives, an individual's deficiencies which interfere with their satisfaction, and conflicting motives. Our physiological needs may be thwarted by droughts, famine, flood, and other physical events. Or their fulfilment may be obstructed by other persons. These are environmental obstructions. Low intelligence, poor memory, lack of leadership, and other personal defects also obstruct the fulfilment of our needs. Conflicting motives, which cannot be fulfilled at the same time, pull us is different directions. Thus conflicts are inevitable in our life.

## Dissociation

The conflicting reaction tendencies may not be harmonised and organised into a unity. They may be separated from the main stream of consciousness. They may be "*split off*" from the consciousness of the personality. They may lead to disintegration of consciousness into separate parts. This is called 'dissociation'. In the normal individual the field of consciousness is generally an unbroken stream of consciousness progressing towards some definite goal. But there are some isolated mental processes, which pursue their ends independently. This division of mind into isolated and independent fragments, which are not integrated into a unity, is called dissociation of consciousness. In a normal mind dissociation is temporary and partial. Both the isolated activities are under the control of the person's mind. Automatic writing, somnambulism, delusion, hallucination, sensorsy anaesthesia, etc., are due to dissociation. But in abnormal persons dissociation is complete. Double personality, triple personality, multiple personality, etc., are due to dissociation of consciousness into isolated fragments, which pursue their goals independently. Dissociated fragments pursue their courses in logic-tight compartments, and are organised into inependent systems. Dissociated or alternating personalities are due to mental disintegation. An insane person is torn between conflicting demands of reality and an unreal, visionary world of day-dream and hallucination.[6]

## Repression

Repression is unconscious suppression of a painful desire, because it cannot be fulfilled. People sometimes react to conflicting motives by "putting out of mind" the painful motive. A person intensely desires to marry his daughter. But he cannot afford to do so. So he does not admit the existence of the difficulty. His desire to marry his daughter is repressed, and he moves about with a seemingly easy and untroubled mind. Repression is ignoring, or not admitting or attempting to forget motives and situations. The repressed desire forms a complex. A complex is an idea or a system of ideas tinged with an affect. It is an emotionally toned idea. It exists in the unconscious or subconscious level of mind. It is expressed in the conscious mind in the form of dreams, day-dreams and the like.

Repression is contrasted with inhibition. Inhibition is conscious suppression. Repression is unconscious. When a student consciously suppresses the desire to go to a movie, and resolves to study hard, he inhibits the first desire. But in repression a person closes his eyes to reality. He avoids the conflict instead of facing it. Repression is injurious to mental health. We should face the conflict, and try to overome it. Repression cannot resolve the conflict.

## Complex

The Psycho-analysts regard a 'complex' as a system of ideas, which is tinged with a painful emotion, and is largely or wholly repressed on account of its painful character. A complex is due to repression which results from conflict. Mental conflict results in repression. Repression leads to the formation of a complex, which is, in some degree, morbid, on account of its lack of harmony with character. Complexes are 'untidy systems' of ideas organised by accidental associations. They are not known and acknowledged by their possessors. They are shut off from attention, memory, and consciousness. They are generated by more or less unconscious and irrational motives. Sentiments, on the other hand, are 'tidy systems' of ideas organised by logical relations. They are not repressed. They are known and acknowledged by their possessors. They are generated by conscious and rational motives.[1]

In certain elderly unmarried women the 'sex complex' does not find a normal outlet, and is, therefore, repressed. The repressed complex may find an indirect expression in a morbid interest in births, marriages, and scandals. Sometimes a complex expresses itself indirectly by means of symbolism. In elderly unmarried women the repressed maternal instinct may find a distorted expression in an exaggerated affection for dogs and cats. A child hated by her step-mother develops a step-motherly complex. Her complex may find expression in unsocial conduct. She may become a delinquent child. She may steal her campanions' articles and indulge in other crimes.

But some psychologists, Drever, Hart, etc., regard a 'complex' as a system of ideas tinged with an emotion. It is not necessarily due to repression and mental conflict. It is not necessarily tinged with a painful emotion. It is not necessarily morbid or abnormal due to unresolved conflict and repression. A hobby is a kind of complex. A person may have a strong 'photography-complex'. A politician may have a strong 'political complex'. A young man may have a strong 'love complex,' which brings a train of ideas about his beloved to his mind, and shuts off other ideas from it.

But generally in modern Psychology the term 'complex' is taken in the psycho-analyst sense of a system of ideas tinged with a painful emotion, and repressed on account of its unpleasantness and lack of harmony with a person's character. Complexes are the cause of neuroses.

Freud maintains that complexes are repressed sex desires. Adler holds that complexes are repressed will-to-power or self-assertive impulse. Both are one-sided. Repressed complexes may be due to repression of all kinds of propensities and desires. Freud makes too much of sex. Adler exaggerates the rôle of inferiority-complex.

### Psycho-analysis : Freud's Method of treatment

Charcot believed that hysteria was a pathological state of the organism. He treated hysteria by the method of hypnosis. His pupil, Morton Prince, used hypnosis in the treatment of multiple or dissociated personality. Janet treated mental automatisms by hypnosis. He found that long forgotten emotional shocks could easily be recalled and described during hypnosis, which were inaccessible in the waking condition. These emotional shocks were cured by suggestions. Janet held that neuroses were due to lowered mental tension or lack of synthetic power and will to overcome the difficulties of life. Sigmund Freud collaborated with Charcot in Paris in the use of hypnosis in the treatment of hysteria. He was struck by hearing Charcot's remark that in all cases of neurosis there was some trouble in the individual's sex life—always, always ! This was a fruitful suggestion. Freud took it up and worked it out. He returned to Vienna and continued the method of hypnosis to treat hysteria. He found some difficulties with the method. Many neurotic patients could not be hypnotised. Hypnosis did not always effect a cure. Charity patients could be cured by curative suggestions during hypnosis. But private patients were too intelligent to get full value from the curative suggestions. Then Freud worked with Breuer, a Viennese physician, and continued the same method of hypnosis. Breuer found that a young female patient felt much better, when she was allowed to "talk out" her emotional difficulties while hypnotized. Breuer and Freud continued this talking out treatment under hypnosis with some success. But Breuer gave up this method of treatment when a female patient declared that she could not part from him, since she fell violently in love with him. But Freud was not discouraged by it. He soon ran into the same difficulty. He held that the psycho-analyst was simply taken as a substitute for the original object of the patient's love. This is called transference. He maintained an impersonal attitude and got rid of the difficulty. Then Freud dropped hypnosis and continued the talking out method without it. He had his subject assume a reclining position and relax and dwell on his or her troubles and their cause. Relaxation with free association was Freud's substitute for hypnosis in the treatment of neurosis. But the credit of discovering this method goes partly to Breuer.

### Freud's Theory of Psycho-analysis

Freud gradually elaborated his theory. He found that neurotic symptoms, dreams, lapses of tongue, lapses of pen, etc., were direct or indirect expressions of repressed desires and complexes predominantly of a sexual nature. So Freud tried to unearth the unconscious sex wishes by the talking out method or free association and interpretation of dreams. With his new methods of free association and dream analysis, Freud could cure many neurotic individuals. He was able to revive experiences that had been repressed, and cure hysterical paralysis, anaesthesias, and neurotic fears and inhibitions. But he found that sometimes his patients, though dismissed as cured, came back after a time with different complaints. He concluded that he could lay bare only some recent repressed complexes. He wanted now to uncover the original complex which was due to some particular emotional shock. Many hysteric women were brought by dream analysis to recall emotional shocks from childhood. They recalled being sexually attacked or seduced by their fathers, uncles, or elder brothers. Freud concluded that what the patient had remembered was some day-dream or phantasy of childhood, which embodied a childish wish of the subject. The day-dream of later childhood was an expression of an unfulfilled wish of earlier childhood. Freud pushed the analysis back to early childhood and revived the emotional attitude of early childhood. Free association was utilized for the emotional revival. Thus Freud discovered the psychoanalytic technique as a method of treatment of neuroses.

Repressed infantile sexuality is the cause of neuroses according to Freud. He lays stress on repression, sex desire (libido), and infancy as the causal conditions of neuroses. They originate in repressed infantile sex desire.[9] Repressed libido (sex) is the cause of neuroses, especially during early childhood. Freud takes the word 'sex'. in a very wide sense. He regards thumb-sucking, biting, things and putting them into the mouth, rubbing and being rubbed, stroked or patted, rhythmical movements of the arms and legs, defecation and urination, as forms of sex gratification. He includes under sex gratification all affectionate behaviour and friendship, and love for art and music. He includes love for father and mother, brothers and sisters, animate and inanimate objects under sex. In other words, he identifies sex with love in the broadest sense. Yet he objects to any attempt to desexualize his *libido*.

## Adler's theory of Psycho-analysis

Adler does not deny the importance of the sex impulse, but he holds that it has not such a comprehensive importance in the child's life as Freud thinks. The self-assertive impulse or will-to-power is the dominant motive of life. It is more thwarted by the social environment than the sex impulse. Inferiority-complex or feeling of inferiority is the cause of neuroses. The phantasies or day-dreams of the individual are not disguised gratifications of the *libido* (sex), but imaginary ways of escape from the sense of inferiority. Dreams also are not direct or symbolical fulfilments of old sex wishes. They relate to the future rather than to the past. They are a sort of rehearsal of some important action to be performed in reality. They reveal the individual's style of life as applied to the approaching crisis.

Neuroses also are caused by inferiority complex. They are cured by removing the feeling of inferiority. The maladjusted neurotic is to be treated by leading him gently to see his inferiority complex and his ingrained way of attaining superiority and thus making him aware of his lack of co-operative power. He should be convinced of his error and made to change his plan of life and gain contact with society. He should be enabled to adjust himself effectively to the social environment.

## Jung's theory of Psycho-analysis

Jung adheres to Freud's technique of free association and dream analysis in the treatment of neuroses. He holds that dreams indicate the patient's unconscious attitude towards his present problem. The analysis gives him an understanding of his present state as well as of his infantile past, and integrates his past experience with his present experience. Jung includes in libido sex impulse (Freud), will for power (Adler), and will to live (Schopenhauer). It is the total vital energy which seeks the goal of growth, power and reproduction. The child's pleasure in taking food arises from the libido, but cannot be called sexual pleasure, since the sex urge has not yet been differentiated from the primal urge to live. Jung holds that Freud was one-sided in his emphasis on psycho-sexuality, or coarse sexuality. His theory of neurosis is different. "A neurosis is a present attempt at adjustment to life, a poor attempt indeed, but at least an attempt at transformation and a new synthesis. The neurosis is to be cured, then, by the analyst's helping along this new synthesis, rather than by his merely unearthing past causes though the latter procedure is of use as a preliminary stage in the treatment.[10]" Freud regarded dreams or neuroses as motivated by repressed sex desires. Adler regarded them as motivated by the will for power. Jung solved the enigma by his doctorine of psychological types. A person, who is motivated by the will for power (Adler), is an introvert, and must focus his interest on the self. But a person, who is motivated by sex desire, is an extrovert, and must focus his interests on the object of love.

### Unconscious Wishes or Motives

Freud holds that the sex wishes banned by the society and ungratified in the waking condition are repressed and become unconscious wishes. They seek direct or indirect fulfilment in dreams, phantasies, neuroses, etc. Repressed sex desires constitute the unconscious. There is a polarity or opposition between the conscious and the unconscious. By nature man follows the pleasure principle ; he seeks for the immediate gratification of his desires. But he is confronted with the realities of his social environment, which compel him to represss his desires to some extent. So, in his day-dreams, dreams, and in the unconscions he follows the pleasure principle ; but he follows the reality principle in his waking life, and conforms to the social codes of morality.

Adler holds that the repressed self-assertive impulse constitutes the unconscious. He does not oppose the conscious to the unconscious. They are not two separate antagonistic entities in the individual, but are bound together as having the same desires and trends.

Jung distinguishes between the personal unconscious and the collective or racial unconscious. The personal unconscious consists of repressed wishes of the individual (Freud), and other experiences, that have been forgotten, being dissociated out of consciousness, and other material unconsciously acquired. The conscious and the unconscious life of the individual develop out of the collective or racial unconscious, which is inherited by way of the structure of the organism. It consists of instincts or innate and primitive ways of acting, and 'primordial ideas', 'archetypes', or primitive ways of thinking. Primitive thinking was symbolical thinking. We also think animistically. We have vague primitive notions of sympathetic magic, and of ghosts, fairies, witches, devils, etc. We have not outgrown this animistic way of thinking. It appears constantly as symbols in our thought.

**Mental Mechanism for resolution of Mental conflict**

Incompatible motives often come into conflict with one another. Conflicting motives which cannot be simultaneouly realized pull us in different directions. Thus conflicts are inevitable in our life.

(1) When we are torn by conflicting motives, we try to remove the conflict by the trial-and-error process. We may try various methods until we succeed in removing the conflict. If a student cannot decide whether he should join Meerut College or Agra College, he should get as much information as he can about both the Colleges, and then decide upon joining one.

(2) The conflict may be removed by compensation. A young man pays greater attention to strenous athletics, when his sex motive is thwarted. An ugly girl emphasises scholarship, when her sex motive is thwarted.

(3) The conflict may be removed by identification. A young man may satisfy his desire for adventure by identifying himself with the hero of a novel or a movie.

(4) Phantasy is another way of removing conflict. A young man whose self-assertion is thwarted, indulges in day-dreaming. He builds 'castles in the air'. He becomes the hero of his day-dream. He is the master of the situation in his world of imagination. Excessive day-dreaming is dangerous. It makes the person lose contact with reality, and generates mental derangement.

(5) The person whose mastery motive is frustrated, belittles others. He is ready to find fault with those who have succeeded where he has failed. He satisfies his egoism by disparaging others.

(6) The person whose egoism is frustrated, blames others. The student, who fails in his examination, lays blame at the door of the 'bad' teacher, 'difficult' text-books, or the 'inconvenient' hours of lectures. He maintains his self-respect by refusing to recognize his short-comings.

(7) An individual may try to escape conflict by projecting himself or attributing his own thoughts or desires to others. He himself suspects his wife's fidelity. But he suspects that

other people calumniate her in public. He attributes his suspicion to others.

(8) A person torn by conflict may adopt rationalization. He seeks good reasons to justify his conduct to himself and others. The minister of a country may adopt a measure for his his own self-aggrandisement. But he may ascribe it to his patriotic motive. A lazy student excuses his lack of study by say ng that he will ruin his poor health if he studies hard.

(9) A person confronted by difficulties reverts to childish reactoins such as sulking, weeping, stamping his feet, kicking objects, etc., which are inadequate to meet the difficult situation. Husbands sometimes dominate their wives and wives sometimes dominate their husbands by sulking, weeping, and threats. These reactions constitute regression. It is reversion to childish or inadequate modes of reaction.

(10) People sometimes react to conflicting motives by "putting out of mind" the painful motive. A person intensely desires to marry his daughter. But he cannot afford to do so. So he does not admit the existence of the diffieulty. The desire to marry his daughter is repressed, and he moves about with an easy and untroubled mind. Repression is ignoring or not admitting or attempting to forget motives and situations. The repressed desire forms a complex. A complex is an idea or a system of ideas tinged with an affect. It is an emotionally toned idea. It exists in the unconscious or subconscious mind. It appears in the conscious mind in the form of dreams, day-dreams, and the like.

Repression is contrasted with inhibition. Inhibition is conscious suppression. Repression is unconscious. When a student consciously suppresses the desire to go to a movie, and resolves to study hard, he inhibits the first desire. In repression a person closes his eyes to reality. He avoids the conflict instead of facing it. Repression is injurious to mental health. We should face the conflict, and try to overcome it. Repression cannot resolve the conflict.

Trial-and-error reactions, compensatory reactions such as identification, phantasy (day-dreaming), belittling others, and blaming others, projection, regression, and repression are the mental mechanism for resolution of conflict. But they cannot resolve the conflict. They are the mental mechanism, which tries to avoid it. The conflict remains unresolved.[11]

9 Woodworth, *Contemporary Schools of Psychology*, y. 150.
13 *Ibid*, p. 182.
11 Munn, *Psychology*, 1956, pp. 139-53.

# INDEX